The Smithsonian Guides to Natural America

THE SOUTHERN ROCKIES

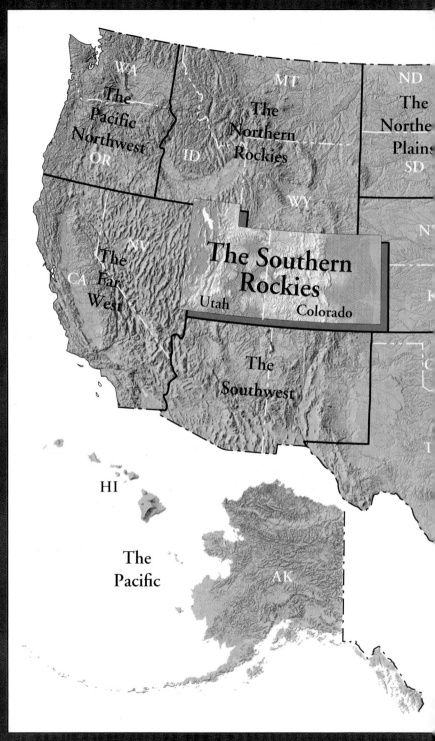

The Pacific Northwest
WA
OR

The Northern Rockies
MT
ID
WY

The Northern Plains
ND
SD

The Far West
NV
CA

The Southern Rockies
Utah
Colorado

The Southwest

HI

The Pacific
AK

MN

WI

MI

The
Great
Lakes

IA

The
Heartland

IL

IN

OH

MO

KY

Central
Appalachia

TN

AR

The
South
Central
States

MS

AL

GA

The
Southeast

LA

FL

SC

NC

The
Atlantic
Coast

WV

VA

MD

PA

The
Mid–Atlantic
States

NY

NJ

Northern
New
England

ME

VT

NH

MA

CT   RI

Southern
New
England

THE SOUTHERN ROCKIES
UTAH – COLORADO

THE SMITHSONIAN GUIDES TO NATURAL AMERICA

THE SOUTHERN ROCKIES

COLORADO AND UTAH

TEXT

Susan Lamb

PHOTOGRAPHY

Tom Bean

PREFACE

Thomas E. Lovejoy

SMITHSONIAN BOOKS • WASHINGTON, D.C.
RANDOM HOUSE • NEW YORK, N.Y.

Front cover: Delicate Arch, La Sal Mountains, Arches National Park, Utah
Half-title page: White-tailed prairie dog, Colorado
Frontispiece: Bryce Point, Bryce Canyon National Park, Utah
Back cover: Blue columbine; Uncompahgre National Forest, Colorado; bobcat

THE SMITHSONIAN INSTITUTION
SECRETARY I. Michael Heyman
COUNSELOR TO THE SECRETARY FOR
BIODIVERSITY AND ENVIRONMENTAL AFFAIRS Thomas E. Lovejoy
ACTING DIRECTOR, SMITHSONIAN INSTITUTION PRESS Daniel H. Goodwin

SMITHSONIAN BOOKS
EDITOR IN CHIEF Patricia Gallagher
SENIOR EDITOR Alexis Doster III
MARKETING MANAGER Susan E. Romatowski
BUSINESS MANAGER Steven J. Bergstrom

THE SMITHSONIAN GUIDES TO NATURAL AMERICA
SERIES EDITOR Sandra Wilmot
MANAGING EDITOR Ellen Scordato
PHOTO EDITOR Mary Jenkins
ART DIRECTOR Mervyn Clay
ASSISTANT PHOTO EDITOR Ferris Cook
ASSISTANT PHOTO EDITOR Rebecca Williams
ASSISTANT EDITOR Seth Ginsberg
COPY EDITORS Helen Dunn, Karen Hammonds
FACT CHECKER Jean Cotterell
PRODUCTION DIRECTOR Katherine Rosenbloom

Library of Congress Cataloging-in-Publication Data
Lamb, Susan.
    The Smithsonian guides to natural America. The southern Rockies—
Colorado and Utah/text, Susan Lamb; photography, Tom Bean;
preface, Thomas E. Lovejoy.
       p.   cm.
    Includes bibliographical references (pp. 254–55) and index.
    ISBN 0-679-76472-0 (pbk.)
    1. Natural history—Colorado—Guidebooks. 2. Natural history—
Utah—Guidebooks. 3. Colorado—Guidebooks. 4. Utah—Guidebooks.
I. Bean, Tom. II. Title.
QH105.C6L35 1996
508.788—dc20   95-9041
                                                                CIP

How to Use This Book

The Smithsonian Guides to Natural America explore and celebrate the preserved and protected natural areas of this country that are open for the public to use and enjoy. From world-famous national parks to tiny local preserves, the places featured in these guides offer a splendid panoply of this nation's natural wonders.

Divided by state and region, this book offers suggested itineraries for travelers, briefly describing the high points of each preserve, refuge, park or wilderness area along the way. Each site was chosen for a specific reason: Some are noted for their botanical, zoological, or geological significance, others simply for their exceptional scenic beauty.

Information pertaining to the area as a whole can be found in the introductory sections to the book and to each chapter. In addition, specialized maps at the beginning of each book and chapter highlight an area's geography and geological features as well as pinpoint the specific locales that the author describes.

For quick reference, places of interest are set in **boldface** type; those set in **boldface** followed by the symbol ❖ are listed in the Site Guide at the back of the book. (This feature begins on page 263, just before the index.) Here noteworthy sites are listed alphabetically by state, and each entry provides practical information that visitors need: telephone numbers, mailing addresses, and specific services available.

Addresses and telephone numbers of national, state, and local agencies and organizations are also listed. Also in appendices are a glossary of pertinent scientific terms and designations used to describe natural areas; the author's recommendations for further reading (both nonfiction and fiction); and a list of sources that can aid travelers planning a guided visit.

The words and images of these guides are meant to help both the active naturalist and the armchair traveler to appreciate more fully the environmental diversity and natural splendor of this country. To ensure a successful visit, always contact a site in advance to obtain detailed maps, updated information on hours and fees, and current weather conditions. Many areas maintain a fragile ecological balance. Remember that their continued vitality depends in part on responsible visitors who tread the land lightly.

C O N T E N T S

PREFACE

The southern Rockies, where the United States makes its closest approach to the vault of heaven and where the continent divides, provide a rich tableau of geology and biology. No wonder, then, that for me as for many others, the southern Rockies were a source of childhood fantasies and vicarious adventure. These were not to be realized until I made the trek to meet my bride-to-be's maternal grandmother, a stalwart lady filled with the wisdom and common sense her family garnered over generations there. It is no wonder that thenceforth no year has been complete without a pilgrimage to this fount of nature.

Colorado and Utah were the last of the lower 48 states to be explored, and the names of the explorers linger on in such landmarks as Pike's and Long's peaks in Colorado and such places as Fremont, Utah. All the great geological surveyors worked here: Clarence King, Ferdinand Hayden, George Wheeler, and the most eminent of them all, John Wesley Powell, whose prescience about water issues echoes to this day. Given the critical role the Smithsonian played in government science and surveying at the time, it is more than appropriate that Smithsonian Butte rises in rocky testament in Utah.

Here are found some of the treasures of the national park system: Rocky Mountain, Zion, Bryce Canyon, Canyonlands, Arches, and Mesa Verde. Colorado and Utah have some of the more spectacular national monuments as well: Dinosaur, Rainbow Bridge, and Great Sand Dunes. For those of a paleontological bent, here are some of the richest fossil-hunting grounds, fodder for the great rivalry between Yale's Othniel C. Marsh and the Philadelphia Academy's Edward Drinker Cope, a bounty of dinosaur gizzard stones (gastroliths), a glimpse of the age when it seems that trilobites ruled the world, and the exquisitely detailed preservation—Florissant Fossil Beds—of what has been so aptly called the "insects' Pompeii."

The geography is dramatic, with plains to the east, and to the

---

PRECEDING PAGES: *Contrasting swaths of golden quaking aspen and dark green spruce pattern Colorado's rugged Sievers Mountains near Aspen.*

west, foothills, then the Rockies themselves, the Colorado Plateau, the Wasatch Line, the Uintas, and, finally, the Great Basin, with the Great Salt Lake within it. In the south, Hispanic place names remind one of the former Santa Fe viceroyalty, and scattered throughout is the legacy of the Native Americans who preceded the European explorers. The Puebloan sites, including the largest cliff dwelling in North America (Cliff Palace in Colorado), present a wealth of opportunity for those archaeologically inclined. The ill-understood causes of the failure of these elaborate and extensive civilizations puzzle us and make us wonder what lessons their decline may hold for today.

In addition to their geological wealth and the glorious colors of the formations, echoing the radiance of the western sunsets, the southern Rockies abound with living things. In some ways, my personal favorites are the tiny flowering plants of the tundra, hunkered low against the cold wind but exquisitely beautiful as they briefly blossom in their cozy microclimates. They are, in a sense, the sophisticate's version of the fabulous spectacle of wildflowers: columbine, lupine, Indian paintbrush in the mountains; and pink vervain, evening primrose, and globe mallow in the plains. Here, too, are one of the oldest living individual organisms, the bristlecone pine, and (because of its huge root systems) one of the largest, the aspen, bespangled with fluttering gilt in autumn. Invisible to us are the microorganisms that make a crust at the soil surface, creating a hospitable environment for the flowers we do see.

The plains, of course, are no longer home to vast herds of bison, gray wolves, grizzlies, or the black-footed ferret, once an inhabitant of prairie-dog towns. Still roaming over plains preserves, however, are herds of North America's own peculiar but handsome pronghorn. (Often mistakenly called an antelope, the pronghorn is actually a family unto itself.) Ferruginous hawks and other raptors soaring overhead are but some of the 200 species of birds found in the region. The prairie is the natural formation we have changed most in North America, but there are still places where we can

---

OVERLEAF: *George Caleb Bingham (1811–79) was widely heralded for his grand panoramas of the West. He painted* **View of Pikes Peak** *in 1872.*

glimpse what westward-moving settlers encountered.

Higher up dwell not only larger forms of wildlife, such as bighorn sheep and elk, but also the plump, whistling marmot. I have always been fascinated by the little pika, which harvests mountain grasses and dries and stores them with as much of an eye to the weather as any farmer. Ptarmigan and horned larks, red crossbills and pygmy nuthatches, mountain bluebirds and black-chinned humming-birds offer a hint of the avian treasures awaiting the keen-eyed birder.

As dry as this country is, it catches water by virtue of its height, which makes for spectacular rivers as well. The Rio Grande, third longest river in the United States, starts here, as do the Colorado, the Yampa, the Arkansas, the South Platte, and the Gunnison, with its spectacular Black Canyon.

As I look forward to a rafting trip down the Green through De-solation and Gray canyons, last summer's memory of the Sangre de Cristo Mountains remains very fresh, and Susan Lamb's wonderfully written guide makes it clear how very much more the southern Rockies hold for future excursions in this part of natural America. That this region could have inspired "America the Beautiful" is obvi-ous. That it did so seems inevitable.

—Thomas E. Lovejoy

Counselor to the Secretary for
Biodiversity and Environmental Affairs,
SMITHSONIAN INSTITUTION

LEFT: *After a winter of heavy snows, native pink geraniums, red paint-brush, yellow groundsel, and purple lupines throng a summer meadow high in the Park Range of Colorado's Routt National Forest.*

SOUTHERN ROCKIES

50   0   50 Miles
50   0   50 Kilometers

WYOMING

NEBRASKA

ROCKY

Greeley

COLORADO

DENVER

COLORADO

MOUNTAINS

Colorado
Springs

Pueblo

PIEDMONT

KANSAS

Rio Grande

Trinidad

OKLAHOMA

NEW MEXICO

TEXAS

INTRODUCTION

INTRODUCTION
THE SOUTHERN ROCKIES

To many people, Colorado and Utah are the essence of the American West. These states encompass the great western landscapes—open plains, magnificent mountains, golden canyons, and stark deserts. Much of this land is unsettled and wild, capturing our imaginations with a vision of reality entirely separate from the one in which most of us live. When we visit such places, our curiosity is rewarded, our delight in the world restored. The rhythms and relationships of the natural world become all-important: the straightforward, cause-and-effect truths of geology, biology, and climate. In Colorado and Utah, these truths are expressed in countless different ways, from spectacular ridges of tundra-clad peaks to mossy seep-spring gardens in deep sandstone ravines.

Colorado and Utah have much in common. Both are lofty states perched thousands of feet above sea level, and both have mountainous, north-south–trending spines—the Rockies of Colorado and Utah's Wasatch Line. They meet along their common boundary on a great stone upland known as the Colorado Plateau, surely one of the loveliest and most intriguing places on the planet. Because of their generally arid climate, Colorado and Utah often share the same plants and animals. Their human stories are largely parallel as well.

It is small wonder that the landscapes of Colorado and Utah inspire superlatives. The landforms that dominate both states are the result of a stupendous, cataclysmic event, the Laramide orogeny (from the Greek *oros*, "mountain," and *genesis*, "creation"), which began about 65 million years ago, at the end of the Age of Dinosaurs. A shearing collision of the earth's two crustal plates carrying the North American continent and the adjoining Pacific Ocean floor warped, twisted, and cracked the land for more than 600 miles east from the point of plate

---

PRECEDING PAGES: *Sunset burnishes the pinnacles of Elephant Canyon in the Needles District of Utah's Canyonlands National Park. Slickrock, or bare sandstone, dominates this region at the heart of the Colorado Plateau.*

contact and raised the Rocky Mountains. Erosion attacked the Rockies even as they rose, and gravel from the mountains piled up thickly on the plains to the east. Although they are heirs to the Rocky Mountains' soil and water, Colorado's golden plains are entirely different: grassy and gently rolling landscapes where lines of cottonwoods mark hidden stream canyons.

West of the mountains, a huge oval section of crust resisted the crushing force of the Laramide to become the Colorado Plateau (an old French word meaning "platter"). Unlike the fractured and folded Rockies, the layers of stone on this 130,000-square-mile platter remained intact—level and neat as a many-layered cake—only rotating a little and rising slightly as well. In subsequent shiftings of the earth's crust, the plateau has been boosted to more than a mile above sea level and fractured a little here and there, but never crumpled. .

The Wasatch Line of central Utah is a long highland composed of tilted ranges in the north and narrow plateaus in the south. The line is an ancient zone of weakness in the earth's surface—geologists report that there have been breaks along it for at least 800 million years—marking the transition between the intact strata of the Colorado Plateau and the splintered landscape of Utah's western desert. After the plate collision that caused the Laramide orogeny, the earth's crust west of the line stretched or extended, splitting in a web of north-south faults. Long slivers of crust moved—some down, some up—to create the valleys and ridges that form the basin and range, Utah's western washboard of a landscape.

The climate of Colorado and Utah is extreme. Overall, both states are dry. To maximize the meager water available, plants and trees have extensive roots and small leaves that are shiny with protective waxes and resins or covered in fine hairs to deflect the sun and wind. Cacti—native only to the New World—have dispensed with leaves, bonding water with gluey substances in the enlarged, thick-skinned stems in which they conduct photosynthesis. Most animals are nocturnal or stay in the shade to reduce the risk of overheating and dehydrating: They venture out in the cooler hours when the sun is low or has set. Human visitors might well learn from them, drinking plenty of water, always wearing sun protection outdoors, and walking during the first and last hours of the day, when the air is coolest, the wildlife most active, and the light on the landscape most revealing.

High as well as dry, Colorado and Utah are cold at night and generally warm in the daytime regardless of season. In some places, plants

ABOVE: *Between the dark tree-islands of spruce and fir in Colorado's glacier-carved La Plata Mountains, corn lilies and white bistort crowd the meadows of Cumberland Basin in the San Juan National Forest.*

and animals must withstand temperature fluctuations of up to 50 degrees in a day. Small, tough foliage helps plants and trees survive these extremes, and many creatures, from reptiles to rodents, estivate (become dormant in hot weather) as well as hibernate (slow their metabolisms in winter). Travelers to the region should come prepared for both hot and very cold temperatures.

Although the two states have generally arid climates, in July and August the southern portions of Colorado and Utah benefit from the monsoons (from the Arabic *mausim*, meaning "season"), spectacular rain- and thunderstorms that originate to the south. On the Colorado Plateau and in the San Juan Mountains, these late-summer storms create sensational displays of wildflowers that are often larger and more colorful than the blossoms of spring. In the winter, the northern parts of both states get lots of snow from storms forming in the Pacific Northwest—a delight for skiers and a hazard for campers.

The plant and animal communities of Colorado and Utah change

ABOVE: *Winter brings an ethereal beauty to the sculpted spires of Utah's Bryce Canyon National Park. Freezing water pries apart the soft limestone, contributing to a rate of erosion that exceeds a foot per century.*

markedly with elevation. At lower levels, where the weather is warmer and drier, grasses and shrubs rustle with mice, snakes, and seed-eating birds. Pronghorn (also called American antelope), coyotes, and mule deer are common. Between 4,000 and 7,000 feet, a sparse, wizened woodland of widely spaced pinyon pines and junipers predominates, and above that are open stands of ponderosa pines on south-facing mountainsides and dense Douglas fir groves on cooler, north-facing slopes. Spruce and fir grow at the next level, and higher still is timberline, the elevation above which trees cannot survive the extremes of cold and wind. Tundra caps many of the mountains in Colorado and a few in Utah as well.

Every mountain in the southern Rockies offers a hundred walks and innumerable meadows, canyons, and desert oases to explore. People have roamed these reaches for well over 10,000 years (perhaps as many as 15,000), from Paleolithic big-game hunters to today's hik-

ers, climbers, campers, mountain bikers, river runners, anglers, leaf peepers, birders, llama trekkers, snowshoers, and skiers, who delight in the extensive public natural areas of both states.

Some lovers of the region, however, lament that the sheer numbers of visitors to natural sites are now spoiling the experience intended by their preservation. Although some places are so crowded that they can no longer be described as very natural, in many cases their sorry condition is the result of inappropriate rather than heavy use. The answer may be not to stay away, but to approach natural areas with gentleness, respect, and adequate information.

Administrators of federal lands have realized lately that distributing the growing number of visitors across a greater area does not diminish negative impacts on resources, it simply enlarges the area affected. To avoid exacerbating the problems of natural areas today, visitors can begin by exploring the classic national parks—Rocky Mountain, Mesa Verde, Arches, Zion—before venturing into less familiar locales. Because well-known national parks are thoroughly interpreted by rangers, exhibits, and trail guides, visitors can learn not only about the geology, biology, and human history of the region but also about ways to spend time there without endangering themselves or the land.

For example, few new visitors recognize the importance of the thin, dark crust on the arid soils of the region. This inconspicuous plant community, known as microbiotic crust (or cryptogamic soil), grows in places sheltered from grazing animals and hikers' boots. Although it resembles dark, dead fuzz, this thin covering is actually a group of lichens, mosses, algae, fungi, and cyanobacteria that absorb water, contribute nitrogen and carbon to the soil, and hold the dirt in place, thereby creating a fragile habitat in which higher plants may succeed. Microbiotic crust is a critical phase in the establishment of vegetation in arid country, and carelessly stepping on it ultimately denudes the landscape and reduces cover and forage for animals.

Colorado and Utah were the last of the lower 48 states to be explored. Except for a few feints across the southern edge of Colorado by military men of the Spanish empire and a little circuit traveled through both states in 1776 by Franciscan missionaries from Santa

LEFT: *A ribbon of green cottonwoods traces the course of the Escalante River in southern Utah. Though scarce, water etches deep canyons into the rocky terrain, which supports a surprising diversity of life.*

ABOVE: *During his exploratory 1869 expedition down the Colorado, a dangling, one-armed John Wesley Powell is pulled to safety with his companion's underdrawers at Utah's Echo Rock.*

Fe, even frigid Wyoming, Montana, and Idaho were better known in the early 1800s. Fear of the rugged mountains, the Spanish, and the Ute, Comanche, and other native peoples kept this area terra incognita until the United States acquired Colorado from France in the Louisiana Purchase of 1803. Then the federal government dispatched military surveys, which relied heavily on the experience of a few mountain men such as Jedediah Smith, William Ashley, Peter Skene Ogden, and James Ohio Pattie, who had trapped along the rivers of the region. Lieutenant Zebulon Pike explored eastern Colorado in 1806, Major Stephen H. Long led a similar expedition in 1820, and Captain John C. Frémont made three trips across northern Colorado and Utah in the early 1840s. In 1847 the Latter-day Saints, or Mormons, established Salt Lake City as a refuge from persecution elsewhere in the country and immediately began to investigate and settle the surrounding area.

Those who officially explored and mapped Colorado and Utah in the final third of the century had an eye for geology as well as geography. The four important surveys were Clarence King's exploration of the 40th parallel, begun in 1867; the Hayden Survey under Dr. Ferdinand Hayden, also authorized in 1867; Lieutenant George M. Wheeler's expedition west of the 100th meridian, which began in 1869; and the semi-official geographic and topographic survey of the Colorado River led by Major John Wesley Powell between 1869 and 1871. Systematic and scientifically sound, the surveys were also splendid adventures, as accounts of them attest. Powell was the most poetic journalist of the four: "When we return to camp at noon," he wrote, "the sun shines in splendor on vermilion walls, shaded into green and gray where the rocks are lichened over; the river fills the channel from wall to wall, and the canyon opens, like a beautiful portal, to a region of glory...."

It is indeed sublime to experience these landscapes in the tradition of romantic adventure established by the early explorers of Colorado and Utah. Unfortunately, particularly in the West, nature is often characterized as tough, primitive, and harsh—a place to test ourselves. In a misguided spirit of independence, hikers set off where there are no trails, demolishing plants and causing erosion. Poorly prepared hikers suffer heat exhaustion or become hopelessly lost in an hour, necessitating costly, intrusive searches and more regulations. Trampled vegetation and disturbed wildlife take years to become re-established, yet four-wheelers roar and "hell-bikers" pedal furiously over the desert, destroying its fragile microbiotic crust. Backcountry explorers should always carry maps, keep track of their location, and restrict off-trail expeditions to bare rock or streambeds.

ABOVE: *Noted artist and naturalist Titian Ramsay Peale painted this watercolor of a bobcat in 1820 when he accompanied the pioneering Long Expedition to record the western plants, animals, and scenery.*

At the other extreme, visitors who regard any discomfort with horror approach natural areas with all the technology of the twentieth century. Four-wheel-drive vehicles tear into remote reaches, bearing campers armed with weed whackers to clear campsites, bug zappers to attract and incinerate insects, and boom boxes and televisions to enliven the quiet night. They lurch off again leaving behind plastic wrapping, food, and exposed human waste. Without realizing the consequences, other visitors insist upon all the amenities of a city wherever they go, creating

more hotels, shops, restaurants, bars, video parlors, and even theaters, which require more roads and parking lots and dams to provide power—all destroying precious habitat and peacefulness. A willingness to rough it a little—by exploring on foot instead of by car, eating a picnic instead of a restaurant meal, packing out everything brought in, and sleeping under the stars—preserves the environment and tends to slow us down and intensify our pleasure in the natural world. After all, this land nourished the Puebloan people, who found everything they needed here for a civilization that lasted a thousand years and still enchants us with its artistry and sophistication.

ABOVE: *Blooming on the prairies each summer, woolly verbena is too bitter for grazing animals but provides a welcome perch for monarch butterflies as they breed on their northward migrations.* **RIGHT:** *Streaked with vivid mineral pigments, a red Navajo sandstone cliff towers over sunlit cottonwoods in the Paria Canyon Wilderness Area.*

The people of the United States are sometimes said to have little common heritage and no connection to the natural world—yet few other societies have set aside as much land for the benefit of the public as ours has in Colorado and Utah. In the past, these shared lands were managed for the production of minerals, timber, grain, and livestock. Today, they are the most effective antidote to the epidemic of stress and social problems in a society increasingly encumbered with noise, crowding, pollution, and haste.

Clearly, we should appreciate the extraordinary resources that we share as citizens and insist that our elected representatives maintain the policies that protect them. Our first responsibility, however, is our individual approach to the natural world. To blunder about the open country of Colorado and Utah without taking the time to understand its climate, topography, flora, and fauna is to call down disaster upon ourselves and the land. As we learn about and conserve the landscape, we understand and conserve ourselves. Or as the poet Gary Snyder says: "stay together / learn the flowers / go light."

COLORADO

PART ONE

C O L O R A D O

In the heart of Rocky Mountain National Park lies Dream Lake. Aptly named, it is a place to watch the dawn awaken mountain, forest, and lake and to savor each emerging sight and sound. Spruce and fir trees murmur in cool breezes, and gray granite boulders lie huddled in the twilight just before the sun appears. Then the first rays strike the dark conifers, painting them a rich emerald and setting aglow bright polychrome lichens splattered on the rocks below them. A chickadee whistles softly, a flicker chatters. The air warms, mist rises from the lake, and a delicate fragrance wafts over the terrain as tiny white and yellow flowers materialize on the mountain slopes. Another day has begun in the rich tapestry that is wild Colorado.

Most people think of the Rocky Mountains when they imagine Colorado. And indeed it is the highest state in the country, with more than 1,140 mountains topping 10,000 feet and 54 peaks above 14,000 feet. The Continental Divide winds along these crests, bisecting the state from north to south and separating streams flowing east to the Gulf of Mexico from those flowing west to the Gulf of California. Eastern Colorado, however, is not mountainous at all. The 200-mile stretch from Kansas to the Rockies— some 40 percent of the state—is golden, undulating prairie. (The state bird, in fact, is the lark bunting, a grassland denizen.) Through the stacked geologic strata of these plains, the mountains burst up, tearing through the orange, buff, and coffee-colored layers whose ragged, colorful edges form foothills called hogbacks. The Rockies surge across Colorado for another 200 miles, a storm-tossed stone ocean of sky-piercing peaks and plummeting depths that support blue spruce and columbine, the state tree and flower. Along the western border with Utah, the land lies almost flat again

PRECEDING PAGES: *In the White River National Forest, golden aspens glow in an autumn sunrise above crystal-clear Maroon Lake near Aspen. Fresh snow dusts the rugged, treeless peaks of the Maroon Bells rising above.*

on the high Colorado Plateau, although sediment-laden streams have etched magnificent canyons into this tableland.

Whether one's idea of Colorado is the broad rangelands celebrated in James Michener's *Centennial*, the mighty Rockies, or the sandstone mesas of the west, rivers bring life to the state. The South Platte, Arkansas, and Rio Grande flow east from the mountains; the Yampa, Gunnison, and Colorado flow west. Their waters trickle, meander, and roar through seven distinct ecosystems: treeless tundra, subalpine forests of fir and spruce or bristlecone pine, montane forests of north-facing Douglas fir or south-facing ponderosa or fire-loving lodgepole pine, pinyon-juniper woodlands, shrublands of brush and wizened oak, and grasslands. Riparian areas line the streams: rich oases of plants, insects, birds, and animals all interconnected with one another and with water. Although wetlands compose only about three percent of Colorado's area, most of the state's wildlife is utterly dependent upon them.

The Pleistocene Ice Age once gripped Colorado's mountains in glaciers, but long grasses flourished on its lower plains, where Paleolithic hunters stalked mammoths and early bison 15,000 years ago. Puebloan people established farming communities in the southwestern canyons 2,000 years before the present, and later groups of hunter-gatherers roamed Colorado: Ute and Shoshone in the mountains; Arapaho, Cheyenne, and Apache on the plains. Colorado's demographics changed during the nineteenth century, when fur trappers and military explorers, then gold prospectors and homesteaders opened up the state. Today, only its southwestern edge remains Native American land.

Currently prosperous, Colorado boasts a diverse economy and bountiful resources for recreation. More than a third of the state is public land. The U.S. Forest Service oversees 14.4 million acres in 11 national forests, mostly in the mountains. The state manages much of eastern Colorado for livestock grazing, and rangelands in the west compose the bulk of the Bureau of Land Management (BLM)'s 8.3 million acres. Scattered throughout, areas of particular significance are the responsibility of the National Park Service.

Visitors come to Colorado for its forested, tundra-topped mountains, where they glimpse its silent creatures—bears, cougars, and elk—and delight in its lush mountain meadows sprinkled with colorful wildflowers. Once here, however, they discover Colorado's diversity: its sunny eastern prairies aflutter with birds, its deep, western canyons where geologic and human history can be read in the sheer sandstone walls. To those travelers willing to listen and observe, any place in Colorado, whether grassland or wetland, sand dune or snowy summit, soon reveals its own remarkable character.

CHAPTER ONE

EASTERN COLORADO:
THE GREAT PLAINS

astern Colorado lies within the Great Plains, the "grassy belly of the continent." From the border with Kansas to the foot of the Rocky Mountains, 40 percent of the state is grasslands. A treeless sweep of prairie, sky, and songbirds, the tawny, undulating plain rises imperceptibly westward toward the distant Rockies. This calming immensity creates the sensation that there is enough time and space and light to consider everything from flower to canyon to cloud, to become absorbed in the world right before our eyes.

Geographers recognize three distinct subregions within Colorado's Great Plains. The high plains (used mostly for grazing and grain production) extend along the border with Kansas. The Colorado Piedmont (where most of Colorado's urban population lives) lies below the Rockies from Denver to Colorado Springs, and the Raton Basin stretches south from Pueblo into New Mexico.

Because eastern Colorado contains no large body of water to moisten or temper its climate, early and late summer are the best times to visit. The rest of the time, the weather tends to be very dry and subject to extremes of wind, heat, and cold. This formidable climate has fostered a short-grass plant community based on blue grama and buffalo grass, resilient and productive plants that support virtually all other life on the plains. They hold the soil together, shading it from the sun and restoring

LEFT: *White prickly poppies and pink bee plants border the scenic auto tour loop through the Pawnee National Grassland, a prime spot to observe the courtship flights and hear the distinctive songs of prairie birds.*

nutrients to it when they burn. Rabbits and pronghorn eat the leaves, burrowing rodents seek the roots, and insects, mice, and birds feast on the seeds. Hawks and coyotes prey on the seedeaters.

From spring through fall, wildflowers carpet the plains. The earliest flowers are short and complete their life cycle quickly, before growing grasses block their sunlight. As the year progresses and the grasses grow higher, taller flowers bloom, wither, and cast their seeds. Thus pussytoes and buttercups are succeeded by penstemons, shooting stars, and mustards, which are followed by evening primroses, lupines, and delphiniums. At length, golden sunflowers loom over the buff-colored landscape.

ABOVE: *A lark bunting, the state bird, alights on a thistle. Welcome harbingers of spring, these migrants breed on the prairie and feast on its insects and seeds.*

OVERLEAF: *Dramatic storm clouds sweep over the Comanche National Grassland. The rain waters the narrowleaf yucca, whose blossoms lure pollinating moths.*

The prairie and its diminishing wetlands support numerous birds. Because there are so few trees in which to perch, several prairie birds, including Colorado's state bird, the lark bunting, sing in flight and nest on the ground. The plains are also on the Central Flyway, a major route for millions of migrating birds. Arriving from points south in spring, some stay to nest and spend the summer while others pause only briefly on their way to breeding grounds farther north. At summer's end, countless birds migrate through on their return journeys.

Swift foxes and mountain plovers are species characteristic of the short-grass prairie because they live only in this flat, open country, where they can see and outpace their predators and prey. With their long legs and bills, mountain plovers look like big brown shorebirds, but they are often found far from water, wheeling about in small flocks and revealing white underwings. Buff-colored "swifties," the smallest foxes in Colorado, den in abandoned burrows and prowl at night. The most common large mammals on the plains today are coyotes, mule deer, and pronghorn. Feared as livestock predators, grizzly bears and packs of gray wolves were completely eradicated from the plains during the last century.

At one time, the Great Plains resembled the Serengeti Plain of Africa in the abundance of its wildlife. Eighteenth-century observers reported that the earth trembled at the approach of bison herds that were five miles

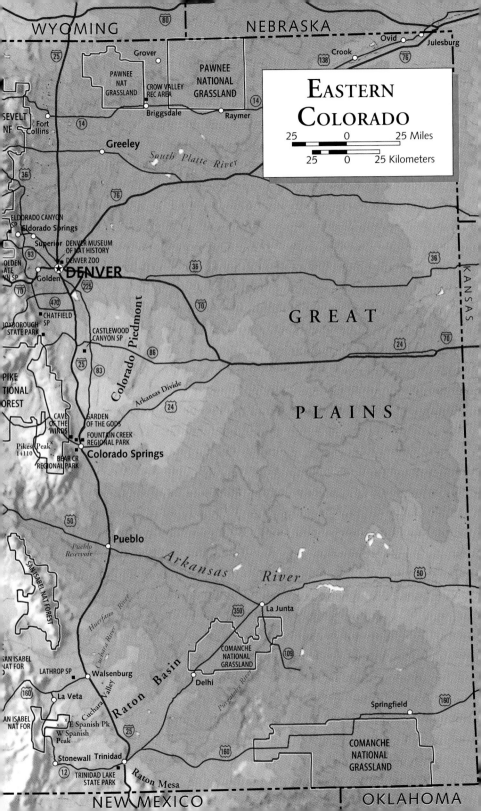

across and ten miles long. Although estimates vary, 50 million bison may have roamed the prairies before the coming of European Americans, who hunted them almost into oblivion. Today bison total perhaps only 70,000 in all of Canada and the United States, but this figure is a considerable increase from a low of a few hundred a century ago.

The native peoples of the Colorado plains differed from one another in many ways, but they all depended upon the meat, hide, and bones of big game—especially bison—for food, clothing, shelter, and tools. In the early 1500s, Apache from the northern part of the continent lived in eastern Colorado, hunting bison on foot with bows, growing crops along streams, and trading with the settled Puebloan people of New Mexico and Arizona. After the introduction of the horse by the Spanish, a number of other peoples displaced by the westward expansion of European Americans moved onto the plains and adopted a similar way of life.

The Great Plains are immense, but public access to them is limited. Along with two national grasslands and a number of state-managed reservoirs, there are several parks in the foothills of the Rockies. The itinerary for this chapter begins in the high plains of Colorado's northeast corner, with some birding along the South Platte River. It continues west through the Pawnee National Grassland to the town of Ault northeast of Denver, next exploring the Colorado Piedmont from Denver to Colorado Springs via side roads. Descriptions of the Raton Basin begin in Walsenburg, highlight the Spanish Peaks, and end with the Comanche National Grassland in the state's southeastern corner.

THE HIGH PLAINS OF EASTERN COLORADO

On the map, Colorado's high plains form a pudgy, inverted L shape from the middle of the state's northern border east to Julesburg, and then south along the entire boundary with Kansas to Oklahoma. The plains occur where layers of sand and gravel shed by the Rocky Mountains are still intact. Erosion has removed these layers closer to the mountains, leaving a line of bluffs that define the western edge of the high plains. As erosion gnaws at them, these bluffs are continually retreating east, leaving oddly shaped buttes on the windy, golden prairie. Writer Hal Borland called this thinly populated country of very small towns and huge ranches "high, wide, and lonesome." With few obstacles in their way, roads, many unpaved, tend to run directly north to south or east to west.

This itinerary begins on the South Platte River Trail Scenic and Historic Byway, a 14-mile loop between Julesburg and Ovid taking Route 138 on the north bank of the South Platte River and County Road 28 on the south bank. Scenic and historic byways in Colorado are marked by roadside signs featuring a blue columbine. This byway follows trails established during the wagon train days of the westward migration and also used by the Pony Express in 1860–61. A pretty line of tall green cottonwoods in an otherwise stark and arid region, the riverbanks are an oasis for birds and other wildlife.

The **Tamarack State Wildlife Area**❖ is more than a dozen miles of river, reservoirs, and wetlands around the town of Crook. Managed primarily for duck hunting in the fall, the wildlife area is closed during April and May for waterfowl breeding. This is a good place to see birds, deer, and small mammals at dawn or dusk. However, the water level in these impoundments varies from year to year, often leaving sloppy mudflats. Because they are intended mostly for anglers and for duck hunters equipped with boats or waders, these areas have few or no trails.

The 125-mile **Pawnee Pioneer Trails Scenic and Historic Byway** runs west from the town of Sterling via Route 14 through the **Pawnee National Grassland**❖. The Pawnee lived primarily in Nebraska and Kansas, but hunted in Colorado occasionally. The national grassland that bears their name is a rolling short-grass prairie with flourishing grasses and flowers, a myriad of bird species, and picturesque buttes. It encompasses 193,060 acres that the federal government purchased between 1933 and 1943 from destitute families desperate to flee the Dust Bowl. Today the **Arapaho**❖ and **Roosevelt**❖ national forests manage the grassland for livestock grazing, wildlife habitat, and recreation. Although it is fenced for cattle and dotted with derelict ranch houses here and there, the Pawnee is a rich habitat for wildlife and excellent birding country.

The Pawnee Grassland is divided into two sections—the **Pawnee Unit** on the east and the **Crow Valley Unit** to the west—both straddling the topographic transition between the high plains and the Colorado Piedmont. The **Pawnee Buttes** in the Pawnee Unit—geologic pagodas of high plains sedimentary layers standing isolated on the surface of the Piedmont—illustrate this transition well. The Pawnee Trails Byway runs just south of the Pawnee Buttes, on bee plant- and sunflower-bordered dirt roads that are muddy in wet weather and bumpy and dusty the rest of the time. To reach the Pawnee Buttes, drive north from New Raymer on the Pawnee Trails Byway, which follows County Road 129, jogging left after four miles to continue north on County Road 127 to County Road 110, which the byway follows west for about six miles. Watch for signs to the Pawnee Buttes Trail.

ABOVE: *On alert for predatory hawks and coyotes, a quartet of black-tailed prairie dogs keeps watch at the entrance to an underground den. Their burrowing improves the grasslands by tilling and aerating the soil.*

From the signposted parking area, the 1.5-mile trail leads through eroded lowlands to the buttes. Depending upon the season, walkers may see prickly poppies, evening primroses, globemallow, pink vervain, and various buckwheats and fleabanes, especially in ravines sheltered from drying winds. The intense light and deep quiet of the prairie can be almost eerie, especially as evening approaches, but yipping coyotes and swooping nighthawks twanging their vibrato call remind visitors that they are not alone.

The buttes are a prime roosting spot for raptors, or birds of prey. Among the most common raptors on the Pawnee are ferruginous hawks, whose name comes from the Latin for "iron" because they are rusty red. With a wingspan of four and a half feet or more, they are the largest members of the hawk family. Other year-round raptors here include red-tailed hawks, marsh hawks, golden eagles, American kestrels, and prairie falcons. In summer, turkey vultures teeter high overhead, raising their long, ragged wings at an angle.

To reach the **Crow Valley Unit,** which is especially popular with birders and mountain-bikers, continue on the Pawnee Trails Byway through Grover to Briggsdale. The Forest Service provides map brochures and bird lists for the 36-mile Pawnee Self-Guided Birding Tour at the

ABOVE: *Usually active at dawn and dusk, three mule deer recline on a grassy prairie hillside in September. Although the bucks are fairly solitary, they may band together before and after the rutting season.*

Crow Valley Recreation Area❖ (where there are campsites and picnic tables), just north of Briggsdale on County Road 77, as well as at its office in Greeley and by mail. Much of the birding tour route is on level, unpaved roads, making it a great mountain-biking route.

All sorts of birds frequent the Pawnee, sitting on fence rails, poking about in ponds, and swooping low over the waving grasses. More than 260 species perform a perpetual savanna symphony of doves cooing, cowbirds gurgling, and hawks shrieking. Mountain plovers are common on the open prairie in summer, as are killdeer, with their keening cry and their habit of pretending to have a broken wing to draw predators away from their nests. Loggerhead shrikes often perch along barbed-wire fences on which they impale their reptile, rodent, or insect prey to be eaten later.

All across the grassland, natural depressions and shallow ponds behind earthen dams collect water for livestock. These playas and stock ponds attract avocets, sandpipers, red-winged blackbirds, and dabbling ducks from the common mallard to pintail and blue-winged teal. Their low voices croaking hoarsely, Wilson's phalaropes arrive in spring to make their nests on the grassy edges of these ponds. They spin like tops on the water to stir up insects and larvae to eat.

Birds are by no means the only wildlife easily observed in the Pawnee.

27

Pronghorn—sometimes called American antelope—keep watch with their enormous dark eyes and bound away when danger approaches, fluffing out the white hair around their rumps to signal other pronghorn. Clocked at 70 miles per hour, pronghorn are the fastest hoofed animals in the world.

Prairie dogs bark to warn one another of danger. Some of their colonies, called towns, cover several acres and are home to hundreds of black-tailed prairie dogs living in burrows organized into territories, or wards. Dusty and bare of plants, prairie-dog towns look barren but play an integral role in prairie ecology. Harvester ants construct glittering quartz-shingled hills in these clearings. Badgers, weasels, coyotes, and foxes eat prairie dogs, and their abandoned burrows shelter long-legged burrowing owls, toads, turtles, rattlesnakes, jackrabbits, and kangaroo rats.

THE COLORADO PIEDMONT

Stretching south from Denver to Colorado Springs, the Colorado Piedmont (a French word meaning "foothill") is a rough rectangle of mile-high country about 150 miles long and half as wide. It separates the high plains on the east from the Rocky Mountains on the west. In this most densely populated part of Colorado, streams of clear water flow down from the Rockies, the climate is relatively benign, and the flat landscape lends itself to roads, railways, and other development near the plains where crops and cattle are raised. With its merry confusion of prairie and mountain flora and fauna, the Piedmont is also the biologically richest part of the state.

When the Rocky Mountains began to lift through ancient sediments about 65 million years ago, layers of those sediments bent up at an angle and eroded from the emerging mountains. Of the ragged edges of bent-up sedimentary layers still fringing the base of the Rockies, the most conspicuous is the red **Dakota Hogback** of 136-million-year-old Dakota sandstone. The Colorado Piedmont is the broad apron of erosional debris that has accumulated below the hogback.

The city of Denver's **Museum of Natural History❖** provides an excellent orientation for local and state natural history. Both the museum and the **Denver Zoo❖** are in the square mile of lawns, trees, and flower beds known as **City Park❖**, which was set aside in the late 1800s as the first of Denver's 4,000 acres of urban parklands. To get an overview of the native flora of the Colorado plains, visit the **Denver Botanic Gardens❖** east of downtown.

Two nearby state parks—Eldorado Canyon and Golden Gate Canyon—illustrate the transition between the Great Plains and the Rocky Mountains. To reach **Eldorado Canyon State Park❖,** take Route 36 northwest from

Denver and turn west onto Route 170 just beyond the town of Superior. The park is eight miles southwest, just past the town of Eldorado Springs. The colorful red and white sandstones at the mouth of Eldorado Canyon were steeply tilted by the rise of the Rocky Mountains. Deeper into the park, dramatic walls of quartzite (metamorphosed sandstone) and granite (cooled magma) more than a billion years old challenge technical rock climbers from the nearby cities. The water issuing from warm springs in Eldorado Canyon is said to be the purest in Colorado.

Golden Gate Canyon State Park❖ is south of Eldorado Springs off Route 93, two miles north of Golden. The canyon, a lovely place to hike, features gentle trails that emerge from pine forests and cross sunny meadows droning with bees and dappled with butterflies, among them huge yellow-and-black-striped tiger swallowtails and the white, increasingly rare, clodius parnassian. Harebells, gaillardia, and brown-eyed Susans bloom among the yarrow and sagebrush. Red-tailed hawks shriek as they spiral upward on warm drafts of rising air, while mule deer, brush rabbits, and irascible blue grouse move soundlessly among the shrubs and high grasses. In front of the visitor center, fat rainbow trout glide serenely around a pond.

The heavy butterscotch scent of ponderosa pine, which emanates from a resin oozed as a defense against pine beetles, drenches both Eldorado and Golden Gate canyons. Ponderosas can grow to 150 feet tall. They are widely spaced, the small plants of their understory groomed by periodic fires. Tassel-eared squirrels eat the tender tips of ponderosa branches and the fungi that grow on the roots, sharing the large seeds in ponderosa cones with red crossbills and Cassin's finches.

Ponderosa forests are veritable aviaries where chattering, drumming flickers swoop among the branches, loose flocks of pygmy nuthatches peep to one another as they forage through the trees, and mountain chickadees rasp *chicka-dee-dee-dee* at all hours of the day. While flashing about in quest of food, black-crested, iridescent blue Steller's jays make a terrific racket of *scraaks* and scary hawk imitations. Brown creepers probe the russet, jigsaw-puzzle bark of ponderosas to pluck out ants, spiders, and spittlebugs. Even decomposing ponderosas offer feasts of insects as well as shelter for birds. In spring, western tanagers with red, yellow, and black plumage, mountain bluebirds, Williamson's sapsuckers, and tiny flammulated owls rear their young in the snug cavities of ponderosa trunks. In those same cavities, dozens of pygmy nuthatches huddle together for warmth in the winter.

Although **Chatfield State Park❖,** 15 miles southwest of Denver off Route 470, does not seem very natural (its 1,500-acre reservoir is popular

with powerboaters), it protects critical habitat for nesting herons and cormorants. Almost 200 other species of birds may be observed at Chatfield, as well as rabbits, coyotes, and deer. The park's 20 miles of trails—most of them paved—and Plum Creek Nature Study Area offer visitors lots of opportunities to learn about local natural history.

From Chatfield, follow the signs five miles south to **Roxborough State Park❖**, where the deep red sandstone of the Fountain Formation eroded into spectacular parallel ridges. Together with the park's variations in elevation, these sheltering hogbacks sustain seven different plant communities ranging from riparian to prairie to oak scrubland, with a forest of pine, fir, and aspen on Carpenter Peak. The park's 12 miles of unpaved footpaths lead from fragrant patches of meadow abloom with Indian paintbrush, golden banner, sand lilies, and sunflowers through dwarf forests of gnarled oaks and mountain mahogany. The creek supports willows, wild plums, hawthorns, and chokecherries. Scrub jays, towhees, and hummingbirds are everywhere—the air is alive with the singing of birds—and golden eagles often sweep overhead. Visitors can observe signs of mountain lions and black bears occasionally, as well as bobcats, mule deer, and snakes.

Roads leading south to Colorado Springs cross the Arkansas Divide (known locally as the Palmer Divide), a broad, gentle highland between the basins of the South Platte and Arkansas rivers. Its high point is about 7,000 feet above sea level, 2,000 feet above the basins below. As a result, more rain falls here, enabling the divide to sustain a forest ecosystem more typical of mountains. Ponderosa pines grow in the coarse, granitic soils shed here from the nearby Rockies.

Five miles south of Franktown on Route 83, **Castlewood Canyon State Park❖** surrounds the 90-foot-deep Castlewood Canyon, which was scoured to bedrock when the dam holding back Cherry Creek burst in 1933. Downstream from the broken dam, a 30-foot waterfall makes a delightful shower on a hot summer day. On the ten miles of trails that wind among creeks and cliffs, kingfishers swoop between cottonwoods growing among huge granite boulders along Cherry Creek, which supports three species of native fish. Tracks of beavers, bobcats, mule deer, and coyotes are pressed into the sand along its banks. Raptors nest in the cliffs and soar above in the sunlight. Tassel-eared squirrels and methodical por-

---

LEFT: *Millions of years ago, the Rockies sheared up through level layers of rock, which were then bent back vertically. Junipers now surround the resulting sandstone fins in the Garden of the Gods near Colorado Springs.*

cupines subsist on the tender parts of the ponderosa pines growing on the plateau above the bluffs.

The city of Colorado Springs lies to the south via Route 83. At **Bear Creek Regional Park**❖ exhibits and naturalist programs focus on Colorado wildlife, and **Fountain Creek Regional Park**❖ features the riparian ecosystems of the Colorado Piedmont. West on Highway 24 is the Colorado Springs city park called **Garden of the Gods**❖, best known for its magnificent spires of red rock. These rusty-colored sandstones—called the Fountain and Red Lyons formations—were deposited between 300 and 240 million years ago and later tilted beyond a perpendicular angle by the uplift of nearby mountains. Several trails lead through pinyon pines, oneseed junipers, and Gambel oaks to scenic vistas of Pikes Peak to the west and the prairie to the east. Garden of the Gods has been designated a national natural landmark because of its diversity of plants, animals, and insects, the result of its location at a biological crossroads where mountain, prairie, and riparian habitats overlap.

Immediately west of Garden of the Gods is **Cave of the Winds**❖, a privately managed attraction (reached via Exit 141 from I-25). Guides lead 40-minute tours along paved paths through chambers illuminated with colored lights. Alternatively, the adventurous may reserve a place on a two-hour "wild tour" through the dark and muddy less developed parts of the cave. During the Pleistocene epoch, acidic water dissolved the limestone along old cracks—joints created by the uplift of neighboring mountains—to create a mile-long series of chambers. Water saturated with dissolved limestone, or calcium carbonate, continued to drip into the chambers, forming stalactites that hang like long stone icicles from the ceiling and sharp stalagmites that point straight up from the floor.

THE RATON BASIN

Beginning about 50 miles south of the city of Pueblo is a third division of the Great Plains in Colorado known as the Raton section or Raton Basin (the name *raton*, Spanish for "rat," was perhaps chosen because pack rats are common in the area). The basin extends south from the Huerfano (Orphan) River into New Mexico and east from the foot of the Rocky Mountains to the bluffs of the high plains. Several patches of this dry,

---

RIGHT: *The wetlands of Lathrop State Park, which provide critical habitat for wildlife, especially waterfowl, lie between the western edge of the Great Plains and the lofty Spanish Peaks on the Rockies' eastern flank.*

Volcanic activity formed the craggy Spanish Peaks (right). Erosion has since worn away the softer overlying rock layers to expose granite dikes of hardened intruded magma (detail at left), which radiate like spreading tree roots.

grassy plateau are capped with basalt flows from vents near the town of La Junta.

The history of this part of Colorado has been documented since the first contacts between Europeans and natives in North America. Lying between Santa Fe, New Mexico (founded in 1610), and the Great Plains, the region was the northern frontier of the Spanish empire in North America, which the Spanish attempted to control with only marginal success.

In 1803, the United States purchased what would become the Louisiana Territory from France. In 1806 Lieutenant Zebulon Pike came west to clarify the newly bought land's boundary with Spain. Pike's expedition pushed up the Arkansas River from Kansas and built a small fort in Pueblo. Although the Spanish government was wary of trade with the United States, New Mexicans generally favored it. After Mexico won independence from Spain in 1821 the Santa Fe Trail was established between Missouri and Santa Fe to foster commerce in the area.

Lathrop State Park❖ is about three miles west of Walsenburg on Route 160. Because of its position between the nearby uplands and lowlands, Lathrop supports five major plant communities within its slight elevational range of 260 feet (from 6,380 to 6,640 feet). Its two reservoirs are surrounded by a narrow band of riparian vegetation including plains cottonwood and crack willow, bounded on the downhill side by acres of mixed-grass prairie. At higher elevations on the hogback ridge to the northwest, a sparse forest of one-seed junipers merges into a pinyon-juniper woodland. Interpretative panels beside an easy two-mile trail along the ridge explain the resulting ecotone, or edge effect. Plants and animals characteristic of all these plant communities mix here, as do shorebirds. When there is a source of water close at hand, as at Lathrop, scrambled ecosystems such as this are especially rich. With a pleasant visitor center, this state park is well interpreted.

Route 12, the Highway of Legends Scenic and Historic Byway—its name a reminder of this region's long history—runs southwest from Route 160 be-

yond Lathrop State Park, passes through the town of La Veta, and continues southwest through the Cuchara (Spoon) Valley, lush ranching country watered by the Cuchara River.

Just south of La Veta, igneous dikes come into view. Some of these walls of lichen-encrusted gray rock rising from slopes clad in low oak woodland are 100 feet high and run for 10 miles or more. They were formed about 25 million years ago, when molten rock, or magma, welled up under this area from deep within the earth. The magma domed up the overlying sedimentary layers and flowed into hundreds of pressure cracks radiating into these surrounding sediments from massive central intrusions called stocks. Erosion has since exposed the dikes by removing the soft sediments surrounding them. The **Spanish Peaks**—gigantic granitic knobs with shoulders cloaked in spruce-fir forests and stands of aspen that turn fiery hues in autumn—are the exposed stocks. West Spanish Peak at 13,626 feet and East Spanish Peak at 12,683 feet are the most prominent features of this part of **San Isabel National Forest❖,** which also includes mountain ranges formed by entirely different geologic processes to the north and west.

Beginning at 9,941-foot Cucharas Pass on Route 12, the unpaved 12-mile Apishapa Scenic Drive offers splendid views of the surrounding mountain slopes and distant prairie, as well as access to hiking trails passing bristlecone pines. Bristlecones survive longer than any other organism on earth. To conserve energy and water, they can retain their tough needles for 40 years. Under especially stressful conditions, bristlecones sacrifice some of the tissue under their bark that circulates water and nutrients to their branches. A gnarled old bristlecone may be more than three-quarters dead—with several eerie, lifeless silver branches—and yet still healthy and growing.

Below the Spanish Peaks, Route 12 descends through Stonewall (named for an outcropping of the Dakota Hogback) and begins to follow the Purgatoire River, which originates in the Sangre de Cristo Mountains to the west. **Trinidad Lake State Park❖** surrounds the lake formed in 1977, when the U.S. Army Corps of Engineers built a dam on the Purgatoire River to control flooding, reserve water for irrigation, and provide a lake for recreational boating. Nine miles of hiking trails around the reservoir take visitors to osprey-viewing areas and to tepee rings left by the Jicarilla Apache.

In the valley of the Purgatoire River, Hispanic farmers from New Mexico founded villages called plazas in the 1860s. Coal mining has been an important economic underpinning of communities in this area since nonnatives arrived, and seams of coal interbedded with sandstones deposited in Cretaceous and Tertiary swamps can be seen in road cuts along Route 12.

From Trinidad, the itinerary takes Route 350—also known as the Santa Fe Trail Scenic and Historic Byway—to La Junta, following the route of the Mountain Branch of the historic Santa Fe Trail. In the 1800s, caravans transported finished goods west via this route and returned east with furs and other raw materials. The completion of the Santa Fe Railroad in 1878 ended commerce on the trail.

Southeast of Trinidad, Raton Mesa (*mesa* is Spanish for "table") is a high, flat, conspicuous tableland, a remnant of sedimentary layers protected from erosion by a caprock of lava that emerged from faults and fissures in the earth's crust less than eight million years ago. Except for Raton Mesa and the similar Mesa de Maya farther east, smoothly rolling grasslands characterize this part of Colorado.

Route 350 enters the **Comanche National Grassland❖** just north of Delhi, about 40 miles northeast of Trinidad. The U.S. Forest Service manages this national grassland, which is divided into two administrative sections: the northern Timpas Unit and the southeastern Carrizo Unit. The Comanche supports a diverse wildlife population, listing 235 species of birds, including eastern and western kingbirds and long-eared, short-eared, great horned,

RIGHT: *Clumps of bunchgrass dot the stark "go-back land" of the Comanche National Grassland. Over time, drought-plagued homesteaders sold the land back to the government, which now manages it for livestock.*

and screech owls; 21 snakes, from prairie rattlers to common water snakes; 13 lizards; 5 species of turtles (ornate box turtles are common here); 5 toads; 3 frogs; the barred tiger salamander; 8 bats; and 52 other mammals, among them bridled weasels, badgers, and gray foxes.

Picket Wire Canyonlands is a scenic sandstone canyon carved by the Purgatoire River (which early Anglo-American settlers pronounced "picket wire"). An eight-mile trail through Withers Canyon affords the only public access to the area. Shallow, blurry imprints along the stony ledges above the Purgatoire in Picket Wire Canyon make up one of the largest concentrations of dinosaur footprints in North America. There are about 1,300 fossilized tracks here, made by carnivorous theropods and plant-eating sauropods at least 150 million years ago.

Also in Picket Wire Canyon are petroglyphs, images carved into rock, which archaeologists attribute to cultures that hunted and gathered in this area from perhaps 5,000 to 300 years ago. The images represent different styles, suggesting that successive cultures made them over that long period of time. The depictions of game animals and abstract symbols are well preserved, having been spared the ravages of vandals in this remote place.

To reach the **Carrizo Unit** of the Comanche National Grassland, take Route 109 south from La Junta and turn east on Route 160 just before Kim. The sunlight-flooded plains of the Carrizo Unit are home to the largest population of endangered lesser prairie chickens in Colorado. Before the dustbowl of the 1930s, before the prairies were plowed, grazed by domestic livestock, and hunted with rifles, these birds were so common that they sometimes formed flocks of more than a thousand. They are rarely seen today, but visitors may observe them in April at their leks, or mating territories. On patches of high, open ground, the males raise the long feathers and purple sacs on their necks, drop their wings and fan out their tails, leap and dance and stomp, boom and cackle, challenging other

ABOVE: *Artists from the Plains tribes probably incised the* **Spotted Woman,** *a petroglyph, into the stony walls of Picture Canyon sometime before* A.D. *500.*

LEFT: *Nests of cliff swallows are clustered in niches above a waterhole in Holt Canyon; the entrances point down to keep the rain from pouring in.*

males and mating with admiring hens. Observers, who may use their own cars as blinds or reserve a Forest Service blind, can obtain maps to well-known lesser prairie chicken leks through the Forest Service district office in Springfield.

Also within the Carrizo Unit is Picture Canyon, 35 miles southwest of Springfield on County Road 18. In this delightful oasis, colorful western tanagers and rufous-sided towhees flutter among leafy oaks and cotton-woods, and swallows build cities of nests under the cliffs. The canyon takes its name from the images drawn and carved on the canyon walls by early cultures. Pictographs, which are drawn or painted rather than carved images, include four-legged creatures daubed in red ocher and a graceful blue gray horse, which must have been put here after the Spanish introduced horses to the area in 1594. Among the petroglyphs is the figure of a woman elaborately decorated with linked circles. Archaeologists believe that people have been camping in Picture Canyon since at least the Late Archaic Period (circa A.D. 0–500). Farmers of the Apishapa culture began to live in villages on the canyon rim about A.D. 1000.

The dusty trail into Picture Canyon is now patterned with the tracks of beetles, lizards, and skunks. Frogs creak in their mucky pools below the boulders, while even at midday the moist earth and many wildflowers exude sweet fragrances. The buckwheat, gooseberries, and wild grapes that grow here were no doubt once gathered by the people of these pre-Columbian communities.

Several other canyons in the Comanche—notably Holt and Sand canyons—also contain rock formations, springs, and the amazing array of plant and animal life associated with water in an arid land. Interested visitors should contact the Forest Service in Springfield or La Junta for directions because these remote areas are not shown on state maps.

Travelers who discover such places on Colorado's Great Plains are likely to have them all to themselves. Peoplewise, the plains are a lonely place; most human development is along the eastern foothills of the Rocky Mountains. However, visitors soon begin to appreciate the presence of wild creatures on these rolling, windswept grasslands. Their sounds and movements become so familiar that returning to civilization can feel like leaving the real world behind.

RIGHT: *Something has to be last. This spire near Holt Canyon in the Comanche National Grassland stands alone, the remnant of a great layer of sediment shed onto the plains from the Rockies and then eroded away.*

NORTH-CENTRAL COLORADO:
RANGES AND PARKLANDS

Massive and magnificent, the Rocky Mountains rear up sharply on the western edge of the Great Plains, then rumple Colorado for 200 miles to the west in a series of mountain ranges alternating with high, flat parklands. Below the rugged, treeless summits of the ranges, the world spreads out in all directions, utterly dwarfed by these titans of stone and sky. Breezes, sharp with the fragrances of pine and elk, rustle ceaselessly through the nodding limbs of the trees. Brooks buzzing with mayflies trickle noisily over granite pebbles.

Colorado's ranges and parklands form a rugged barrier stretching south from the Wyoming border two-thirds the length of the state to Route 50. The state's central spine is a series of mountain ranges that include the Laramie, Mummy, Medicine Bow, Front, Park, Gore, Tenmile, Sawatch, and Elk. This landscape formed when the squeezing pressure of tectonic forces began to bend and break the worn-down roots of two earlier mountain ranges into narrow blocks, pushing some of the blocks as high as 25,000 feet. Layers of sediments atop the blocks simply draped over them in the process, creating a combination of broken and arched strata called a faulted anticline. Between the blocks that rose to become mountain ranges, other blocks dropped down and developed into broad, level meadowlands called parks.

LEFT: *Shaped by strong timberline winds into a "flag" or "banner" tree whose limbs are splayed to one side, this gnarled spruce overlooks the rugged Collegiate Peaks Wilderness Area near the Continental Divide.*

Spring in the Colorado Rockies is wet and windy. The fair, mild weather of late spring gives way by late June to warm days with sensational thunderstorms almost every afternoon for two or three months in a row. September and October tend to be sunny but cold at night, because the thin, dry air of these mountains does not retain heat well. Although most visitors come to Colorado during the long, warm days of summer, the Rocky Mountains are more typically a cold-weather place where deep winter lasts from October well into March. Because winter storms come from the west, the western mountains receive the heaviest snowfall; similarly, the western sides of most Colorado peaks get more snow than their eastern flanks. Rain and snow falling on the Rockies are a vital source of water for the cities of the Front Range: Fort Collins, Denver, and Colorado Springs.

Where strong sun falls on the shrubbery at lower elevations, desert plants such as sagebrush and Apache plume thrive among pinyons and junipers. The higher they grow in these mountains, the more plant communities are influenced by cold. Douglas firs are more common than ponderosas in the damp ranges of western and northwestern Colorado, shrouding the mountains above the pygmy forest. Dark, spiky Engelmann spruces and subalpine firs take over until the highest ridges, where there are blankets of tundra.

People have known Colorado's mountains for millennia. Ice Age hunters ventured into the Rockies for mammoths and *bison antiquus*. After the demise of these huge creatures, small bands of archaic people continued to hunt in the high summer pastures for *bison bison* (a smaller animal than *antiquus*), elk, deer, pronghorn, and bighorn sheep. To funnel game into kill sites, these ancient hunters built stone walls and blinds that have been dated to 6,000 years ago. Little is known about the human presence in these mountains until the period of contact between Europeans and Native Americans, which began peacefully when French and Anglo-American mountain men trapped beaver here in the early 1800s. The Cache la Poudre ("stash the powder") River takes its name from this era, when French trappers stowed their extra gunpowder on its banks.

The itinerary for this chapter follows a serpentine route, starting north and west of Rocky Mountain National Park in the Medicine Bow and Flat Tops mountains and then looping back to the park itself and Mount

OVERLEAF: *In Colorado's San Isabel National Forest, swaths of willows turn a burnished gold each fall. Here they flourish in the moist, wetland conditions around the beaver ponds on Cottonwood Creek near Holywater.*

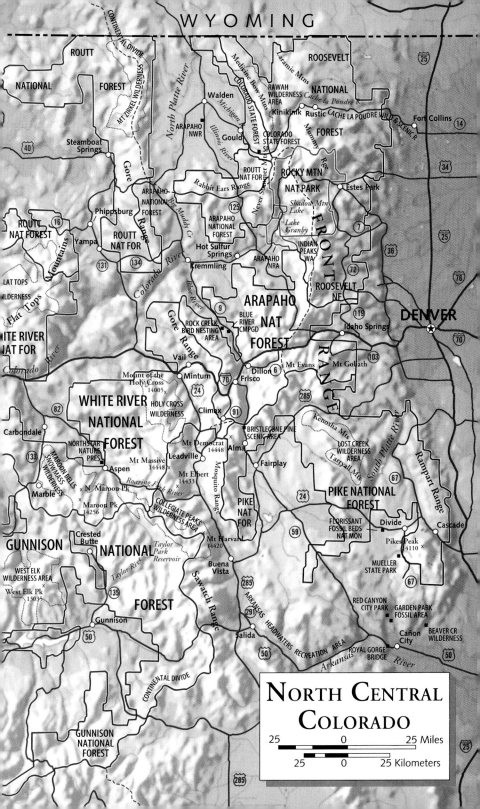

NORTH CENTRAL COLORADO

25   0   25 Miles

25   0   25 Kilometers

Evans, which together make up the Front Range. Next we explore the heart of Colorado's Rockies heading south to historic Leadville and west to Aspen and the Maroon Bells country. Continuing west, the route winds through mining country and the headwaters of the Arkansas River, culminating atop Pikes Peak.

NORTH OF ROCKY MOUNTAIN NATIONAL PARK

The Laramie, Mummy, and Front ranges form ramparts extending south from the Wyoming border to Colorado Springs. Although these ranges look impenetrable, deep canyons slicing through them provide passage-

ABOVE: *Small, social creatures closely related to chinchillas, pikas spend their summers providently, sun-drying flowers and grasses for winter food.*

RIGHT: *Pikas inhabit talus slopes where frost-shattered rock accumulates, such as the Nokhu Crags above Lake Agnes in the Colorado State Forest.*

ways to their heights and to the open parklands behind them. The river canyons also expose cross-sections of the faulted-anticline mountains with their cores of ancient schists and granites.

Travelers may see this geologic story along Route 14, the Cache la Poudre–North Park Scenic and Historic Byway, which climbs into the ranges northwest of Fort Collins, crosses 10,276-foot Cameron Pass between the Medicine Bow and Never Summer Mountains, and finishes in the parkland basin of North Park—the same route to summer game pastures that Stone Age hunters took for thousands of years.

The route follows the **Cache la Poudre Wild and Scenic River❖,** the only river in Colorado so designated. This status protects the river from dams, but the term *wild* is something of a technicality because in summer the Cache la Poudre is often crowded with rafters and anglers. In several campgrounds along its banks, "camp-robber birds" such as Clark's nutcrackers scold from the trees and rufous and broad-tailed hummingbirds hover around feeders hung from motor-home awnings. At the **Big Bend Campground** on Route 14 near Kinnikinnick, there is a wayside exhibit and bighorn sheep viewing area.

The Laramie Mountains are on the north side of Route 14 in the north-

ern part of **Roosevelt National Forest❖**, which like all public lands in Colorado contains dozens of day hikes and backpacking trails. The Green Ridge Trail is a 34-mile round-trip jeep and mountain-biking road running north on Forest Road 177 from Lost Lake, which is off County Road 103 east of **Cameron Pass**. It leads to a high mountain ridge between 9,400 and 10,200 feet, through meadows glorious with wildflowers in July—bistort, rose-colored paintbrush, and purple aster—and finally to stands of lodgepole pine providing sweeping views of the Medicine Bow Range to the west. The Green Ridge Trail meets Forest Road 162 leading east to the Red Feather Lakes, which are popular with anglers. (A more direct route to these lakes is up County Road 69 from Rustic.)

Terminal moraines (mounds of debris left behind by retreating glaciers) lie heaped around Cameron Pass, and just beyond the pass off Route 14 is another good place to look for bighorn sheep. A five-mile hike up the American Lakes–Crags Trail, in the **Crags Scenic Area** of the **Colorado State Forest State Park❖**, leads to a lovely alpine basin surrounded by sheer slopes where bighorns often graze. Another steep, half-mile trail leads from the same trailhead area along a shady brook to **Lake Agnes**. Shrubs bearing white elderberry blossoms and mertensia (mountain bluebells) grow in moist but sunny patches. The volcanic dike that impounds Lake Agnes forms spectacular pinnacles to the north and leads to a talus slope busy with bleating pikas, small-eared gray members of the rabbit family that are about the size of guinea pigs. Lake Agnes lies just below the ruggedly picturesque Nokhu Crags, which are the northern peaks of the Never Summer Mountains.

The main part of the Colorado State Forest State Park extends northwest, across the west side of the windswept Medicine Bow Mountains; the eastern flank of the Medicine Bows is within the **Rawah Wilderness Area** of the **Roosevelt National Forest❖**. These splendid peaks harbor many lakes and streams amid U-shaped, glacier-carved valleys. Wind and fire are important players in the drama of the Medicine Bows. Gnarled krummholz gnomes huddle against lashing gales from 11,000 to 11,500 feet in the stunted forest growth often found at timberline. Below this elderly elfin woodland, subalpine forests form spiky ruffs, and a ribbon of lodgepole pine "fire forest" bands the slopes lower still, growing where high-intensity fires or lack of moisture have virtually eliminated all other trees.

Around the town of Gould, the Cache la Poudre–North Park Scenic and Historic Byway emerges from the mountains into North Park, a flat, down-dropped basin about 35 miles wide and 45 miles long that is the northernmost of four such large, intermountain parklands in Colorado. Lying at about 8,000 feet between the Medicine Bow Mountains to the east, the Park Range to the west, and the Rabbit Ears Range to the south, the basin is a patchwork of private and public property.

One of the best places in the state to observe moose is northeast of Gould in the Colorado State Forest State Park. There is a moose-watching platform on County Road 41 off Route 14, along the willow-lined Michigan River. In the 1970s, land managers successfully introduced moose—which were naturally expanding their range south over North America—into this area. Today moose browse in the cool high-elevation wetlands, nibbling tender willow shoots. The lower meadows of the Colorado State Forest State Park are also good places to watch for elk early in the morning or at dusk. Moose and elk are closely related members of the deer family, but moose are distinguished by huge flat antlers and long, horselike heads with droopy lips. Standing up to seven feet tall and weighing as much as 1,400 pounds, moose are the larger of the two. Elk, also known as wapiti, look more like huge reddish mule deer with short pointed muzzles. They bugle in the fall rutting season, uttering shrill screams that sound like whinnying horses.

Route 14, the scenic byway, continues to angle across North Park along the verdant bottomland of the Michigan River. Where there are no streams in this basin, the land is very dry and covered only in grasses and sagebrush. Although North Park receives little rain during its short, warm summer, streams from the surrounding mountains meander across it to form the headwaters of the North Platte River, which flows north into Wyoming. These streams make the basin a surprisingly rich habitat for birds and an important stop for migrating waterfowl, but the wildlife areas in North Park, artificial impoundments managed by the state of Colorado for hunting and fishing, are not particularly attractive.

The U.S. Fish and Wildlife Service, however, has developed scenic wetlands in the **Arapaho National Wildlife Refuge❖** along the Illinois River to serve as feeding and nesting area for ducks and Canada geese. More than 5,000 ducks may appear in late May in this refuge, which is south of Walden on Route 125. Early morning and late afternoon are the best times for viewing American avocets, black-crowned night herons, eared and pied-billed grebes, willets, soras, Forster's terns, gulls, and coots. As in other wetlands in Colorado, white-tailed prairie dogs and big Richardson's ground squirrels live here, sharing their towns with burrowing owls that stare solemnly from the mounds around the rodents' dens.

Sage grouse—among the most entertaining birds in North America—live in the upland hills of North Park year-round. Between late March and early May, they gather at dawn on courtship grounds called leks, where the males puff up their throat sacs and strut, making noises like a coffee percolator, to impress female grouse. Of the several leks in North Park, one of the easiest to find is the **Coalmont Lek❖** on County Road 26 southwest of Walden via Route 14.

The Park Range forms the western wall of North Park. Until about 11,000 years ago, glaciers lay heavily on the range, and it still bears the imprints of the Ice Age: cirques (deep, bowl-shaped recesses), arêtes (saw-toothed ridges between adjoining cirques), and U-shaped valleys. The Park remains a snowy range; winter storms from the Pacific Northwest encounter it before other mountains of the Rockies, and its western slope receives much more precipitation than its eastern, lee side.

To cross the Continental Divide atop the Park Range, take County Road 24 west from Route 14 to Forest Road 620, then drive west on Forest Road 60 over 10,180-foot **Buffalo Pass.** Because it receives an annual average of 25 feet of snow, the pass is open only during the summer. The road climbs out of the arid rangeland of North Park through meadows abloom with false hellebore (also known as skunk cabbage) and aspen-cloaked mountainsides, to a campground in a subalpine forest brightened with lupine and raspberry-colored paintbrush. Tiny downy woodpeckers whinny and tap on the trees, and white-crowned sparrows whistle almost constantly. Violets, columbine, and yellow fawn lilies border open patches in the woods; delicate meadow rue sways in sheltered places.

Mount Zirkel Wilderness Area crowns the gently rolling, glacier-flattened crest of the Park Range, where the Continental Divide Trail passes through a blend of subalpine forest and alpine tundra amid outcroppings of pink granite, lumps of white quartz as big as elephants, and blocks of banded gneiss. Sedges grow in soggy places together with marsh marigolds, bog orchids, and king's crown sedum. Grassy meadows sprinkled with alpine avens and candytuft contain patches of "pink snow," where communities of algae, fungi, bacteria, and protozoa grow in the summer. (A pigment in the protective coats of the algae tints the snow pink at the highest elevations and orange or green lower down.)

LEFT: *Along the moist western slopes of the Park Range, thimbleberry carpets an aspen grove in the Routt National Forest. Its raspberrylike fruit is savored by both resident wildlife and itinerant humans.*

Dotted here and there are "tree islands"—gnarled spruces bunched together with rings of gooseberries and little spruce around their feet. Tree islands are refuges. The tightly bunched conifers shelter and support each other in the wind, and their dark trunks absorb heat, moderating the temperature and increasing the humidity within the island as they melt the snow around them. Delicate rust-colored mushrooms pop up in their shade, and their dense thickets and supply of seed-bearing cones make them important shelters for birds and other animals. In summer's warmth, the silvery gray bark of the spruce is as fragrant as incense.

ABOVE: *Although they range widely throughout sagebrush country, sage grouse are dowdy and secretive. They compensate for this low profile with showy courtship rites each spring.*
RIGHT: *Called the Cradle of the Wilderness, Trappers Lake lies in the White River National Forest's Flat Tops Wilderness Area; in 1919 it became the first federal land so designated.*

Travelers who prefer not to drive their vehicles on the dirt road over Buffalo Pass can take Rabbit Ears Pass by heading southwest from Walden on Route 14, then west on Route 40. The Rabbit Ears are the remains of a volcanic plug, formed where magma—molten rock—erupts through a passage to the earth's surface. After the eruption ceases, the magma hardens. Erosion then removes the soft material surrounding the hardened rock and exposes it. In this case, the volcanic remnants stick up like a pair of rabbit ears, forming the western end of the Rabbit Ears Range, a wall of rocks across the southern end of North Park.

The town of Steamboat Springs is on Route 40 on the other side of Buffalo Pass at the western foot of the Park Range. Now a year-round recreation center, this ranching town is named for once-noisy hot springs that emerge from deeply buried hot rocks via faults in the Dakota sandstone. The springs' waters contain minerals, including aromatic sulfur, believed to be therapeutic. Indeed, a soak in any of the more than 150

hot springs in the Steamboat area is a treat after a long hike up to the Continental Divide from Fish Creek Falls (see below), after a mountain-bike ride on the Continental Divide Trail from Rabbit Ears to Buffalo Pass, or after downhill or cross-country skiing around the Steamboat Springs ski village (three miles south of town).

Four miles east of Steamboat Springs on the Fish Creek Falls Road (Forest Road 320), **Fish Creek Falls** plunges almost 300 feet over rocky ledges, spraying cool mountain water on summer visitors strolling paths lined with wildflowers such as fireweed and Jacob's ladder and with fragrant ceanothus bushes. Chipmunks with striped faces scamper through the low woodland of Gambel oak as they compete with similar-looking ground squirrels (minus the facial stripes) for treats from passersby. Mourning cloak butterflies—chocolate with creamy edges and blue spots—flutter among the willows along Fish Creek.

Black-billed magpies swoop between the fence posts surrounding rangeland here. These splendid, metallic-black and white birds measure 20 inches from their ebony beaks to the tips of tails that are more than half the length of their bodies. Loud, raucous, and seemingly fearless, they astonished the intrepid explorer Meriwether Lewis when they raided the plate right under his nose. Because they are scavengers that will eat almost anything, including carrion, magpies play an important role in any ecosystem.

South of Steamboat Springs via Route 131, the Flat Tops Scenic and Historic Byway, or Route 16, begins in the town of Phippsburg and winds west on the northern perimeter of the **Flat Tops Wilderness Area**❖ in the **Routt National Forest**❖. The Flat Tops Mountains are domes pushed up by the collision of tectonic plates that formed the other Rockies, but this range is flat because volcanoes in the region buried its peaks in sheets of lava. Later, glaciers scooped wide amphitheaters into their blocky headlands.

In the open topography of this range, it is easy to spot soaring raptors such as red-tailed hawks and the ospreys that fish in its many lakes. Ospreys—flamboyant two-foot-long hawks—hover 50 to 100 feet above the lakes, suddenly plunge feet-first to yank fish out of the water, and then strenuously flap away, carrying their struggling prey into the trees.

Below the high, tundra-clad tops of the mountains, aspen groves color the slopes a delicate green in spring, brilliant yellow and orange in the fall. Aspen roots survive for centuries, even when the trees have been shaded out by pines and firs. When the conifers are removed by fire or logging, the aspens sprout again from their extensive root network. The spectacular aspen groves of the Flat Tops, the result of huge fires that burned here in the 1800s, are a good example of this process.

Forest Road 205, a spur heading south of the scenic byway, leads to the Flat Tops Wilderness Area and to **Trappers Lake,** where a trail follows the shore through grassy slopes and sharp-scented spruce noisy with scolding chickadees and the occasional horselike bugling of bull elk in the fall.

After retracing the scenic byway, follow Route 134 southeast of Yampa, crossing the Gore Range via 9,527-foot Gore Pass. Near the town of Kremmling (south on Route 40), Big Muddy Creek joins the Colorado River in the basin of Middle Park, a small, similar cousin of North Park. In this semidesert scrubland, low sagebrush hills rise above lush, green riverbanks. The town of Hot Sulphur Springs marks where water heated far below and mineralized with eggy-smelling sulfur reaches the surface along faults. Hogbacks of Dakota sandstone—the eroded edges of hard rock layers that have been turned up by bulges of the earth's crust—further illustrate the tectonic forces at work in this area.

THE FRONT RANGE AND ROCKY MOUNTAIN NATIONAL PARK

The Dakota sandstone hogbacks in Middle Park mark the edge of the **Front Range,** the largest faulted anticline in Colorado. (Technically, the Front Range extends from Wyoming to Colorado Springs and includes the Mummy and Rampart ranges and the Tarryall and Kenosha mountains, in addition to the mountains above Denver that most people call the Front Range.) When the Laramide orogeny (mountain building) began about 65 million years ago, this long slice of 1.75-billion-year-old rock rose 15,000 or 25,000 feet, bending up the layers of rock above it—such as the Dakota sandstone—at extreme angles. Sedimentary layers even bent over backward in places where the ancient core rocks, relieved of the pressure of the depths where they formed, expanded along thrust faults. The area around Kremmling is heavily faulted, and in some cases older rocks overlie younger ones.

Nestled at the foot of the Front Range, the **Arapaho National Recreation Area❖** is northeast of Middle Park off Route 34. This busy place encompasses several reservoirs on the Colorado River—the largest are Lake Granby and Shadow Mountain Lake—popular with sail- and powerboaters. Arapaho also includes 14,000 acres of forested slopes, where trailheads lead into the **Indian Peaks Wilderness Area❖.**

Route 34 (Trail Ridge Road) leads from the Grand Lake entrance into **Rocky Mountain National Park❖,** the splendid crown of the Front Range. Encompassing 265,727 acres of tundra, coniferous forest, and subalpine wildflower meadows as well as streams, more than 150 lakes, 900 species of plants, and a wide variety of wildlife, the park is probably the best place to develop an overall understanding of and affection for the Rockies. Trail Ridge Road (Route 34 within the park) leads through the delicate tundra that covers nearly a third of the national park. Several pull-outs along this 50 miles of paved road allow contemplation of grand mountain vistas as well as intimate views of tiny tundra plants. Because the tundra is fragile, walkers should be careful to stay on designated trails.

The Continental Divide snakes 40 miles through Rocky Mountain National Park from La Poudre Pass in the north to 13,138-foot Ogalalla Peak in the south, separating the waters flowing east that eventually reach the Gulf of Mexico from those flowing west. One of the most important rivers

In poor habitats, rose paintbrush (above) draws nutrients from the roots of other plants; wild lupines (below) actually enrich the soil with nitrogen.

RIGHT: *In Rocky Mountain National Park, the lofty Front Range towers over meadows of yellow gaillardia and purple locoweed.*

in the western United States, the Colorado, rises in the Never Summer Range on the west side of the park to flow 1,450 miles to reach the Gulf of California. Within the park the Colorado is a modest stream, easy to reach from several pullouts along Route 34, the main road north from the Kawuneeche Visitor Center near Grand Lake. For a better view hikers can also climb the Colorado River Trail for 7.3 miles from its marked trailhead (10 miles north of Grand Lake on Route 34) to the source of the river in the marshy Kawuneeche Valley. Otters and moose (reintroduced to the park in 1978) as well as burgeoning herds of elk and deer may be spotted along the river's willow-lined banks.

The park's headquarters and eastern entrances, near the town of Estes Park, are only a two-hour drive from Denver via Route 36, making Rocky Mountain a popular place for hikers, campers, and anglers in summer and for cross-country skiers and snowshoers in winter. A hiker's paradise, the park contains 355 miles of trails ranging from short and level to rugged, several-day treks into breathtaking wilderness. Self-guided interpretative trails begin at Bear Lake (half a mile around an alpine lake), Never Summer Ranch (one mile round-trip to a 1920s dude ranch), Moraine Park (an easy quarter-mile nature walk), Sprague Lake (a half-mile level route), and Coyote Valley (one mile). The Bear Lake, Sprague Lake, and Coyote Valley trails are accessible to wheelchairs. In addition, short trails lead from scenic overlooks along Trail Ridge Road (Route 34).

Above the twisted ruff of stunted krummholz (from the German for "twisted wood") trees at timberline, rare alpine vegetation

ABOVE: *Stony outcroppings create important microhabitats high in Rocky Mountain National Park. Here mats of specially adapted flowers hug the sunny side of lichen-covered rocks along the Tundra Nature Trail.*

cloaks the mountains. Preserving this extensive tundra—a Lapp word for the treeless reaches of the Arctic—was one of the main reasons for creating this park in 1915. In the area above timberline, plants are small and hug the ground, often forming cushion-shaped mats to survive in cold, dry, and ferociously windy conditions. Such plants take decades to develop and are very delicate, yet alpine tundra in summer bloom (late June) is surprisingly rich and vivid: blue alpine phlox, pink moss campion, and yellow snow buttercups huddle among more subtly colored lichens and mosses. Although the ground at this elevation absorbs heat from the intense sunshine (there is twice as much ultraviolet radiation here as at sea level), the wind whips the warmth away only a few inches above the tundra.

Although not always conspicuous, certain wildlife is well suited to this environment. Clucking like chickens, white-tailed ptarmigan eat the dwarf willows of the tundra, while flocks of brown-capped rosy finches poke about on the ground for seeds and insects. Horned larks and water pipits in-

ABOVE: *Each summer herds of elk move from sheltered woodlands up to the 12,000-foot-high alpine pastures along Trail Ridge Road in Rocky Mountain National Park. Above the tree line, snowbanks persist all year.*

vestigate soggy places and snowbanks for the bugs they harbor. Deer, mountain goats, a protected population of mountain bighorn sheep, and herds of magnificent elk graze the tundra, and northern pocket gophers till its soil. Pikas scurry about the rock piles, while fat yellow-bellied marmots bask in the alpine sun.

During the summer, rangers at various visitor centers offer diverse programs emphasizing the park's major themes: glacial geology, the effect of elevation on communities of plants and wildlife (especially the tundra), and the importance of biodiversity.

After leaving Rocky Mountain National Park, follow the Peak to Peak Scenic and Historic Byway (Route 7 south and then Route 72 south of Ferncliff). County Road 102 (Brainard Lake Drive) leads west from Route 72, just north of the hamlet of Ward, into the 73,391-acre **Indian Peaks Wilderness Area❖,** which overlaps the southern boundary of Rocky Mountain National Park and the northern boundary of the Roosevelt

National Forest. Between June 1 and September 15, permits are required to camp here because Indian Peaks is Colorado's most popular wilderness area. At elevations ranging from 8,400 to 13,500 feet, miles of delightful trails wind through forests and meadows, along brooks, and through tundra. The area is named for the 13,000-foot mountains within it that bear the names of Native American tribes: Navajo, Pawnee, and Paiute peaks.

The Pawnee Pass Trail starts at Long Lake and climbs through an evergreen forest to exquisite Lake Isabelle, which is cradled among alpine crags and glaciers. The trail passes from sunny meadows blooming with hot pink elephantella in midsummer into stands of spruce, where delicate wood nymphs nod demurely next to thickets of pale-leaved bilberry. Extravagant bouquets of magenta Parry's primroses crowd brooks that rush down mountainsides and froth through mountain bluebells and bittercress while cabbage white butterflies flutter about in shafts of sunlight. Through the dense, shadowy forest, high-rumped snowshoe hares in their chocolate-colored summer coats lope on huge white feet. Like tiny brown cones, oval growths on spruce twigs show where gall aphids have injected chemicals with their eggs, stimulating the growth of the tree's tissue to provide a protective, edible housing for their larvae. Yellow-, rose-, and salmon-colored paintbrush splash the meadows around the lakes.

Long Lake Fen is a soggy meadow on the southeast side of Long Lake. From seeping through limestone, the water here is very alkaline. Horsetails and flat-leaved willows rim the fen, which is dotted with hummocks of sphagnum moss and rare sedges and rushes. Bluish hair grass is common, and cotton grass (actually a sedge), with its tufts of white fibers, grows here as well. Sedges store carbohydrates in their rhizomes, cylindrical stems that grow horizontally underground and send up new shoots.

To visit **Mount Evans,** take routes 72 and 119 south, then I-70 west to Idaho Springs and Route 103, the Mount Evans Scenic and Historic Byway. This unpaved byway—closed in winter—climbs 6,724 feet in 28 miles to the summit of 14,264-foot Mount Evans. From here, travelers can see from 14,255-foot Longs Peak, 50 miles north of Mount Evans, to 14,110-foot Pikes Peak, about 60 miles to the southeast. En route to the top are many places to stop and enjoy the view or to hike into the Mount Evans Wilderness Area, which contains all of the mountain except for the

LEFT: *Bull elk shed their antlers each winter and grow a new set by late summer to defend harems of up to 60 cows during the fall rutting season. During the rest of the year bulls live apart from cows and calves.*

road. Two designated scenic areas—Abyss Lake and Mount Goliath—invite invigorating strolls, and a short walk from the Mount Goliath turnout is the northernmost stand of bristlecone pines in Colorado.

Mount Evans is a batholith—formed about 1.7 billion years ago as an intrusion of magma into rocks lying very deep below the earth's surface—that has been faulted, uplifted, and eroded down twice. Its magma cooled very slowly, hardening into a granite containing large crystals of black mica, clear quartz, and pink and white feldspar. Lifted above the high-pressure depths where it formed, this granite expanded, and tectonic stresses cracked it in many places. Weathering has caused the mica exposed along these cracks to swell and pop off surrounding minerals so that big pink spherical boulders develop.

Mount Evans is a good place to observe the various plant communities that develop at different elevations. At the foot of the mountain, ponderosa pines and Douglas firs predominate, but at about 10,000 feet, the nature of the forest changes to a mix of Engelmann spruce, lodgepole pine, aspen, and bristlecone pine (depending upon exposure) frequented by pine martens, weasels, and elk. Mount Evans supports the only arctic tundra—as opposed to alpine tundra—in Colorado. Arctic tundra is very wet, marked by many water puddles.

THE MOSQUITO AND SAWATCH RANGES

West of Idaho Springs on I-70, take Exit 216 for a chance to go over, not under, the Continental Divide. Detouring around the interstate's Eisenhower Tunnel, Route 6 climbs the scenic **Loveland Pass** where krummholz clings to steep mountain slopes below bare, glaciated peaks. Travelers can pause at the 11,992-foot summit of the pass for solitary walks on the continent's windy rooftop, where the only sound is the sighing of the wind and the squeaking of pikas. Old man of the mountain, an alpine sunflower with exceptionally large blossoms for a tundra plant, blooms here in profusion among patches of dwarf willow.

Route 6 to the town of Dillon continues southwest. From here birders may enjoy driving north on Route 9 for eight miles to the **Blue River Campground❖,** there turning southwest for 2.5 miles to the trailhead for the **Alfred M. Bailey Bird Nesting Area❖,** a 1.5-mile hike. Though a small area, it supports 80 different bird species in habitats ranging from riparian, meadow, and cliff to aspen, lodgepole pine, and subalpine forest.

South on Route 9 from Dillon leads to an easy hike in the Pike National Forest among the "fourteeners" of the Mosquito Range and a stand of an-

ABOVE: *Growing only above 7,000 feet, stiff-needled bristlecone pines prefer coarse, rocky soil exposed to wind and sun, conditions perfectly met in the Bristlecone Pine Scenic Area in Pike National Forest.*

cient bristlecone pines. The road follows the Blue River (impounded in Dillon Reservoir) below the eastern walls of the Tenmile Range, crosses 11,541-foot Hoosier Pass, and then continues along the South Platte River below the Mosquito Range. From the hamlet of Alma, Park County Road 8 heads west up Buckskin Gulch to the Kite Lake Campground at 12,000 feet, where a trail leads over tundra and scree to **Lake Emma** and to the summit of 14,148-foot Mount Democrat. On the way to Kite Lake is a signed road to the **Bristlecone Pine Scenic Area❖.** A mostly level mile-long trail goes to Windy Ridge, where gnarled 800-year-old trees persevere despite sun, wind, and freezing winters.

The Mosquito Range is draped with sedimentary layers that are neatly cross-sectioned at Horseshoe Mountain Cirque, west of Fairplay. These mountains and the Blue and South Platte rivers were heavily mined with pickax, pan, and sluice. Since the 1860s, Fairplay has boomed now and then as a gold mining town.

South Park, a down-dropped block southeast of Fairplay, is filled with

65

sediments from the Mosquito Mountains to the west and the Front Range to the east. It supports a grassland about 30 miles wide by 40 miles long, a good summer range for elk and other grazing animals and, until the nineteenth century, a favorite hunting ground of the Ute people. The Tarryall Mountains are on its northeast side; here hiking trails lead into the **Lost Creek Wilderness Area**❖ from county roads north of Route 24.

ABOVE: *Each spring white-tailed ptarmigan molt from their pure white winter plumage to mottled brown breeding plumage. They frequent the rocky tundra above the tree line in summer, feasting on tasty tidbits of dwarf willow.*

RIGHT: *In Pike National Forest, sunrise brightens the crest of a cirque above Lake Emma, a glacial tarn ringed by "fourteeners" near the Continental Divide in the Mosquito Range.*

This region's mining history is abundantly evident around Leadville. From Alma Junction, just south of Alma, those with four-wheel drive can reach Leadville via the very rugged Park County Road 12 over 13,186-foot Mosquito Pass. Other visitors can resume the itinerary at Frisco, south of Dillon, by turning southwest on I-70 to Exit 195 and taking Route 91 south. On the way to Leadville, Route 91 passes the world's largest molybdenum mine at Climax. Interested travelers may tour this mine, where half of the world's molybdenum is extracted. For those just passing through, exhibits in the parking lot explain the geology of the ore body.

The town of Leadville got its start when prospectors working their way up the Arkansas River in the winter of 1859–60 found "color"—gold—in the gravels of the river near the village of Granite. Their discovery brought more prospectors, who panned up the Arkansas and its tributaries with little to show for their efforts. Legend has it that they were ready to give up when a fellow from Georgia named Abraham Lee dug down in the snow to dip water from a little creek to boil for coffee. With a whoop, Lee yelled, "Boys, I've got all California in this here pan!" He located a rich concentration of gold nearby and staked his claim. By the middle of the next summer, 8,000 to 10,000 hopeful prospectors were camped along the stream, panning for gold, and the town that would become

Leadville was established to serve them.

In all but a handful of places, a 100-mile-long mountain barricade blocks travel between the valley of the Arkansas River and points west. The Sawatch Range, the highest in Colorado, embraces 15 peaks higher than 14,000 feet, including the three highest mountains in the state: 14,433-foot Mount Elbert, 14,421-foot Mount Massive, and 14,420-foot Mount Harvard. The Sawatch is so high that permafrost—permanently frozen subsoil—has persisted here to depths of 100 feet since the last Ice Age.

With heavy summer rains, hail, sleet, and lots of snow, the Sawatch Range is a soggy crest of mountains year-round. Not surprisingly, the area is good for skiing, as attested by world-famous resorts in Aspen and nearby Vail. From Route 24 south of Leadville, Route 82 crosses the Sawatch Range over **Independence Pass,** at 12,095 feet the highest crossing of the Continental Divide (closed in winter). There are sweeping vistas from the pullout at the top of the pass, and a short footpath through tundra is musical with the songs of white-crowned sparrows. Timberline, the upper limit of the subalpine forest, is very obvious on the surrounding mountains.

Independence Pass divides the **Collegiate Peaks Wilderness Area**❖ of the **Gunnison**❖, **San Isabel**❖, and **White River**❖ national forests on the south from the Hunter-Fryingpan Wilderness Area of the White River National Forest to the north. About a mile west of Independence Pass, a trail leads north to Independence Lake—the source of the Roaring Fork River—from a parking area on the north side of Route 82. The trail passes four alpine lakes surrounded by boggy land where marsh marigolds—a favorite food of elk—bloom all summer.

West of this trailhead, Route 82 dives down the canyon of the Roaring Fork River. En route to the town of Aspen, the **Roaring Fork Braille Trail**❖ on the south side of the road follows a guide line with 22 interpretative signs (in Braille and in print) along a quarter-mile loop trail through spruce-fir forest. Built in 1967, this trail was the first of its kind in the world and has served as the model for more than 60 such trails in the United States alone.

The Roaring Fork River flows through the Grottos, a sinuous slot canyon of water-polished granite about eight miles east of Aspen. Although the river's course has changed, pools still form in the old river bottom. The canyon's smooth stone walls seem almost flexible, a testament to the power of time and flowing water. From the roadside pullout marked for the Grottos, a short trail leads along the river to smooth boulders where visitors relax in the sun to the sounds of the river and forest.

On the east end of the valley just outside Aspen, a glacial moraine once dammed the Roaring Fork. The **Northstar Nature Preserve❖** protects the meadow that formed as the resulting pond filled with sediments. It is a good spot to watch for hawks and red foxes, which prey on the meadow voles in this grassy clearing.

Aspen is in a glacial valley surrounded by magnificent peaks. City parklands border the Roaring Fork River, which passes right through town. In the 25-acre **Hallam Lake Nature Preserve** on the edge of Aspen, the **Aspen Center for Environmental Studies❖** is an excellent place to get a close look at live birds of prey undergoing rehabilitation from injuries. Naturalists handle screech owls and golden eagles, trumpeter swans nest on Hallam Lake, and staff programs and exhibits teach visitors about local ecology. Visitors should call ahead for hours and schedules.

The town is named for the many tall slender trees with white bark and triangular leaves that bedeck the slopes around it. Aspens, members of the *Populus* family (the same as cottonwoods), resemble but are not closely related to birches, which are in the *Betula* family. Aspen leaves are attached to their twigs with flat, floppy petioles, or leaf stems, that allow them to flutter in the slightest breeze and led to one species' Latin name, *Populus tremuloides*, or quaking aspen. They often reproduce by sending saplings up from their roots, so that genetically speaking, a grove of aspens may be considered one individual. In fall, when aspens change to fiery reds and yellows, family patches take on the same hue, creating a brilliant patchwork among the surrounding dark green conifers.

South of Aspen, the beautiful but forbidding Maroon Bells rise up within the **Maroon Bells–Snowmass Wilderness Area❖** in **White River National Forest❖.** Towering above Maroon Lake at the end of a U-shaped valley surrounded by other mountains are the enormous pyramid peaks of 14,156-foot Maroon and 14,014-foot North Maroon, their tilted quartzite layers tinged the color of dried blood by iron oxides. Climbing accidents have given these mountains the nickname Deadly Bells. In this classic glacier country, with its spectacular sheared-off peaks and hanging valleys, snow accumulates to great depths and then thunders down the steep sides of the mountains leaving avalanche chutes, wide swaths denuded of trees.

The more than 100 miles of trails that wind throughout the Maroon Bells–Snowmass Wilderness Area may be reached from several points around it (details are available at the ranger office on Hallam Street in Aspen). In summer, visitors must take a shuttle bus to the popular trails around Maroon Lake from the parking lot at the start of Maroon Creek Road off Route 82 just west of Aspen. The lake's appeal is particularly evi-

dent in summer, when the surrounding meadows are ablaze with pink wild roses, white thimbleberries, and purple monkshood. Weasels undulate like russet ribbons through the thick green grass and cow parsnip, and the scent of Colorado dogwood, intoxicatingly sweet, wafts down from aspen groves on the slopes above. Black-chinned hummingbirds visit red and yellow paintbrush, and yellow warblers flit among the trees. Muddy "slides" show where beavers have gnawed down aspens and dragged them to their lodges in the lake.

The main trail leads past Maroon Lake through woods and piles of rocky talus to Crater Lake, in the wilderness area. Because so many visitors take this beautiful walk, some of the animals are almost tame. (Offering them a potato chip, although tempting, is a terrible idea—human foods are the worst possible fare for a wild animal, and feeding them makes them sick, dependent, and aggressive.) With great nonchalance, yellow-bellied marmots play and sun in the wilderness area. Sometimes called whistle pigs, these furry, cat-sized rodents chirp to one another when they sense a threat. Marmots live in harems of several females with a single male, spending eight months of the year in their burrows. All summer they gorge on green plants and rest, accumulating fat to see them through their long winter hibernations. Pikas, on the other hand, do not hibernate. They are busy haying all summer, gathering grasses and flowers that they scatter on rocks to dry for winter food. These little lagomorphs (members of the rabbit family) have round ears and almost no tail. Prey for weasels, coyotes, and hawks, they squeak or bleat to warn one another of danger.

During the winter, when this landscape is cloaked in deep snow, cross-country skiers can experience the winter wilderness on a trail system established in the mountainous triangle between Vail in the north, Aspen to the west, and Leadville to the east. This high country lies within the **Holy Cross Wilderness Area❖,** second in popularity only to the Indian Peaks. The wilderness area is named for an unusual feature on the northwest face of a dark, pointed 14,005-foot granite peak called the Mount of the Holy Cross, where crevices intersect to form a 1,500-foot-high cross. Snow stays in these crevices well into summer, emphasizing the visual effect. Hikers making the popular but arduous 12-mile round-trip to view the cross should stay on the

---

LEFT: *Ferdinand Hayden, leader of the 1871 geological survey of the Rockies, named these mountains "Maroon Bells" for their shape and color.*

OVERLEAF: *Fast-growing aspens colonize slopes denuded by avalanche or fire, as here near Maroon Lake in the White River National Forest.*

trail and be especially mindful of the principles of low-impact hiking. To reach the trailhead, take Route 24 south from I-70 for 2.8 miles and turn west on Forest Road 707 just past Minturn. Start hiking from the Half Moon Pass Trailhead, 8.5 miles up the road near the Half Moon Campground.

From Carbondale (northwest of Aspen via Route 82), the West Elk Loop Scenic and Historic Byway—Route 133—runs south. Shortly before McClure Pass, Forest Road 314 leads east through a deep valley with almost vertical aspen-covered walls to the little town of Marble. From the end of the road, a footpath follows flower-lined Yule Creek to gaping quarries in the mountainside, where stonecutters hacked out the high-quality marble used in the Lincoln Memorial and the Tomb of the Unknown Soldier. In an astonishing metamorphosis, Leadville limestone, squeezed and heated by igneous material welling up beneath it, has been transformed from muddy gray to brilliant sugary-white marble.

Following Route 133 to the west and Route 135 to the east, the West Elk Scenic and Historic Byway encircles the West Elk Mountains of **Gunnison National Forest❖.** The mountains lie within a rugged area about 30 miles in diameter, mostly within the roadless **West Elk Wilderness Area❖,** which includes 13,035-foot **West Elk Peak.** In the northern part of the range, basaltic pinnacles remain where lava once erupted through conduits and flowed into radiating cracks in the surrounding sediments, forming basaltic dikes. Coarse layers of volcanic ash, boulders, and lava blanket the southern sides of the range.

Although parts of the West Elks are almost brutal hiking terrain, throughout the summer these cool mountains receive scattered showers that sustain lovely streams and wetlands. Ponds sparkle in the sun, full of mosses, algae, larvae, and insects such as water striders and water boatmen. Mosquitoes buzz around the water, and ladybugs bumble over the spreading white blooms of nearby mountain parsley. Dainty fairy slippers grow in boggy areas, yellow potentilla and bright fireweed in the meadows, and chickweed and rose crown sedum among the rocks. Vibrating the air, tiny hummingbirds probe scarlet gilia and paintbrush for nectar, while pocket gophers leave mounds of tilled earth, later imprinted with the hooves of deer, elk, and bighorn sheep.

To the east (take County Road 12 east below Paonia Reservoir), the byway follows Route 135 through spruce forests to cross 9,980-foot **Kebler Pass,** a favorite area for viewing the bright fall colors of red and orange oaks and golden patches of aspen among the evergreens. This road leads into the high valley resort of Crested Butte, where mountain-biking is pop-

ABOVE: *Extravagant displays of fluffy white mountain parsley, yellow composite flowers, and purple Jacob's ladder brighten the moist summer meadows below East Beckwith Mountain in Gunnison National Forest.*

ular in summer, skiing in winter. In this part of Colorado, sagebrush-bunchgrass persists up to 8,000 feet, purple lupine lines the roadsides, and wild strawberries grow in the shade along with maidenhair ferns.

In snowy or inclement weather, continue south on Route 135 to the town of Gunnison and turn east on Route 50 to cross the Sawatch Range over 11,312-foot Monarch Pass, which is open year-round. In summer, continue south of Crested Butte on Route 135 only as far as the hamlet of Almont, then turn northeast up Forest Road 742 toward **Taylor Park** and **Taylor Park Reservoir❖.** This pleasant, shady drive leads up the valley of the Taylor River among the forested foothills of the Sawatch Range, where families come to fish in small streams and lakes, to camp, and to stay in simple, old-fashioned resorts. From campgrounds and lodges, easy trails wind along brooks and through the woods.

Moist, cool places at high elevations are sometimes habitats for rarely seen amphibians such as tiger salamanders, boreal toads, and northern leopard frogs. The boreal toads have a pale stripe down their back, walk rather than hop, and make a soft chirping sound, and the northern leopard frogs are sleek, dark-spotted creatures that grumble, purr, and squawk in cacophonous chorus. Unprotected by fur, fangs, or feathers, such amphibians are a very vulnerable form of life. Although many of them lay thousands of eggs at a time, their delicate eggs require a watery habitat. Because streams and ponds are being tapped, diverted, and contaminated at a rapid rate all over the world, the populations of various amphibians are in decline globally, in many cases disastrously. Recent studies implicate several culprits, among them water pollution and acidification, habitat destruction, and predation by introduced species of snakes and fish. One of the most alarming studies documents a connection between increased exposure to ultraviolet-B radiation (due to thinning of the atmosphere's ozone layer) and massive die-offs of toad and frog eggs.

On the east side of Taylor Park Reservoir, Cottonwood Pass Road (Forest Road 209) leads to a particularly scenic crossing of the Sawatch Range. From Taylor Park to the summit of the pass, the road is not paved but is suitable for passenger cars; east of the pass, the road is paved (closed in winter). Cottonwood Pass Road leads past several trailheads into the **Collegiate Peaks Wilderness Area❖,** a formidably rugged hiking prospect; visitors should check with the Forest Service office in Gunnison for locations and advisories. From 12,126-foot **Cottonwood Pass,** hiking and cross-country ski trails run both north and south to intersect the Colorado Trail. At the summit of the pass, a tundra pond surrounded by dwarf willows is a good place to watch and listen for ptarmigan. On the east side of the pass, beavers have built dams in many places along Cottonwood Creek. More than any other creature except human beings, beavers alter the world around them. They eat leaves and twigs and cut down trees, exposing the ground to sunlight, which stimulates the growth of a thicket of other plants, which in turn provide cover and food for more animals.

SALIDA TO PIKES PEAK

From the town of Buena Vista, Routes 285 and 291 follow the Arkansas River south to Salida; Route 50 then traces the river as it flows east. The Arkansas—the most popular river in Colorado for recreation, particularly rafting, kayaking, and fishing—offers hot springs and good bird-watching opportunities. The **Arkansas Headwaters Recreation Area❖** includes 148 miles of the river and its banks from just south of Leadville to the **Pueblo Reservoir❖.**

Looming up for miles on either side of the Arkansas River in Royal Gorge are dark, swirling metamorphic rocks called schists and gneisses, shot through with pink granite intrusions. These rocks are the ancient, gnarled roots of the mountain range that dominated this region 1.7 billion years ago, which geologists say rivaled the Himalayas. From Route 50 eight miles west of Canon City, a winding road leads to the private **Royal Gorge Bridge**❖ (fee charged) over the deepest part of the chasm, where the river is 1,053 feet below the rim. Sightseers can take an incline railway that is said to be the steepest in the world to the bottom or an aerial tram across.

From Canon City, the **Gold Belt National Backcountry Byway**❖ offers three different routes north to the Florissant Fossil Beds. These old, often narrow mining roads twist up through a patchwork of BLM and private land where ghost towns nestle in spectacular scenery. All three branches of the byway begin in scrubby foothills and grasslands, climb through ponderosas or Douglas firs into subalpine forests, and finally reach stands of hardy limber and bristlecone pines. The westernmost branch of the byway, called High Park Road, follows Route 9 north from just west of Royal Gorge. The first part of it—Skyline Drive—offers thrilling views to the south of Royal Gorge and its bridge from the crest of the Dakota Hogback. The road continues north through rolling hills with views of Pikes Peak and Mount Pisgah and traverses the open rangeland of High Park, a basin that was once grazed by Texas longhorns favored by rustlers and is now a good place to look for mule deer.

The central and eastern branches of the byway are especially narrow and twisting and cannot accommodate vehicles more than 25 feet long. The central branch due north of Canon City is known as Shelf Road because of one stretch notched into a cliff that is straight out of an acrophobic's nightmare (four-wheel drive is recommended, particularly in wet weather). Places of interest along the road include the first oil well west of the Mississippi, drilled here in 1862. Unfortunately, there is little to see at the famous **Garden Park Fossil Area**❖ except the geologic formation (explained in interpretative panels) where the Great Dinosaur Race took place from 1877 to 1889. During those years, two rival paleontologists, E. D. Cope and O. C. Marsh, excavated neighboring outcroppings of Jurassic badlands, finding nearly complete skeletons of allosaurus, apatosaurus, camarasaurus, ceratosaurus, diplodocus, haplocanthosaurus, and stegosaurus in a passionate, widely publicized competition.

The byway continues to Garden Park, a smaller and lower version of the intermountain parks that characterize the northern Colorado Rockies. At **Red Canyon City Park**❖, vermilion sandstone spires, freestanding walls, and bluffs of the Dakota Hogback jut above the dark green pinyon-juniper forest. Red Canyon is a delight to rock climbers and day hikers alike, and trestle tables under the trees make it a pleasant place to stop for a picnic. As the road continues north, it narrows into a deep canyon and

the nerve-wracking stretch that gives Shelf Road its name.

The byway's eastern branch—Phantom Canyon Road—runs along Eightmile Creek, providing access to hiking and camping in the BLM's 26,150-acre **Beaver Creek Wilderness❖.** This area centers on the confluence of East and West Beaver creeks and ranges from pinyon-juniper woodland to subalpine forest dissected with streams; bighorn sheep and mountain lions are sometimes seen here. A short way up the road is the **Indian Springs Trace Fossil Site❖,** where the rock bears tracks and burrows made by horseshoe crabs and trilobites when it was still mud, 450 million years ago. The route then continues through enchanting Phantom Canyon, where narrowleaf cottonwoods, willows, alders, thimbleberries, and wild roses grow along Eightmile Creek.

Phantom Canyon and Shelf roads converge in Cripple Creek, a historic mining town turned gambling mecca for busloads of people from Colorado Springs and beyond. Florissant Road continues northwest to the **Florissant Fossil Beds National Monument❖,** which preserves some of the most exquisite geologic specimens in the world—fragile bees, butterflies, ants, and dragonflies trapped by volcanic ash in an "Insects' Pompeii." About 35 million years ago, rivers of volcanic mud dammed this mountain bowl, forming a swampy lake. For half a million years thereafter, nearby volcanic eruptions dusted this ancient Lake Florissant with fine ash, which carried insects into the lake and entombed its fish as well. The ash later compacted to form shale in which these Eocene-Oligocene life-forms were preserved so gently that even the delicate veins of insect wings can still be seen. Mudflows also buried enormous redwood trees around the lake, along with birches, beeches, hickories, willows, and palms. Both leaf and insect fossils are on display in the visitor center, and several self-guided footpaths lead to petrified redwood stumps in the woods and sunny meadows, which deserve their French name of *florissant,* meaning blooming.

The itinerary now travels east on Route 24 to the town of Divide, then south on Route 67 to **Mueller State Park❖,** where 85 miles of nature trails wander through 12,103 acres of field and forest. On Mueller's higher slopes, trails enter parklike forests of firs, aspens, blue spruces, and pines chattering with chickarees. Bald outcrops of pink granite offer perfect perches for resting and gazing at distant valleys and mountains. Blue

---

LEFT: *Youthful ponderosa pines overlook an ancient stump of the extinct giant sequoia species* Sequoia affinis *at Florissant Fossil Beds National Monument. The stump petrified in volcanic mud some 35 million years ago.*

ABOVE: *In the late 1880s horsedrawn carriages toiled five hours to climb Pikes Peak; by 1901 a cog railroad reached the summit much faster.*

grouse, robins, and white-breasted nuthatches rustle about in the forest, and mule deer and rabbits are common. Mueller is large and wild, with open, sunny forests where wild plums and chokecherries attract bears in autumn; aspen buds, catkins, and birds' nests lure the animals here in spring. However, Mueller's importance as bighorn habitat was what induced the Nature Conservancy to buy the preserve, a former cattle ranch, and then make it available to the state of Colorado. The permanent bighorn herd numbers about 40, and the larger Pikes Peak herd migrates to Mueller in winter to stay through spring lambing.

Returning north on Route 67 to Divide, the way turns east on Route 24 to the Pikes Peak Highway in the **Pike National Forest❖.** From the town of Cascade at the foot of **Pikes Peak,** this 18-mile unpaved toll road (closed in winter) climbs 7,700 feet—a greater vertical increase from foot to summit than any other mountain in Colorado—through forests, meadows, and reservoir-filled mountain valleys to stark tundra. En route to the summit of Pikes Peak, scenic viewpoints and picnic areas provide access to fishing spots and trailheads. On this isolated mountain, the climate is so

ABOVE: *Motorists now ascend Pikes Peak in minutes, but it takes hours for marathoners to run the 14-mile trail to the summit and back.*

harsh and dry that many of the trees are stunted and twisted into krumm-holz. Even aspens grow in mashed mats here as a result of the wind, heavy snow, and bitter cold of long, hard winters.

Pikes Peak is a batholith similar to Mount Evans, but its uplifted granitic core is only about a billion years old. The granitic rocks of Pikes Peak are weathering into rounded pink boulders, exposing bits of Colorado's state mineral, a green feldspar called amazonite. Possibly the most famous mountain in the United States, Pikes Peak was named for Lieutenant Zebulon Pike, the leader of a U.S. Army expedition sent west in 1806 to determine the southern boundary between the recently acquired Louisiana Purchase and New Mexico, then a part of the Spanish empire. The sight of Pikes Peak heartened weary pioneers as they crossed the prairies in wagon trains, and the view from its 14,110-foot summit led Katharine Lee Bates to write the poem that begins, "O beautiful for spacious skies, for amber waves of grain, / For purple mountain majesty, above the fruited plain," and was later put to music. It seems entirely fitting that this glorious view should have inspired our nation's most gentle and nature-oriented patriotic song, "America the Beautiful."

81

CHAPTER THREE

SOUTHERN COLORADO: THE HIGH COUNTRY

The San Juan Mountains stretch 120 miles from west to east in Colorado's southwestern corner. Their more than 10,000 square miles could enclose Vermont. Their average elevation is 10,000 feet, and they encompass more land above that elevation than any other range in the country. Geologist Halka Chronic has nicknamed the San Juans "the land of fire and ice." About 65 million years ago, the same collision of crustal plates that was compressing and folding the Rockies caused huge domes of varicolored sedimentary rock to buckle up here. Much later, volcanoes erupted for an intensely violent period lasting 30 million years, covering these domes with lava, ash, and debris. Glaciers then carved the buried mountains into graceful bowls, U-shaped valleys, and cirques that combined to isolate arêtes (ridges). Streams of meltwater scored deep canyons in the exposed rock.

Standing in the path of moisture-bearing clouds from the gulfs of Mexico and California, the mountains of southwest Colorado receive the majority of their moisture in the summer while blocking that moisture from the northwest part of the state. Countless brooks trickle together to become rushing torrents churning down steep slopes. As part of the Continental Divide, the San Juan Mountains are the source of the San Juan and Dolores rivers, which join the Colorado River to the west in Utah, as well as of the Rio Grande, which flows southeast.

LEFT: *In the Yankee Boy Basin near Ouray, frequent summer showers produce lush bouquets of delicate blue columbine, Colorado's state flower. Here they flourish just below the treeline of the San Juan Mountains.*

At about 7,000 feet, the Rio Grande flows into the San Luis Valley and then turns south into New Mexico. A high, flat basin between abrupt mountain ranges, the San Luis Valley is a product of the Rio Grande Rift, which runs from central Colorado into Mexico. The rift began to form between 30 and 20 million years ago, as the forces of plate tectonics lifted all of Colorado almost a full mile. In the San Luis Valley area, the crust bulged upward, stretching with considerable tension. Blocks of crustal material rifted (split apart) and rotated up on one side to form the Sangre de Cristo and Culebra ranges, and the San Luis Valley dropped down between them and the San Juans. The rifting of the earth's crust produced torrents of lava that buried the land in black basalt and interbedded with sand and gravel washed down from the surrounding mountains, creating enormous reservoirs for groundwater.

This itinerary takes a variety of scenic byways as it loops through the San Juan Mountains, visiting Telluride, Durango, then the Rio Grande watershed, the La Garita Wilderness, and the wildlife refuges of the San Luis Valley. The route ends at the dramatic Great Sand Dunes National Monument.

THE SAN JUAN MOUNTAINS

Glaciers scooped pyramidal peaks and sharp ridgelines in the San Juan Mountains. Combined with brutal weather conditions, the steepness of these slopes keeps the summits of the San Juans almost bald of vegetation down to about 11,000 feet. On the upper slopes each summer, however, a few hardy, matlike perennials and serendipitous annuals leaf and flower. Compared with the rest of the state, the San Juans are soggy mountains. In July and August, heavy monsoon rains arrive from the Mexican Pacific coast and the Gulf of California. Below the frigid tundra, these rains produce some of the most spectacular wildflower displays in the western United States, when high meadows of brilliant emerald grass are crowded with blue columbine (Colorado's state flower), raspberry- and lemon-colored paintbrush, purple polemonium, and towering cow parsnip. Above these jewel-like basin meadows rise big naked gray mountains with dazzling white crowns of snow.

Along with many streams and lush meadows, slopes in the San Juans below 11,000 feet support spruce but almost no lodgepole pine. Deep

---

OVERLEAF: *Autumn snow squalls and blazing aspens announce the end of the brief summer season in the San Juan Mountains near Telluride. By winter, the ponderosa pine will lose a third of its needlelike leaves.*

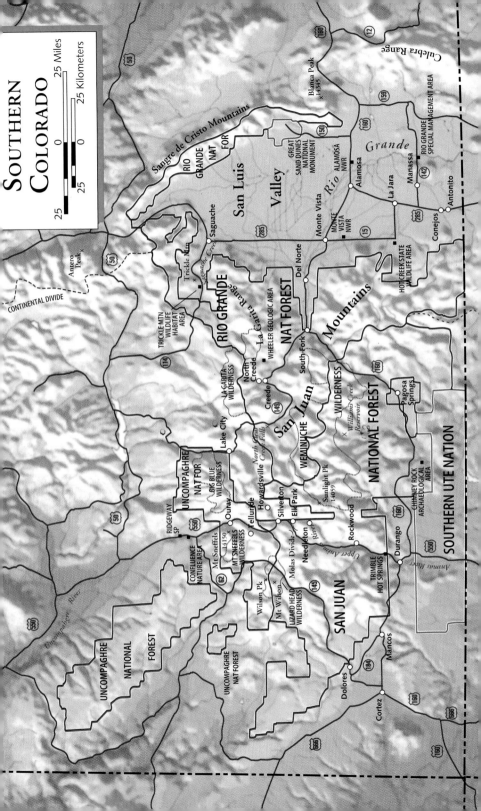

SOUTHERN COLORADO

25 Miles
0   25 Kilometers

Culebra Range

Sangre de Cristo Mountains

Antero Peak ×

CONTINENTAL DIVIDE

Blanca Peak ×14,345

RIO GRANDE NAT FOR

GREAT SAND DUNES NATIONAL MONUMENT

Grande

RIO GRANDE SPECIAL MANAGEMENT AREA

San Luis Valley

ALAMOSA NWR

Alamosa

Manassa

La Jara

Antonito

Conejos

Saguache

Saguache Creek

Trickle Mtn ×

Monte Vista

MONTE VISTA NWR

Del Norte

TRICKLE MTN WILDLIFE HABITAT AREA

RIO GRANDE

La Garita Range

HOTCREEK STATE WILDLIFE AREA

RIO GRANDE NAT FOREST

San Juan Mountains

WHEELER GEOLOGIC AREA

South Fork

La Garita

North Creede

Creede

NAT FOREST

La Garita WILDERNESS

LA GARITA WILDERNESS

Lake City

Pagosa Springs

WILDERNESS

Williams Creek Reservoir

WEMINUCHE

San Juan

NATIONAL FOREST

BIG BLUE WILDERNESS

North Clear Creek Falls

Howardsville

Silverton

Elk Park

Sunlight Pk 14,059

UNCOMPAHGRE NAT FOR

RIDGEWAY SP

Ouray

Telluride

Rockwood

CHIMNEY ROCK ARCHAEOLOGICAL AREA

SOUTHERN UTE NATION

Mt Sneffels ×14,150

MT SNEFFELS WILDERNESS

CONFLUENCE NATURE AREA

Molas Divide

Needleton

Upper Animas

Trimble Hot Springs

Durango

Uncompahgre River

UNCOMPAHGRE NATIONAL FOREST

Wilson Pk ×

Mt Wilson ×

LIZARD HEAD WILDERNESS

UNCOMPAHGRE NAT FOREST

SAN JUAN

Animas River

Mancos

Dolores

Cortez

ABOVE: *Near Creede in the Rio Grande National Forest, nimble bighorn sheep ewes browse the shrubs along a precipitous cliff at Spring Creek. Their soft-centered hoofs provide good traction on such steep sites.*

snow in winter causes frequent avalanches, which cut bare swaths into dense stands of trees. Mule deer, elk, bobcats, mountain lions, black bears, and snowshoe hares thrive at this elevation, where the chirping of marmots and pikas is a common refrain, and there is even an occasional rumor of a grizzly bear sighting.

The nineteenth-century prospectors who found gold and silver in the San Juan Mountains brought an end to Ute autonomy by developing mines, mining roads, and shantytowns that have since been abandoned. Today tourism is the main industry, especially in spas fed by hot springs such as the ones at Ouray. Along with hiking and mountain biking in summer and skiing in winter, many visitors simply drive through the mountains in summer and autumn, enjoying the scenery on paved byways or rough Jeep trails. Walking and driving need not be mutually exclusive, however, because on every road there are pullouts where travelers can park and take a stroll through the crystalline air and spectacular scenery of these magnificent mountains.

Ridgway State Park❖, a few miles north of town on Route 550 in the foothills of the San Juan Mountains, surrounds a reservoir formed just below the confluence of Dallas Creek and the Uncompahgre River. One of the

ABOVE: *Where the clang of pickaxes echoed in a frenetic mining boom a century ago, the shrill whistles of marmots now ring. The slopes of the San Juans between Ouray and Telluride were plucked smooth by glaciers.*

newest of Colorado's state parks, Ridgway is a model for barrier-free parks all over the country. A short path designed with accessibility in mind leads to the **Confluence Nature Area,** a small preserve where hawks and owls roost in tall cottonwoods. Pinyon-juniper woodland and sagebrush-grassland surround most of the lake. Birds and flowers are particularly abundant in April and May, and views of the snowy, resplendent San Juan Mountains to the south are all the more delightful from this warm, sheltered spot.

The unpaved, twisting Owl Creek Pass Road (County Road 8) heads east from Route 550 across from Ridgway State Park to the little-known **Uncompahgre Wilderness Area❖** on the northern edge of the San Juans. At the top of 10,114-foot **Owl Creek Pass,** a turn south on Forest Road 860 for several miles leads to signed trailheads. (The Uncompahgre can also be accessed from the south.) Mount Sneffels soars to 14,150 feet in the **Mount Sneffels Wilderness Area❖** on the northern edge of the **Uncompahgre National Forest❖** just south of Ridgway. The wilderness area can be reached via several trails and unpaved tracks from Routes 62, 145, and 550, which encircle it. Although very steep and rugged, roads and trails in these mountains transport the traveler into a fabulous world of majestic peaks, tundra and dark spruce forests, green meadows and gurgling brooks.

THE SAN JUAN SKYWAY

The San Juan Skyway Scenic and Historic Byway follows Routes 62 and 145 from Ridgway to Telluride, a quaint Victorian mining town now famous for winter skiing. Chairlifts from the ski area make the slopes above town accessible for downhill and cross-country skiing in winter and for hiking or scenic viewing in the summer.

ABOVE: *Pine grosbeaks travel in flocks except in spring, when these large finches pair up for breeding. It takes the males about two years to develop their dusty red adult plumage.*

RIGHT: *Slow-growing spruce have almost crowded out the sun-loving aspens along the course of the West Dolores River below Lizard Head Pass.*

Ten miles southwest of Telluride in the **Uncompahgre**❖ and **San Juan**❖ national forests is the **Lizard Head Wilderness Area**❖, named for a prominent shaft of stone poking up above the cliffs and humped shoulders of the mountains around it. Although the three "fourteeners" in this wilderness—14,246-foot **Mount Wilson,** 14,159-foot **El Diente Peak,** and 14,017-foot **Wilson Peak**—are considered extremely difficult to climb because of their loose rock and exposed pitches, most of the area is gentle, open country that is pleasant for walking and cross-country skiing. Of the 35 miles of hiking trails in Lizard Head, most are accessed from Lizard Head Pass Viewing Area, one mile south of Trout Lake on Route 145.

Route 145 continues southwest to Dolores. (For information about the Colorado Plateau country south and west of Dolores, see Chapter 4.) Below town, turn east on Route 184 to run south of the **La Plata Mountains.** Although these mountains show the mining scars that their name suggests (*plata* is Spanish for "silver"), they are still wild and beautiful. Bistort-strewn meadows ripple below clattery talus fields and naked gray ridges. Pockets of forest grow in protected amphitheaters. The higher, treeless slopes of these mountains are marvelous for watching the night sky in crisp, clear air where no artificial lights diminish the splendor of a million brilliant stars. A section of the

LEFT: *In the Needle Peaks near Durango, tundra-clad Mountain View Crest offers hikers spectacular views of the Weminuche Wilderness Area.*
RIGHT: *With fine leaves resembling needles, ground-hugging habits, and a short tundra growing season, pink mountain heather blooms just after snowmelt, in July and August.*

Colorado Trail and other trails are accessed via several forest roads from Mancos. Llama trekking, which can be arranged in Mancos, is popular in the relatively remote La Platas—llamas carry the food and gear while their human companions hike unencumbered.

The San Juan Skyway continues east on Route 160 to Durango, formerly a mining and railroad town and now a base for river-runners, hikers, mountain bikers, skiers, and sightseers keen to experience the mountains. White-water rafting and kayak trips launch here for 20-mile trips down the Animas River into the **Southern Ute Nation❖** (permits required). A narrow-gauge railway puffs along the Animas River from Durango north to Silverton and back, stopping at Elk Park and Needleton to drop or collect hikers who wish to explore the Weminuche Wilderness Area to the east.

The 460,000-acre **Weminuche Wilderness Area❖**—shared by the San Juan and **Rio Grande❖** national forests—is the largest in Colorado. It covers very high country, averaging 10,000 feet above sea level and containing three "fourteeners": 14,083-foot Mount Eolus, 14,082-foot Windom Peak, and 14,059-foot Sunlight Peak. The most famous features in the Weminuche Wilderness are probably the Needle Peaks, named for their high, inaccessible summits that stick up above the Chicago Basin. The wilderness area encompasses a vast realm of tundra-cloaked, U-shaped valleys separated by knife-edged ridgelines. Summer thunderstorms soak the Weminuche regularly, booming and crackling in its curved granite amphitheaters.

In addition to the trailheads along the train route, there are other points where visitors can enter the Weminuche on foot or on horseback. To reach the network of trails around Mountain View Crest (just southwest of the three fourteeners), drive 9.5 miles north from Durango on County Road 250 and turn east on Forest Road 682 to Henderson Lake, where a signed trail leads to the wilderness boundary. From the town of Pagosa Springs (about 50 miles east), a 14-mile drive north on Fourmile

LEFT: *Native only to North America, bobcats are soundless, efficient hunters by night or by day, preying on rodents, rabbits, and hares; their territories can encompass 75 square miles—at any elevation.*

RIGHT: *At sunrise on the Fourth of July, winter ice still floats on aptly named Ice Lake in the San Juan National Forest near Silverton.*

Road leads to a very pleasant 6-mile (round-trip) day hike to Fourmile Falls. The Weminuche Trail starts from the end of Poson Park Road near **Williams Creek Reservoir❖,** which is also north of Pagosa Springs. Forest Service staff in Durango, Pagosa Springs, or Creede can advise hikers about the many other trails that traverse the Weminuche.

The **Chimney Rock Archaeological Area❖** is worth a side trip east of Durango via Route 160. A thousand years ago on Chimney Rock—a high mesa with two chimneys (stone pinnacles) on top of it—ancestors of the Pueblo people built homes and kivas, or ceremonial rooms. In the six square miles of the archaeological area are more than 200 Puebloan structures of the type found around Mesa Verde near Cortez on the Colorado Plateau, as well as a Great House that appears to be the work of Puebloan people from Chaco Canyon, New Mexico. Researchers think that this site was used for ceremonies and for archaeoastronomy, the observation of celestial events by people of the past. During the "lunar standstill" that occurs every 18 years, the full moon rises between the twin stone pillars of Chimney Rock, an impressive event that can be viewed only from the Great House.

The San Juan Skyway leads north from Durango on Route 550 up the valley of the Animas River, which is flanked by interesting, tilted sedimentary strata. From **Trimble Hot Springs❖** 6 miles north of Durango, the river is placid enough for canoes to paddle about 10 miles downstream. However, in the 28 turbulent miles from Silverton to Rockwood, the Upper Animas boils through a beautiful, remote, and dangerous canyon that only experienced white-water rafters and kayakers should attempt.

North on Route 550, the picturesque old mining town of Silverton with its Victorian clapboard houses lies surrounded by talus slopes gaudy with red

and ocher outcroppings and mine tailings. To reach the Continental Divide Trail from Silverton, drive east on Route 110 to Howardsville and take Forest Road 589 up Cunningham Gulch for 4.5 miles to the end of the road. A three-mile trail leads west from Forest Road 585, off Route 550 just west of Silverton, to **Ice Lake,** an ethereal mirrored pool in the talus above timberline. Dark chestnut marmots twirl their tails as they scamper among the rocks around its shores, and shiny green hummingbirds whir over wine-red penstemon and purple-fringe phacelia.

From Silverton to Ouray, the San Juan Skyway is known as the Million Dollar Highway because blasting this 22 miles of winding road into the mountainsides made it one of the most expensive highways ever built in this country. Unpaved Camp Bird Road leads from just south of Ouray to **Yankee Boy Basin** in the **Uncompahgre National Forest❖,** a gorgeous destination for four-wheel-drive and mountain-biking trips. Here Twin Falls—depicted on the label of a famous Colorado beer—froths into a meadow thick with blue and white columbine, red penstemon, yellow paintbrush, and purple larkspur. Spruce and fir forests cover the mountainsides, and puffy white clouds sail among high peaks of gray rock shrouded in snow. At the ecotone—the edge where meadow and forest blend—grow elderberry shrubs, mertensia, and common juniper. American dippers plunge for larvae in streams lined with dwarf willows. Badgers hunt the meadows, while pine martens—and some say wolverines—patrol the wooded slopes above the basin. The Blue Lakes Trail climbs from Yankee Boy Basin to the Blue Lakes and spectacular Mount Sneffels in the Mount Sneffels Wilderness Area.

Trails into the **Uncompahgre Wilderness Area❖** from its southern side branch from the BLM's unpaved 65-mile Alpine Loop National Backcountry Byway between Ouray and Lake City. From Route 550 south of Ouray, the byway leads east toward Lake City on rocky and perpendicular old mining tracks. (Two-wheel-drive passenger cars can just manage the section from Silverton to Lake City.) Breathtaking walks and scenery are around every corner on the Alpine Loop, which traverses a massive landscape beneath a vast and awe-inspiring sky. In many places, the tundra is soggy most of the summer; water trickling from snowbanks is tinged pink with the spores of algae. Water-loving marsh marigolds and

LEFT: *Summer sun melts the high snowbanks that feed Twin Falls in the lush Yankee Boy Basin, where a patchwork of subalpine forests and moist meadows provides habitat for a diverse mix of plants and animals.*

Parry's primroses grow thickly in such spots, while pink moss campion and wild candytuft dot the thinner, drier soils, and different colors of lichen—gray, orange, and lime green—splotch the charcoal rocks all around. The highest point of the byway, in the precipitous western section, is 12,800-foot **Engineer Pass,** a sharp ridge surrounded by red, brown, and buff frost-wedged talus at steep angles of repose. **Engineer Peak** is a nunatak, a jagged peak that stayed above the smoothing force of Ice Age glaciers. The Alpine Loop is open from late May or early June (depending on weather) to late October.

RIO GRANDE COUNTRY

The **Rio Grande,** arguably the most famous river in the West, has probably inspired more romances than any other river. The very name Rio Grande conjures up images of doomed Spanish explorers, singing cowboys, and proud Pueblo and Apache people, all depending on the river in the indifferent vastness of the desert Southwest. The third longest river in the United States at 1,885 miles, the Rio Grande begins as a collection of clear streams seeping together from snowbanks below Stony Pass, just east of Silverton at about 13,000 feet. From here the river flows east between the San Juan Mountains to the south and La Garita Range to the north. Winding down steep mountain canyons, it picks up volume and finally tumbles into the broad San Luis Valley, where it spreads out, slows down a little, and turns south to New Mexico.

The scenery along the Rio Grande changes with the seasons. At higher elevations, the new leaves of willows, alders, and birches often emerge rusty-colored, changing to bluish green in summer and then to yellow or brown in the fall. Lower down or in sheltered places, cottonwoods as tall as 50 or 60 feet add their fluttery, lime green foliage to the palette in spring, their rich golden leaves in autumn.

Cold air from its upper reaches flows down the course of the Rio Grande, stressing the plants and animals that live along it. Hardy shrubs that not only survive but bear fruit and seeds on its banks include chokecherry, hackberry, wild plum, river hawthorn, box elder, and hazelnut. Because water creates habitat regardless of temperature, a community of sedges, rushes, mosses, and suspended plants such as watercress and algae is alive with insect larvae, fish fry, and tadpoles. Herons and egrets stalk frogs and salamanders in the eddies, dippers push themselves along the streambed, and willow flycatchers, Wilson's warblers, and belted kingfishers nest in the trees along the river.

ABOVE: *Opportunistic omnivores, sociable coyotes live and hunt in packs and eat anything from berries and grasshoppers to snakes, rabbits, and even deer. They are fine runners and when pressed can leap up to 14 feet.*

The **Rio Grande National Forest❖** encompasses the entire watershed of the Rio Grande in Colorado, including those sections of the San Juan and La Garita mountains on the eastern side of the Continental Divide, and the west side of the Sangre de Cristo Mountains on the eastern edge of the San Luis Valley. This national forest is extremely varied, including high, rocky crags, forested slopes, bizarre formations eroded from volcanic ash, grassy meadows, and sagebrush-covered foothills.

East on Route 149 from Lake City, the Silver Thread Scenic and Historic Byway crosses 11,361-foot Slumgullion Pass and bends south through Spring Creek Pass. About seven miles south of Spring Creek Pass, a quarter mile in on Forest Road 510, North Clear Creek pours over an abrupt escarpment of eroding basalt in a dazzling torrent of foaming white water called **North Clear Creek Falls❖.** Forest Service biologists began to introduce moose here during the winter of 1991–92, the first of a planned five-year release of a hundred animals. The moose released here are Shiras, one of four subspecies in North America. Shiras are especially well adapted to drier areas.

The **La Garita Wilderness❖** is north of Creede. Two roads lead north—up West Willow Creek and up East Willow Creek—from North Creede to the heads of a number of wilderness trails. La Garita is a rocky

place of talus slopes and glacial moraines, although there are spruce-fir forests and mountain meadows as well. Because it is far from population centers and is free of snow only six or eight weeks a year, it is one of the less-visited wilderness areas in the state. Summer rain showers are frequent, and these mountains can be quite cold at night. The rain fosters lush meadows that attract lots of wildlife and replenishes streams and several lakes offering good fishing.

The **Wheeler Geologic Area** hides in the dark spruce-fir forest within the La Garita Wilderness Area. Wheeler is a pale, lavender-and-white badlands of loosely packed volcanic ash and tuff, eroded into strange and unexpected formations that have been compared to an enchanted city of walls, mosques, and fluted columns and to an army of stone sentinels atop ancient castles. To reach the trailhead, drive 7.3 miles east of Creede on Route 149 and turn north up Forest Road 600 for 10 miles. A 14-mile unpaved, four-wheel-drive road and trail (open from July to mid-October) leads from this point to within half a mile of the formations, and several footpaths wind among them. Although the site is not far from Creede, the road is so bad that even driving to Wheeler is a half-day expedition.

From Creede, the itinerary continues east on Route 149, joining Route 160 at South Fork. The Forest Service offers educational brochures for self-guided drives in the nearby mountains and foothills. The Ride through the Rockies Tour, beginning on Forest Road 360 off Route 160 just south of South Fork, loops southeast past Crystal Lakes and back through South Fork east to Del Norte on Route 160, taking visitors through an area that was heavily logged in the early 1980s to arrest an infestation of spruce bark beetle. The resulting clear-cuts are good places to look for elk and deer and to observe the slow process of reforestation.

The Forest Service also recommends driving north from Del Norte on English Valley Road to look for wildlife on the Animal Lovers' Tour. Below Eagle Rock is a sign explaining where to look for bighorn sheep. Pronghorn, mule deer, and coyotes appear along the road, which leads from shrubland through pygmy-forest–clad hills up to crags where cliff-dwelling birds such as golden eagles, white-throated swifts, and rock doves roost.

The local mix of valley, foothill, and mountain is promising terrain for wildlife. **Trickle Mountain Wildlife Habitat Area❖**, off Route 114 west

---

LEFT: *In the arid San Luis Valley, a yellow-flowered plains prickly pear cactus thrives in the boulders along an ancient lava bed. Just beyond, the Rio Grande River flows sedately from Colorado into New Mexico.*

101

ABOVE LEFT: *Because its unusually large eyes are adapted to hunting in dim light, this immature black-crowned night heron will rest during the day but perch over water to watch for swimming prey at dawn or dusk.*

of Saguache, above the northwest corner of the San Luis Valley, embraces an exceptionally rich combination of habitats. The area covers 147,230 acres of the Rio Grande National Forest and BLM and private land varying 5,000 feet in elevation from 14,269-foot Antero Peak to the foothills below. Many streams water it, including the tightly meandering Saguache Creek on the area's southern boundary. Wandering about on grassy, undulating mesas and hills etched with stream canyons, a hiker with binoculars has a very good chance of seeing some of the mule deer, pronghorn, and several hundred bighorn sheep here. Occasionally, bobcats, mountain lions, or black bears appear, and elk are spotted here as well. Ordinarily, these animals would not be so close to one another, but the mosaic of habitats around Trickle Mountain brings them together.

The eastern San Juan and La Garita Mountains—huge glacier-carved domes on the western side of the San Luis Valley—have not been discovered by great numbers of visitors and are ideal for those seeking solitude and wildness.

THE SAN LUIS VALLEY

Descending east on Route 160 from the rugged San Juan Mountains toward Alamosa, travelers may be astonished to find themselves on a 50-mile-wide, almost perfectly flat plain surrounded by high ranges. The **San**

ABOVE: *Northern-migrating sandhill cranes pause on the frozen wetlands of the Monte Vista refuge in the San Luis Valley. These courting adult "sandies" have painted their feathers orange with rusty mud.*

Luis Valley is a buff-colored, stream-laced shrubby grassland that extends 100 miles from north to south, right through the middle of Colorado's border with New Mexico. The valley is a product of the Rio Grande Rift, which is also responsible for the Sangre de Cristo and Culebra ranges defining the valley's eastern side.

Because the San Luis Valley is a high desert, its elevation averaging more than 7,500 feet above sea level, temperatures fluctuate wildly from minus 50 degrees to 90 degrees Fahrenheit. The rain-shadow effect of the nearby mountains reduces precipitation to an average of only seven inches per year. Growing here are grasses and shrubs tolerant of drought, grazing, and salt, such as four-wing saltbush (or chamiza), sagebrush, snakeweed, and rabbitbrush (also called chamisa locally). Amazing as it might seem considering the harsh weather conditions, green fields of wheat, barley, and alfalfa wave in the ever-present breezes too, irrigated with water pumped from wells and the Rio Grande.

The San Luis Valley is part of Colorado's most Hispanic region. The village of Antonito (on Route 285 south of Alamosa) lies only about 100

OVERLEAF: *In this subtle autumn still life, dried flower sepals, golden grasses, and yellow rabbitbrush harmonize with the burnished leaves of the Fremont cottonwoods along Medano Creek at the Great Sand Dunes.*

miles due north of Santa Fe, which was founded in 1610. Spanish efforts to control the northern frontier of their empire brought several military expeditions through the San Luis Valley, including one in 1779 led by New Mexico governor Juan Bautista de Anza, who had founded San Francisco, California, only a few years earlier. Although the Spanish granted vast tracts of land on this northern frontier, actual settlement was very limited. In the second half of the nineteenth century—well after independence from Spain—many more Hispanic farmers settled in southern Colorado in self-sufficient groups consisting of large families who raised mostly livestock. Our Lady of Guadalupe in the town of Conejos—the oldest church in Colorado—dates from this period.

The San Luis Valley is important to migrating waterfowl. The U.S. Fish and Wildlife Service created the **Monte Vista National Wildlife Refuge❖**, six miles south of Monte Vista on Route 15, using irrigation canals and wells. However, the **Alamosa National Wildlife Refuge❖**, southeast of Alamosa via Route 160, lies within the oxbows, wet meadows, and stream corridors of the Rio Grande's natural floodplain. Both wetlands support ducks, Canada geese, herons, ibis, and killdeer, along with beavers, mule deer, and coyotes. Grebes, egrets, rail, avocets, stilts, and kingfishers nest here, as well as northern harriers, Swainson's hawks, and red-tailed hawks. Prairie falcons and American kestrels are year-round residents. In winter, 20,000 ducks, rough-legged hawks, and bald and golden eagles remain in the San Luis Valley area. Self-guided auto tours wind through both refuges, and there is a hiking trail along the Rio Grande in the Alamosa.

Every March, bird lovers travel to the San Luis Valley to see thousands of northward-migrating cranes and their endangered foster children, whooping cranes. Cranes, elegant five-foot-tall birds with wingspans of seven feet, now and then pause while eating the grain in fields to raise their heads and utter haunting, gurgly cries. In the mid-1970s, biologists hoped to increase the number of whoopers by placing their eggs in the nests of sandhill cranes. Although whooping cranes did hatch, they were confused by growing up in the nests of another species and have not bred successfully.

In a small canyon due west of La Jara off Route 15, the **Hot Creek State Wildlife Area❖** offers a shady respite from the scorched plain of the San Luis Valley. Hot Creek flows from a warm spring in hills several miles to the west, cutting through dark sheets of basalt in this shallow canyon oasis before joining crooked La Jara Creek and eventually the Rio Grande. Within this canyon, frogs hop among the cattails and tall grasses growing along the braided stream, and wild roses and currants bear colorful fruit in autumn. Cliff swallows stick their mud nests onto rock overhangs and swoop about catching insects hatched in the water. Kingfishers perch in the willows over beaver-dammed pools; black-crowned night herons stare with their brilliant red eyes from cottonwood snags. White yarrow, purple fleabane, and deep-pink mallow bloom in cool patches of soil and grass along the canyon wall. At its upstream end, the canyon opens out into rangeland dotted with stands of ancient cottonwoods where great horned owls hoot at night. Hot Creek is a small area, but its concentration of birds and plants make for a delightful morning or afternoon walk.

East of Manassa on Route 142, also known as Los Caminos Antiguos ("the ancient roads") Scenic and Historic Byway, is a good place to begin an easy trip on the Rio Grande by raft, canoe, or kayak. The river and the level rangeland on either side of it for 30 miles north of its entry into New Mexico is included within the BLM's **Rio Grande Special Management Area❖.** For a short time after they launch, river-runners can see the Sangre de Cristo Mountains to the east beyond crumbly black mesas that are the remains of lava flows. Closer to the New Mexico border, the banks of the river become walls of basalt, enfolding rafters in a more intimate world.

The Sangre de Cristo Mountains rear up a mile and more along a still-active fault scarp to form the eastern wall of the San Luis Valley. This thin, crescent-shaped, jagged range has been proposed for wilderness designation. It is extremely rugged, including seven dark, intimidating fourteeners, among them granitic 14,345-foot Blanca Peak at its southern end. Weather is harsh in the Sangre de Cristos: Afternoon thunderstorms may occur 100 days a year, sharp winds howl across the San Luis Valley and buffet the mountains in any season, and the sun bears down intensely. The mountains get their name, which is Spanish for "blood of Christ," from the red stain splashed on their crests by the setting sun.

Continue east on Route 142 and north on Routes 159 and 150 to reach the **Great Sand Dunes National Monument❖,** in the northeastern corner of the San Luis Valley, where light comes to play. In the morning, golden dawn creeps onto the dunes to tickle the ripples gently and then all at once charge in a blaze up the slopes. A bully at noontime, the sun allows those caught on the sand no escape from its searing heat. With evening, the light is playful again. Purple shadows dance, and when the moon rises its silver glimmers and spins over the dunes.

Great Sand Dunes is also where people come to play. Because breezes smooth the sands every day, the National Park Service sees no reason to prohibit running, rolling, jumping, dancing, or drawing on the miles of fine, dark sand within the monument (the dunes cover 39 square miles in all). Howling teenagers throw themselves headfirst down the steep leeward sides of the dunes. A man with a saxophone pauses at the edge of an acoustically promising bowl and blows. Children lie on their backs on the cool, dew-moistened surfaces, waving their arms up and down to make angels in the morning. Moonlight skiers schuss down the whispering slopes.

The Great Sand Dunes lie at the western foot of the Sangre de Cristos, where a low pass in a crook of the mountains funnels the winds coursing east across the San Luis Valley. As they rise and crowd into the narrow passage, the winds slow and drop coarse sand picked up from the valley floor. The sand forms a dune field that is 700 feet high in places, the tallest in North America. Over time, the dune field stays in roughly the same place, probably because shifting winds occasionally push it back away from the mountains and because groundwater and streams keep the sand moist and heavy.

Although the dunes look practically lifeless—and compared to their surroundings they are—several creatures thrive on them: giant sand-treader camel crickets, circus beetles, and Great Sand Dunes tiger beetles (found nowhere else). Kangaroo rats—which metabolize their water from their food—and coyotes, bobcats, and rabbits leave their tracks in the sand. Delicate ricegrass and blowout grass grow in pockets on the lee sides of the dunes, as do prairie sunflowers and scurfpea.

The waters of Medano Creek, which flows along the southeast side of the dune field, sometimes move invisibly through the sand instead of flowing on top of it. Still, there is plenty of water to sustain the brightly colored cottonwoods where magpies quack gruffly to one another in the afternoons. Green-tailed towhees scrabble among the rabbitbrush in the low, level grass, and a pinyon-juniper woodland grows on the hills above the dune field.

In the vastness of the sky and grandeur of the mountains, nature makes its presence felt in the San Luis Valley, and little distracts the mind from contemplation. A privately supported colony of international religious and cultural groups lives at **Crestone,** north of the Great Sand Dunes. Its members come here to study and practice the principles of peace and harmony where the timeless and enduring landscape puts human concerns in perspective.

RIGHT: *Blowout grass and Indian ricegrass are among a handful of plants that can survive the windy, shifting surfaces of the Great Sand Dunes, which nestle at the base of the Sangre de Cristo Mountains.*

PRINCE BOOKS

109 E. MAIN STREET NORFOLK 622-9223

111882   Reg 1 10:35 am 05/04/96

S SMITHSONIAN GT NA   1 @ 19.95   19.95
SUBTOTAL   19.95
TAX   .90
TOTAL   20.85
CASH PAYMENT   21.00
CHANGE   .15

Mon-Fri 9-8, Sat 10-8, Sun 11-5

WESTERN COLORADO: BASIN AND PLATEAU

W est of the Rocky Mountains, Colorado is a high but horizontal landscape. Instead of the craggy peaks and glacier-carved valleys of the Rockies, the southwest corner of the state features the uplifted Colorado Plateau, a tableland deeply grooved with canyons like the palm of a rancher's hand. In the northwest, converging streams carve the rolling Uinta and Wyoming basins into patterns called dendritic (from the Greek *dendritos*, "pertaining to a tree") because on a map they look like branching trees.

Western Colorado, where evaporation exceeds precipitation, is technically desert. Yet although they are dry, the Colorado Plateau and basin country are not especially hot. Temperatures may reach 90 degrees on a summer afternoon, but mornings and evenings are cool enough to provoke a shiver. Walking is pleasant in this open, airy topography. Dry air means clear, strong light, which reveals a countryside clad only meagerly—here in sagebrush and a few sparse grasses, there in a pygmy forest stunted from lack of moisture and soil. Yet there is life here, life that has adapted to the dryness, to the corresponding swings of temperature, and to the paucity of soil.

Overall, western Colorado is covered with a pinyon-juniper woodland averaging only 20 to 30 feet high. Just as in the Rocky Mountains, however, there are other plant communities, determined mostly by their elevations above sea level and the availability of water. At the higher elevations, ponderosa pine and Douglas fir predominate. Sagebrush and bunchgrass

LEFT: *Sandstone-topped Independence Monument, a 450-foot monolith, towers above Colorado National Monument, where rock layers are draped over a fault and now form the rim of the Uncompahgre Plateau.*

are typical of lower, drier, hotter elevations. Complex riparian ecosystems fringe the streams.

Both the plateau and the basin country are lonely places where few people live today. Yet they were once the homeland of two of North America's most successful and sophisticated cultures, the Puebloan to the south and the Fremont to the north. The Puebloan people abandoned their communities in Colorado about A.D. 1400, the Fremont a little earlier, after at least 1,000 years of settled life here.

Today, much of western Colorado—mostly public land administered by the Bureau of Land Management, the National Park Service, or the state of Colorado—is accessible to the public. Beginning in the southwest corner of the state on Route 666, this chapter visits Puebloan sites at Ute Mountain Tribal Park and Mesa Verde National Park. From Cortez, the itinerary meanders north to Grand Junction, a land of spectacular canyons and mesas including Colorado National Monument and paleontological sites. The route then leads north on 139 to the lonesome northwest corner of the state for a circuit around basin country that finishes at Browns Park National Wildlife Refuge.

THE COLORADO PLATEAU

Ever since the uplift of the Colorado Plateau, the Colorado River and its tributaries have been inexorably dissecting it, exposing its neatly layered strata in canyons and mesas that are both forbidding and intimate. Eight to ten centuries ago, Puebloan people built their homes in the natural alcoves of canyon walls and on mesas. The town of Cortez, in the southwest corner of Colorado, is a good base for visitors who want to explore a number of important Puebloan archaeological sites. Many of these beautiful stone villages, especially those tucked into sandstone alcoves, are well preserved and convey a vivid picture of the Puebloan way of life. Because parks containing Puebloan sites have been protected from other development, they are also good places for nature walks and observations.

The Ute Mountain Nation takes its name from Sleeping Ute Mountain, which is visible on the skyline northwest of the capital, Towaoc (12 miles south of Cortez off Route 666). The **Ute Mountain Tribal Park**❖—a large preserve of Puebloan cliff dwellings—is on an unpaved road off Route 666, directly across from Route 160. A fee is charged for visits to the park, which must be made in the company of a Ute guide and reserved in advance through the tribal office in Towaoc. Because these excursions take some planning and last most of a summer's day,

few travelers take the trouble to visit this fascinating park.

The Ute Mountain Tribal Park encircles the southern end of Mesa Verde, a high green tableland tilting slightly to the south. As a result of this tilt, streams of runoff water carved deep canyons in the southern edge of the mesa itself. Puebloan people then built intricate villages in the canyon walls and atop the mesa. Today, Ute guides take very small groups of visitors about 30 miles over bumpy dirt roads up the side of Mesa Verde. Once atop the mesa, visitors follow their guides along rough footpaths, climbing up and down long ladders to ancient Puebloan ruins. Although they are crumbling now, these stone villages are much as the Puebloan people left them. In cavelike niches dissolved into the cliffs by seeping water, rough rock walls as high as 30 feet lean at precarious angles. Ancient wooden beams designed to support these walls and mostly fallen roofs rest at crazy angles inside. Corncobs and potsherds are scattered everywhere, and except for the chirping of juncos and the rustle of the wind in the trees, all is quiet. Because there are no paved footpaths or other modern conveniences at Ute Mountain Tribal Park, it is easy to imagine the people of the past.

Sharing the tableland with the tribal park is **Mesa Verde National Park❖**, an impressive site accessible from a road leading south from Route 160, 10 miles due east of Cortez. More than 4,000 Puebloan sites have been found here, including cliff dwellings from the thirteenth century, some of which have been meticulously excavated and stabilized. Mute and intriguing, each is a stone honeycomb of rooms with shared walls; archaeologists speculate that some once housed more than 200 people. Representing earlier stages of Puebloan culture on the mesa above are pit houses (roofed subterranean chambers) from the Basket Maker phase, dating from as early as A.D. 550.

Mesa Verde National Park is a very different experience from Ute Mountain Tribal Park. In contrast to the handful who seek out the tribal park, tens of thousands of visitors descend on Mesa Verde every summer. Self-guided trails to clusters of ruins in the national park are paved, and most are fully accessible, although some are quite steep. Food and drinks are available at the four main visitor destinations: Morefield Village (the campground), Far View Visitor Center, Wetherill Mesa, and Chapin Mesa, where the museum is located. The museum's artifacts and dioramas offer

---

Left: *Built by the Puebloan people eight centuries ago, circular kivas, subterranean ceremonial rooms, are part of Balcony House, a large dwelling built into a sandstone cliff alcove at Mesa Verde National Park.*

ABOVE: *A pronghorn buck grazes on BLM lands near Rangely. Able to see for 4 miles, it bolts away from threats at up to 70 miles per hour.*
RIGHT: *In the shadow of the San Juans, the Dolores River winds north across the Colorado Plateau.*

answers to questions about everything from Puebloan pottery styles to the history of southwest archaeology.

Wetherill Mesa, reached by a side road to the right just past the Far View Visitor Center, is named for the Wetherill family of nearby Mancos. Richard Wetherill is credited with discovering Mesa Verde's Cliff Palace when he was out looking for stray cattle one snowy afternoon in 1888, although the antiquities of the region were already fairly familiar to the Anglo settlers of the area. The road to Wetherill Mesa is open only in the summer, when visitors can drive its 13 miles to see several cliff dwellings including Step House, Kodak House, and Long House.

After the visitor center, the first stop on the main park road is the ruins at Far View on the broad expanse atop the mesa. Here people farmed at 7,630 feet above sea level for more than 400 years, from about A.D. 800 to 1200. Anthropologists have compared archaeological evidence with the traditions of today's Pueblo people to deduce that Puebloan beliefs were integrated into all aspects of everyday life. Prayers and ceremonies bonded these ancient communities together in observance of the cycle of seasons and the rites of passage of members of their society.

One of several main clusters of ruins at Mesa Verde is at the end of the park road to Chapin Mesa. Tucked into an alcove in the wall of Spruce Canyon, the well-preserved **Spruce Tree House** contains 114 rooms and 8 kivas; a self-guided nature trail winds along nearby cliffs to a splendid example of prehistoric rock carving, a 12-foot petroglyph. **Cliff Palace**—with 217 rooms and 23 kivas the largest cliff dwelling in North America—overlooks Soda Canyon, as does the smaller **Balcony House,** where visitors must climb a 32-foot ladder and crawl through a narrow tunnel. Trails lead to various overlooks where hikers can get a better perspective on the extraordinary architecture as well as see into the canyons, thick with Gambel oak and Douglas fir, where Puebloan people once hunted mule deer and rabbits and gathered pinyon nuts and juniper berries.

The heyday of Puebloan civilization at Mesa Verde lasted from about A.D. 1100 to 1300, and most of the cliff dwellings were constructed in the mid-1200s. By 1300, however, Mesa Verde stood empty. Archaeologists believe that a combination of drought, crop failure, and social stresses ended Puebloan society here after seven centuries of occupation.

At the **Crow Canyon Archaeological Center❖** on Route 666 just

117

north of Cortez, travelers who have made arrangements in advance can participate in excavations of Puebloan sites lasting several days. Alternatively, day programs enable visitors to examine artifacts, watch archaeologists at work, and even learn to use an atlatl, or spear thrower.

A large, circular great kiva and several smaller kivas, including one with painted walls, are preserved at the BLM's **Lowry Indian Ruins National Historic Landmark**❖ (25 miles north of Cortez on Route 666, then west 9 miles from Pleasant View). Built by the Puebloan people in the eleventh century, Lowry once included at least 40 rooms arranged in three stories. Hikers use Lowry as a trailhead into the BLM's **Cross Canyon Wilderness Study Area**❖, where there are many Puebloan ruins and extensive stream canyons that support lush riparian ecosystems. The sighing of the wind and the howling of coyotes only enhance the peaceful solitude here.

WESTERN CANYON COUNTRY

There are a number of different ways to explore western Colorado en route to Grand Junction. In spring, the adventurous can run all or part of the Dolores River below McPhee Dam, which is just north of the town of Dolores. The 46-mile stretch from Cahone in the upper part of the canyon north to Slick Rock on Route 141 is an exciting excursion through challenging white water that takes two or three days. The 48 miles from Slick Rock north to Bedrock (on Route 90 near Paradox), which also takes two or three days, is a more placid experience through a twisting, secluded canyon with sheer sandstone walls. For those on a tighter schedule, some of the companies serving the Dolores also offer day trips. Such a voyage is literally an immersion in the geology, flora, and wildlife of the plateau country, offering the time, peace, and quiet to take it all in. Because the Dolores is a desert river, the best time to raft it is from mid-April to late June, when the dam is releasing the most snowmelt.

The Unaweep-Tabeguache Scenic and Historic Byway follows Route 145 from Placerville to Naturita and then Route 141 from Naturita to Whitewater. From just past Uravan to Gateway, Route 141 parallels steep, scenic, sandstone-walled Dolores Canyon to the west. On the eastern side of the byway is the Uncompahgre Plateau portion of Uncompahgre National Forest, which is accessible by unpaved roads leading east. Pre-Columbian and Ute petroglyphs speak from the cliffs and boulders of the Uncompahgre Plateau, and several informational signs along the road highlight the natural and human history of this area. The Uncompahgre Plateau is an oval highland some 25 miles wide that extends about 100 miles, from near Montrose to northwest of Grand Junction. Tectonic stresses have lifted it twice—first about 300 million years ago and then as recently as 28 to 8 million years ago—only for erosion to wear it down each time. At present, erosion is attacking the red sedimentary layers that overlie its deeper granite. Streams groove both its southwest and northeast sides, creating remote hiking spots.

As Route 141 turns east at Gateway, it enters Unaweep Canyon at the north end of the plateau. Unusual because streams flow from both ends of it (*Unaweep* is a Ute word meaning "canyon with two mouths"), the canyon is about a mile wide, 40 miles long, and 2,500 feet deep. About 8 miles east of Gateway, the BLM's **Unaweep Seep❖,** a designated area of critical environmental concern (ACEC), sustains a verdant 55-acre hillside marsh where plants seldom seen west of the Rockies flourish. A rare species of butterfly and the violet it feeds upon live here as well, but because access to the area is restricted, travelers are unlikely to see either.

In its 130 very challenging miles, the **Tabeguache** (Ute for "place where the snow melts first") **Mountain Bike Trail❖** crosses the Uncompahgre Plateau between Montrose and Grand Junction. As it passes through all the major ecosystems in this region—including sagebrush-bunchgrass, oak chaparral, pinyon-juniper woodland, ponderosa pine, aspen, and spruce-fir—the trail offers fabulous views of the surroundings: Grand Mesa, the West Elk Mountains, and the Black Canyon of the Gunnison to the east and La Sal Mountains to the west. Also a great route for hikers, the Tabeguache Trail connects with the **Kokopelli Trail❖,** another mountain-bike route, between Grand Junction and Moab, Utah.

On the eastern side of the Uncompahgre Plateau, Route 50 leads east from the town of Montrose to **Black Canyon of the Gunnison National Monument❖** (on Route 347), a gothic fantasy carved by the Gunnison River into streaky, grayish to purplish brown cliffs marbled with pink granite. At Chasm View, its narrowest point, the canyon is a mere 1,100 feet across. For millions of years, the Gunnison River was caught between eruptions of the West Elk Mountains to the north and the San Juan Mountains to the south. Finally, the river's course became entrenched between the two, dropping almost a hundred feet per mile. This drop gives the Gunnison River enough velocity to carry tremendous loads of abrasive sediments and scour deeply through layers of volcanic and sedimentary deposits into the dense, hard schist and gneiss of the region's 1.7-billion-year-old "basement rocks."

The national monument encloses the deepest and steepest 12 miles of

119

LEFT: *Soaring on six-foot wingspans, ecologically important turkey vultures cruise the Colorado Plateau scavenging carrion and garbage by smell.* RIGHT: *Although it looks puny from the rim, the Gunnison River gouged through bedrock to carve the monumental Black Canyon of the Gunnison.*

Black Canyon, where escarpments of hard, twisted rock such as the Painted Wall—at 2,300 feet the highest cliff in Colorado—are awe-inspiring reminders of the age and power of the planet. At Devils Lookout, visitors seem to stare right into the tangled bowels of the earth. The canyon's walls are weathered and rough, with long vertical spires. Just under the rim, white-throated swifts, violet-green swallows, and iridescent ravens glide and glint in shafts of sunlight while the river roars audibly far below.

Cold air flowing down Black Canyon at night, and reduced sunlight on its north-facing slopes, have reversed its life zones to some extent. A stunted forest of Gambel oak, serviceberry, and mountain mahogany intermingled with sagebrush-grassland grows at 8,000 feet on the warm, dry plateau above, while Douglas firs and aspens find niches in side canyons below the rim. Grouse feed on the sagebrush and scrub jays, bluebirds, and Clark's nutcrackers on the seeds, berries, and insects of the rim. Blue-gray gnatcatchers swoop among the bushes, and peregrine falcons and canyon wrens live in the cliffs. Although there are a number of short walks on the rim of the national monument, the terrain is so precipitous that no marked trails lead into Black Canyon. Rock climbing is permitted, but this is no place for amateurs.

The dams that are temporarily slowing Black Canyon's erosion are upstream to the east, in the **Curecanti National Recreation Area✦**. From

OVERLEAF: *Near Grand Junction, a sturdy Utah juniper clutches the sandstone rim of Colorado National Monument's sheer eroded cliffs, which were uplifted along a fault above the Grand Valley of the Colorado.*

LEFT: Colorado's largest predator, the mountain lion has become a controversial symbol of tension between wilderness and civilization. RIGHT: In Colorado National Monument, fragile fingers of fog outline the ancient sandstone spires along the rim of Monument Canyon.

Cimarron on Route 50, there is a short access road to Crystal Lake, which is so narrow that it is limited to hand-carried watercraft. Farther along Route 50 near the town of Sapinero, Blue Mesa Dam backs up the Gunnison River to create 20-mile long Blue Mesa Lake, a shiny blue reservoir surrounded by the stark slopes of the West Elk Mountains.

Ute people once hunted deer and rabbits and gathered grass seeds, roots, and serviceberries in the area of Blue Mesa Lake. They probably came as the seasons dictated, following game and ripening plants into the mountains from spring into summer and passing back through as the weather in the high country cooled. Evidence of a human presence here goes back 10,000 years, and remains of wickiups (brush huts) radiocarbon-date to between 5,000 and 7,000 years ago. Today the lakes of the Curecanti National Recreation Area are stocked with game fish for anglers. Sailors, wind surfers, powerboaters, and water-skiers ply this watery playground all summer, and during the snowy season, cross-country skiers watch for wintering elk and bald eagles.

GRAND JUNCTION AND ENVIRONS

Heading north and west, Route 92 between Hotchkiss and Delta intersects Route 65 (the Grand Mesa Scenic and Historic Byway), leading north across Grand Mesa and providing access via numerous unpaved side roads to lakes, campgrounds, and trails. Cross-country skiing is popular on the mesa in winter; the northern, glaciated end boasts the **Powderhorn** downhill ski area.

All 53 square miles of Grand Mesa, the largest table mountain in the

country, lie within the **Grand Mesa National Forest❖.** The rims of this stupendous conifer-clad upland are more than 10,000 feet above sea level and a mile above the surrounding valleys. Although lava flows hundreds of feet thick protect its sandstones from erosion, the Colorado and Gunnison rivers, flowing on either side of Grand Mesa, are steadily whittling away the purple shale at its feet.

Hundreds of natural and enhanced lakes dot the rolling top of the mesa, attracting a prodigious number of birds and other wildlife, including elk, mule deer, red foxes, black bears, and mountain lions. Grand Mesa's cool subalpine forests, grassy meadows, and good fishing also attract many human visitors throughout the summer, but hikers may still find solitude as well as breathtaking views of the surrounding lowlands, cliffs, and mountains on the ten-mile Crag Crest Trail, which has steep drop-offs on both sides. Leaving the mesa, Lands End Road on its western tip, a spur of the Grand Mesa Scenic and Historic Byway, is a thrill-a-minute plunge down switchbacks to the valley floor. The unpaved road descends through a cross-section of plant communities, including aspen groves and oak woodlands that are yellow and salmon-colored in autumn.

The town of Grand Junction gets its name from its position at the confluence of the Colorado and Gunnison rivers. It is surrounded by orchards

LEFT: *A fierce collared lizard, which preys on smaller lizards, basks at Rabbit Valley Fossil Site.*

RIGHT: *In remote Rattlesnake Canyon, this natural formation is one of eight arches that have weathered into the sandstone rim of a nearby side canyon.*

and fertile farms irrigated by the rivers. On either side of Grand Valley, different rock layers form imposing cliffs. To the north, sandstone caps the sheer brownish-purple Mancos shale of the Book Cliffs. The BLM administers most of the Book Cliffs area, dry sagebrush country with slopes covered with pinyons and junipers. The Grand Junction BLM office provides map brochures describing hiking and camping spots here, such as the **Little Book Cliffs Wild Horse Range❖,** where 80 elusive wild horses run free.

Colorado National Monument❖, one of the state's most exquisite examples of sandstone escarpments and canyons, is southwest of Grand Junction off Route 340. Its 32 square miles feature golden cliffs and canyons carved into the northeastern edge of the Uncompahgre Plateau overlooking Grand Valley. This hiker's paradise offers both short and long trails into the canyons. The air is pungent with sagebrush and pine and echoes with the trill of the canyon wren. Trickles of water seep from the sandstone walls, creating tiny gardens of mosses and flowers. At the bottom of some canyons grow tall cottonwood trees, their leaves turning bright green to golden with the seasons. A few fortunate hikers may catch a glimpse of desert bighorn sheep or spot signs of secretive mountain lions.

The most conspicuous rock layer in Colorado National Monument is the cross-bedded Wingate sandstone, which forms soaring red cliffs several hundred feet high with rounded tops of Kayenta and Entrada sandstone. Although erosion has removed other strata that once overlay these sandstones along the rim, the upper layers are still present in the southern section of the monument, farther back from the edge of the plateau. These layers include the Jurassic Morrison Formation, which has yielded gastroliths—dinosaur gizzard stones—as well as a 60-foot-high dinosaur fossil just outside the monument's southern boundary.

The ancient sandstone walls of Colorado National Monument are rough-

ABOVE: *In contrast to the scattered trees usually found at this elevation, water-loving Fremont cottonwoods cluster in thickets along the Yampa River at Deer Lodge Park in Dinosaur National Monument.*

ly even with the Book Cliffs—composed of much younger Mancos shale—on the other side of Grand Valley. Clearly, there has been considerable displacement of these rock layers. Geologic measurements show that the Uncompahgre Plateau has uplifted 6,700 feet relative to the Book Cliffs.

The BLM's **Rattlesnake Canyon**❖ is only 13 miles from the western boundary of Colorado National Monument, but the dirt road to it is so rocky and rutted that a four-wheel-drive vehicle can take two hours to reach the trailhead. (There is also a seven-mile hiking trail to Rattlesnake Canyon—ask for directions at the BLM office in Grand Junction.) The driving route begins on the West Glade Park Road at the intersection with Rim Rock Drive. After .2 miles, turn right at the dirt track signposted "Black Ridge Road" and follow it for 13 miles to a spectacular promontory with a panoramic view of the surrounding valleys and cliffs. From this point, a half-mile red sandstone trail winds down through scented cliffrose and Mormon tea to a side canyon whose southwest rim is perforated with eight natural stone arches, the densest concentration outside Arches National Park in Utah.

Because it is so remote, Rattlesnake Canyon is a peaceful place, a perfect spot to watch the antics of fence lizards as they raise and lower themselves on their forefeet, showing off their bright blue bellies. Biologists speculate that the push-ups help these little insectivorous lizards look fierce—aiding them in defending their territories and impressing potential mates—or keep cool by raising their bodies off the sun-warmed stone.

Another approach to Rattlesnake Canyon is by day hike from **Horsethief Canyon State Wildlife Area❖,** a deep-red sandstone chasm carved by the Colorado River. Commercial outfitters in Grand Junction offer one- and two-day rafting trips from the town of Loma (about 15 miles west of Grand Junction) 26 miles through **Ruby Canyon❖** to the Westwater Ranger Station in Utah. Splashing through white water on a hot summer day somehow enhances the wild magnificence of western Colorado: the pervasive aroma of sagebrush, the sound of birds calling, and the massive presence of the rock formations here.

Because of the many fossils found in this part of Colorado, the BLM calls the area around Grand Junction the Dinosaur Triangle. At the BLM's **Dinosaur Hill❖,** just off Route 340 between the Colorado National Monument and the town of Fruita, a one-mile trail encircles a site where paleontologists excavated apatosaurus, brachiosaurus, and other dinosaur fossils around the turn of the century. At the **Rabbit Valley Paleontological Area❖,** off I-70 west of Grand Junction just before the Utah border, visitors may see fossils that are actually in the process of excavation at a dinosaur quarry. Along Rabbit Valley's quarter-mile Trail through Time, signs explain ancient twig and branch impressions, the limb and backbone of a camarasaurus, and fossil hash (lots of little bits of bone). This stark place of rocks, rabbitbrush, and lizards tends to be very sunny and hot.

Three miles down an unpaved road on the other (south) side of I-70 from Rabbit Valley, the BLM's **McDonald Creek❖** is in a cool, shady desert canyon where Fremont people painted and carved mysterious pictures. Within 1.5 miles of the trailhead are four of their rock art panels, which evoke a strong sense of the people who lived here a thousand years ago. The canyon is full of fruit-bearing shrubs—serviceberry, barberry, and skunkberry—as well as other plant and animal food sources. Because the BLM managers felt that McDonald Creek would be its own best interpreter, there are no trails or signs indicating the pictographs.

NORTHWEST BASIN COUNTRY

Few visitors find their way to the northwest corner of Colorado above Grand Junction. The Uinta and Wyoming basins merge here, in dry BLM

ABOVE: *A summer storm approaches the Yampa River as it winds below Duffy Mountain near the town of Craig. Such bends, called meanders, form when a watercourse slows as it crosses a relatively level plain.*

land without any well-known attractions except **Dinosaur National Monument❖,** which most people enter from Utah (see Chapter 6). Yet there are beautiful and interesting (albeit lonesome) places to visit in Colorado's northwest basin country where hiking, camping, and picnicking are permitted (the staff of local BLM offices can suggest specific places depending upon the season and weather conditions).

Here, lobes of the Uinta and Wyoming basins extend into Colorado from Utah and Wyoming, meeting to form a low arc across Colorado's northwest corner that separates the southern Rockies from the middle Rocky Mountains of Utah. The term *basin* refers to the underlying geologic structure of this area, which was flooded by Lake Uinta between 50 and 40 million years ago. The sediments of this ancient lake are known today as the Green River shale and are considered one of the most important energy reserves in the world. Like monstrous mechanical grasshoppers, oil pumps dot this gently rolling rangeland, which is also grazed by cattle and pronghorn.

Route 139 from the Grand Junction area north to Rangely ascends 8,268-foot Douglas Pass, high enough for colorful aspens in the fall, and then descends into long, narrow Canyon Pintado. Although it is heavily grazed by cattle and ornamented with a big gas pipeline, the canyon gains a moody beauty from its isolation. Fremont petroglyphs dated circa A.D. 800 through 1150 appear on boulders at the mouths of many of its side

ABOVE: *Above the cottonwood-lined Yampa River in Dinosaur National Monument, pinyon pines and junipers dot a hogback ridge (an eroded edge of sedimentary rock bent up at an angle) created by the Uinta Uplift.*

canyons. The BLM has placed explanatory panels along the road to help visitors find petroglyphs, and adventurous travelers may want to investigate promising boulders for images of disconnected humanlike figures, zigzags, and game animals.

Visitors may also take I-70 east from Grand Junction and Route 13 north from Rifle along the Grand Hogback, the feature that defines the local, western boundary between the Rocky Mountains and the Colorado Plateau. Here, sandstone and shale layers pushed up by the rising of the White Mountain Plateau have been eroded into a ragged ridgeline. Just above Rifle, turn on Route 325, where a dam across a natural gap in the hogback creates **Rifle Gap Reservoir❖**, popular for waterskiing. Through a narrow canyon four miles north of the reservoir is **Rifle Falls State Park❖**, sometimes called Colorado's Hawai'i, where the diversion of Rifle Creek in the 1920s created three 80-foot waterfalls. The spray from these cascades supports a remarkably luxuriant habitat in this otherwise dry region. Short trails lead to a green wall of mosses, ferns, and monkeyflowers, where frogs croak and salamanders crawl among slimy boulders.

Returning to Route 13 and continuing north to Craig, this path crosses the Yampa River. In its more than 200 miles, the Yampa wanders west across the Wyoming Basin from its swift headwaters in the Flat Tops Mountains to its confluence with the Green River in Dinosaur National

Monument. Outfitters offer one- and two-day trips on the 53-mile segment of the Yampa between Craig and Juniper Hot Springs, through rocky, sun-drenched, sagebrush-covered hill country where mule deer, elk, and bald and golden eagles may be spotted.

In the very northwestern corner of Colorado about 75 miles west of Craig via Route 318, dramatic **Irish Canyon** slices through the Uinta Uplift, a cross-section of Colorado's geologic history that dates back more than two billion years. The five-mile road north through the canyon passes successively younger, tilted layers of sugary red quartzite, limestones, and other seafloor sediments that were once deeply buried. After the wrenching tectonic uplift of the Uinta Mountains, erosional debris from the uplift covered this, its eastern edge. An ancestor of Vermilion Creek dug a course across the debris and cut down into the hard layers below it to carve Irish Canyon. Erosion then removed the rest of the soft debris surrounding the hard rocks of the uplift, enabling the present Vermilion Creek (on the east side of the uplift) to extend its length upstream in a process called headward erosion. The head of the creek crept so far west that it met its ancestor, the stream that originally carved the canyon. The present Vermilion Creek pirated, or captured, the waters of this older stream, so that it no longer flows through Irish Canyon. The canyon is a scenic and intriguing place to hike or stop for a picnic. The Fremont people may once have used it as a "game drive," herding deer or pronghorn into its narrow passage so that they could be hunted more easily. A short interpretative trail leads to Fremont petroglyphs on boulders at the canyon's southern entrance: triangular-bodied, human-like figures with long lines scrolling out from their heads.

On Route 318 only a few miles west of Irish Canyon is the **Browns Park National Wildlife Refuge❖,** an unusually lovely federal bird sanctuary where a wide, meandering river bordered by mature cottonwoods is set against a background of tilted rock strata. The U.S. Fish and Wildlife Service is attempting to restore the natural floodplain of the Green River, altered by a dam upstream in Flaming Gorge, by pumping water to flood the banks of the river in a pattern similar to the one that occurred before it was dammed. Great Basin Canada geese nest here, as do redheads, mallards, and other ducks.

At the **Gates of Lodore** in Dinosaur National Monument (just south of the wildlife refuge off Route 318), the Green River plunges between towering walls of the same dark red quartzite seen at Irish Canyon (and also at Flaming Gorge). This spectacular section of the river is beloved by river-runners, and several companies offer trips through the Gates of

Above: *Sprinkled with hardy juniper trees, rolling BLM grasslands in Colorado's Big Gypsum Valley afford fine views of the snow-clad La Sal Mountains, which rise almost 13,000 feet just across the border in Utah.*

Lodore. For those on a brief visit, there is a short trail near the campground and a compact nature guide that identifies the flora of the pinyon-juniper ecosystem here. (More information on Dinosaur National Monument appears in Chapter 6.)

Although from the windows of an air-conditioned car the landscape of western Colorado looks sere, those who take a walk, mountain-bike ride, or river trip here soon fall under the spell of this ancient Fremont and Puebloan homeland.

133

UTAH

PART TWO

U T A H

At sunset, the rockbound landscape of southeast Utah and Arches National Park glows golden, exposing the very bones of the earth. This is the perfect time to visit Delicate Arch, one of the best-known symbols of the state, when it frames a vista of burnished slickrock and purple sky like some ancient ceremonial passageway. On such evenings, canyon wrens pour out their sweet, melancholy decrescendo, and pine-scented breezes course audibly like ocean waves through towers and swales of stone.

Arches lies in Utah's portion of the Colorado Plateau, where flowing water has carved alluring canyons and intricate labyrinths out of thick layers of angular sandstone, shale, and chalky limestone. Lying mostly from 4,500 to 6,500 feet above sea level, the plateau is dominated by scraggly pinyon pines and junipers twisted by the dry winds.

In the center of the state the Wasatch Line, a geologists' term for the state's backbone of snowy northern mountains and narrow southern plateaus, runs from Idaho to Arizona, dividing Utah's 85,000 square miles roughly in half. These highlands separate eastern Utah's share of the Colorado Plateau (drained by the Colorado River) from the Great Basin of western Utah, where streams pool in shallow, salty lakes with no outlet to the sea. Meeting the Wasatch Line at a right angle are the Uinta Mountains, which include 13,440-foot Kings Peak, the highest mountain in Utah. Although dark forests shroud much of the Uinta Mountains and Wasatch Line, there are sunny meadows and bare rock outcroppings as well. Altogether, Utah's ten million acres of highlands rear up into storm tracks to wring some moisture from the sky, making them a cool refuge for people and wildlife in summer and a playground for skiers in winter.

PRECEDING PAGES: *In Dead Horse Point State Park, an ancient Utah juniper overlooks Meander Canyon, where the Colorado River has cut neat cross-sections through the thick sedimentary layers of the Colorado Plateau.*

Most of the western third of Utah is fault-ridden basin and range, a corrugated landscape of narrow, north-south–trending mountain ranges separated by long basins. Gravels shed by the sharp-ridged ranges of ancient Paleozoic limestones are slowly filling up the flat basins. The Great Salt Lake Basin in the north is much broader and larger than others in Utah, containing a permanent lake that shimmers under the intense desert sun, its waters up to eight times saltier than the ocean.

Utah is a rain-starved state, the second driest in the country after Nevada. Dry air gains and loses heat quickly, which means that daytime temperatures may soar above 100 degrees and drop to 50 at night in some places in the summertime, and plunge from 70 to 20 degrees in the winter. Native flora and fauna have adapted; plants often have small leaves that appear blue because of insulating fuzz or olive green because of resinous or waxy coatings. Animals tend to move about only at night or at times when the sun is low.

Ice Age hunters pursued ancient bison and mammoths across Utah when it was a lush landscape of tall grasses and lakes. As the climate warmed and dried, hunters of smaller game prevailed for thousands of years until a benevolent climate cycle and the knowledge of how to grow corn fostered the rise of the Puebloan and Fremont civilizations. These settled people prospered and grew in numbers until the strain of repeated droughts caused the disintegration of their societies, to be followed yet again by hunter-gatherers. After the mountain men of the 1820s and other early explorers, people of the Mormon religion settled Utah in 1847. In no other state is natural history so intertwined with the story of its modern people: The sego lily is the state flower because Mormon pioneers ate its bulbs to stave off starvation, and Utah's bird is the seagull, which in 1848 saved settlers' crops from a plague of crickets.

Of Utah's land, 80 percent is managed by government agencies for public use. Of this, 64 percent is federal land, two thirds of which is managed for livestock grazing by the Bureau of Land Management (BLM). Utah's eight national forests encompass 15 percent of the state. In addition to five national parks, the National Park Service administers six national monuments and a national recreation area.

In Utah, visitors should save road travel for midday, when the sun is so strong that it drains the landscape of its color and hikers of their strength. The best times to walk are dawn and dusk, when the sun is gentler, the landscape hauntingly beautiful, and the air so still that sounds usually missed— the clink and rattle of rocks underfoot, the twittering of bats overhead, and the faint swish of junipers and sagebrush in the distance—are audible.

UTAH'S WASATCH LINE AND UINTA MOUNTAINS

The Wasatch Line is a great splintering break in the earth's crust that runs down the middle of Utah slightly northeast to southwest, splitting the state in half. Its heights offer sweeping panoramas of vast basins, fissured tablelands, and ridged deserts. One of North America's most notable landforms, the Wasatch Line manifests itself in the northern half of Utah as a row of craggy, fault-block mountains called the Wasatch Range. On its eastern side, this range is a ramp slanting up toward the sky, only to drop precipitously on its western front. In the southern part of Utah, the Wasatch Line transmutes into the wider, flatter high plateaus, which are steep-sided and deeply dissected by river canyons.

Unlike most of the ranges in the region, the ancient Uinta Mountains run east-west, forming a fat bulbous bridge of stone between the northwestern edge of Colorado and north-central Utah. A huge pile of brick-colored quartzite more than 20,000 feet thick, the Uintas were deposited as sand in a trough of shallow water and then compressed during the creation of the Rocky Mountains about 65 million years ago. The Uinta Uplift is a squeezed-up dome measuring 150 miles from east to west and 35 from north to south. Its rounded knobs have since been deeply carved by glaciers, forming scalloped, half-dome ridges and soft green valleys; but the rock of the Uintas is so hard that it weathers very slowly, producing little soil.

LEFT: *Winter only reluctantly gives way to spring on the higher, southern ramparts of the Wasatch Range. May brings a light dusting of snow to aspens along the Mount Nebo Scenic Loop in the Uinta National Forest.*

Compared with the rest of the state, Utah's highlands are verdant because storms from the Pacific Northwest carry abundant rain and snow to the northern mountains in winter and spring. At Brighton, a ski resort near Salt Lake City, snowfall averages more than 400 inches a year, and January is the wettest month. By contrast, the southern plateaus receive much less moisture and the wettest seasons are summer and fall, when moist air masses from the Gulfs of California and Mexico produce bursts of warm rain. Although it is only a thousand feet higher, Brighton receives more than three times as much rain and snow as Bryce Canyon in the southern plateaus.

In Utah's highlands temperatures can fluctuate from pleasantly warm to very cold over the course of any 24-hour period, so plants and animals must be able to cope with freezing virtually any night of the year. As a result, tundra caps the upper elevations of the mountains, while dark subalpine forests of spruce and fir bristle between about 9,000 and 11,000 feet, as well as down in some lower, shady canyons. For six or more months a year, these subalpine forests are deep in snow.

Below the subalpine zone, dark, dense woodlands of Douglas fir cloak the slopes of Utah's northern mountains. At the same elevations on the southern slopes of the Uintas and the southern plateaus, ponderosa pines create more open, parklike forests. Where fires have cleared the Douglas firs in the northern highlands, lodgepole pines and bright groves of aspens appear. Generally in the southern reaches, only the aspens invade such sunny spaces. Hundreds of bird species live in these warmer forests between 7,000 and 9,000 feet, where several bushes of the rose family produce fall berries, and many seeds can be found in cones.

Oak chaparral prevails from about 6,000 to 7,000 feet in the Wasatch Range, creeping up higher along sunny ridges and fingering into lower elevations along canyons. Chaparral is a stunted-looking plant community, containing lots of shrubs, small maples, and gnarled mountain mahogany as well as spindly oaks. At similar elevations in the Uintas to the east and on the high plateaus to the south, pinyon-juniper woodlands dominate.

The Wasatch Range, high plateaus, and Uinta Mountains fall almost entirely within six national forests, although they also include national, state, and local parks. All are well developed for visitors, featuring scenic drives,

---

OVERLEAF: *At the edge of the Table Cliff Plateau, the Claron Formation—composed of the same soft limestone found at Bryce Canyon—has eroded spectacularly around the Paunsaugunt Fault below Powell Point.*

ABOVE: *Shy forest denizens, black bears learn early to scramble up nearby trees when interrupted in their foraging for roots, berries, grubs, and carrion.*

RIGHT: *Growing from the same vast root base, clonal stands of identically colored aspens cascade down steep slopes near Guardsman Pass in the Wasatches.*

campgrounds, and hiking trails. This itinerary begins on Scenic Byway Route 89 in the north-central part of Utah, swings east of Salt Lake City into the Uinta Mountains and then heads south nearly the full length of the state (roughly parallel to Interstate 15) through the Uinta, Manti–La Sal, Fishlake, and Dixie national forests. Route 89 is again the main route through the scenic high plateaus to Bryce Canyon National Park and Cedar Breaks National Monument.

THE NORTHERN HIGHLANDS

On the western side of the Wasatch Range is an exceptionally long, abrupt escarpment called the Wasatch Front, which runs 210 miles from Soda Springs, Idaho, to Nephi, Utah. Movement along the Wasatch fault zone—east side up, west side down—began 38 to 25 million years ago and continues today. Numerous hot springs, frequent earthquakes, and the presence of igneous rocks reveal its seismically active nature. Although erosion has been wearing it down ever since the beginning of its uplift, the Wasatch Front still soars splendidly more than a mile above the cities below.

The Wasatch Front is subject to intense levels of sun, wind, and avalanche-producing snow. Subalpine and Douglas fir forests cling to its steep slopes in patches separated by expanses of tundra or rocky grassland. White snow lingers late into spring on its gray stone parapets, dotted with tufts of deep-green woodland and paler green clearings. In autumn, the oaks and maples of the chaparral lower down change color, blanketing the laps of the mountains with bright red and yellow shawls.

For more than a century, Utah's industrious Mormon settlers have de-

ABOVE: *The largest members of the deer family, Shiras moose are increasing their range in Utah, including the Bear River Range. Usually solitary, they sometimes band together after the rutting season.*

pended upon the resources of these northern mountains—originally for timber to build their cities and rangeland to raise their livestock, more recently for recreation. The Wasatch National Forest (later the **Wasatch-Cache National Forest❖**) was established in 1906 to restore the watersheds of mountains already devastated by logging, fire, and grazing.

A good way to visit the northernmost part of the Wasatch-Cache National Forest is to travel from Logan northeast up Route 89, the Logan Canyon Scenic Byway, into the Bear River Mountains. The range is named for the Bear River, which runs along the western foot of the mountains from its source in Idaho. The scenic byway twists up the sheer-walled, fossil-laden limestone canyon of the Logan River to its highest point, 7,800 feet. East of this summit, an overlook offers a pretty view of exceptionally blue Bear Lake; the shoreline is almost all privately owned and not accessible to most travelers.

During the last Ice Age, glaciers carved valleys and ridges into the block-faulted Bear River Mountains, and trickling water continues to dissolve their limestone into a karst topography of many caves and sinkholes. Backpacking trails in the **Mount Naomi Wilderness❖** north of Route 89 lead hikers into a delightful landscape where warbling vireos flit

ABOVE: *Below Mount Naomi in the Bear River Mountains, summer vegetation along White Pine Creek is ideal forage for moose, which tug up the aquatic plants with their rubbery lips and nibble at streamside shrubs.*

from flowery meadows into stands of maples, aspens, and Douglas or subalpine fir. A few moose browse the willows along streams in the wilderness area, which is named for 9,979-foot Mount Naomi, the highest peak in the Bear River Mountains. To the east beyond the wilderness area, more trails wander through U-shaped valleys, tundra-clad cirques exposing tilted limestone strata, and blue mountain lakes. A pleasant walk along the one-mile Limber Pine Trail leads to a natural bonsai garden of contorted limber pines (including five trees twisted together) and grand vistas of neighboring valleys and mountains.

At such higher elevations, elk bugle their challenges during the rutting season and then move lower to escape the deepest winter snows and find forage. Travelers interested in seeing these magnificent animals in their shaggy winter coats may want to take an excursion to the **Hardware Ranch Game Management Area**❖ near Hyrum off Route 101, which runs east from Route 89 south of Logan. Here, employees feed wild elk in the winter to keep them from ravaging the local range and crops, and drive horse-drawn sleighs full of bundled-up visitors out to view them.

Southwest of Logan via Route 89 lie the Wellsville Mountains, separated from the Bear River Range by the Cache Valley. The **Wellsville Mountain**

Wilderness❖, which encompasses the highest peaks of the Wellsvilles, is a lovely place for day hikes, affording sweeping views of the surrounding wetlands and distant mountain ranges. It is also famous as a place to see migrating hawks. From here, Hawkwatch International monitors raptors on their southbound migrations during September and October.

From Mantua, south on Route 89 from the Wellsvilles, the unpaved Willard Peak Scenic Backway climbs 14 miles south, to 9,500-foot

Inspiration Point in the Wasatch-Cache National Forest. The peak provides a hawk's-eye view of the Great Salt Lake, the Bear River Range to the north, and the Wasatch Range to the south. At this point, travelers may wish to visit the **Bear River Migratory Bird Refuge❖,** just west of Brigham City, or the Raft River Mountains on the border with Idaho (see Chapter 8).

Before continuing south to explore the rest of the Wasatch Range, travelers can journey to the Uinta Mountains by driving east from Salt Lake City on Interstate 80 to Exit 148 and following Route 248 southeast to Kamas, where Route 150, the Mirror Lake Scenic Byway, begins. This approach to the Uintas winds along the Provo River, through rugged, forested mountains popular with visitors and bustling with resorts and campgrounds, to the **High Uintas Wilderness Area❖.** Campgrounds at the foot of the Uinta Mountains may be reached by roads leading north from Route 40. The advantage of this southern route is that it also leads to the Flaming Gorge National Recreation Area and to Dinosaur

ABOVE: *Spring finds a male western bluebird—a tiny, five-inch-long cousin of the robin—perched on a ponderosa twig.*

RIGHT: *At sunrise, pale reflections from the snow on Mount Timpanogos brighten the waters in Deer Creek Reservoir State Park.*

National Monument, both areas where the innards of the Uinta Mountains are exposed in scenic canyons (see Chapter 6).

The High Uintas Wilderness Area, the largest in the state, is Utah's Eden, a quiet realm where nature's rhythms are relatively undisturbed except by hikers and a few grazing cattle. The High Uintas are vast and mostly unspoiled, a paradigm of ecological diversity. Three fourths of Utah's bird species have been sighted in these mountains, where extensive old-growth forests support a number of rare birds, from eight-inch-long saw-whet owls (which rasp like a saw being sharpened), to pileated

ABOVE: *Hardy yellow monkeyflowers cling to rocks above the rushing waters of Cascade Springs in the Wasatch Mountains. Each day seven million gallons of water flow from these springs into the Provo River.*

woodpeckers twice that size, to fierce northern goshawks. Grouse whortleberry cloaks the floor of the subalpine forest here, and the Uintas are the only place in Utah to support extensive stands of lodgepole pine. The state's largest elk and moose populations roam the Uintas, browsing in the grassy meadows and along streams thick with willows. Mountain lions, black bears, and bighorn sheep live here too, but are seldom seen.

This wilderness area embraces some of Utah's highest mountains—including its very loftiest, 13,440-foot Kings Peak—and tundra stretches 60 miles without a break, covering more than 300 square miles. Heavy winters produce enough snowmelt to fill more than 2,200 small lakes and countless streams abounding with fish and river otters, as well as marshy bogs unusual for arid Utah. Many trails lead into the High Uintas from Route 150, but because of the deep snowpack, the hiking season lasts only from the beginning of July to the middle of September. Even during the summer months, rain showers drench many afternoons. Hikers wishing to visit the High Uintas can contact the Forest Service office in Vernal, Kamas, or Roosevelt to check on trail conditions before entering the wilderness area.

THE CENTRAL MOUNTAINS

The Wasatch Mountains (part of the Wasatch Range) form a magnificent backdrop to the metropolitan area that includes Ogden, Salt Lake City, Orem, and Provo. All the roads into the canyons of these mountains make very scenic drives and lead to lovely places where shady walks wander among bigtooth maples and aspens, along gentle paths bordered by bracken and creeping barberry to waterfalls and hidden ravines. Bright aspens, with dark spruces poking up through them, flutter on the upper slopes. Staff at park and Forest Service offices and campgrounds can describe their favorite walks or provide Forest Service maps showing many short trails.

Although they are some of the most heavily used national forest lands in the country, the Wasatch Mountains have kept much of their natural character because of the four large wilderness areas within them. The **Twin Peaks❖** and **Mount Olympus❖** wilderness areas are accessible from Route 190, which runs east from I-15 up Big Cottonwood Canyon to the **Brighton Ski Resort❖**. Route 210 heads east from I-15 up Little Cottonwood Canyon to the ski resort at **Alta❖**, providing access to both the Twin Peaks and **Lone Peak❖** wilderness areas. Also running east from I-15, up through American Fork Canyon, is Route 44, which leads to the Lone Peak and **Mount Timpanogos❖** wilderness areas.

Together, these wilderness areas comprise almost 70,000 acres of spectacular mountain scenery and a number of popular hiking trails, which are fairly strenuous because the Wasatch Mountains are high and steep. Several peaks in the range exceed 11,000 feet and are snowbound much of the year. In summer, melting snow sustains water-loving flowers such as Parry's primroses, columbine, forget-me-nots, and pennyroyal in damp meadows alternating with slopes of spruce and fir. Busy pikas and big, sunbathing marmots stare at passing walkers in midday, and mule deer, elk, and moose graze silently at dusk. Occasionally, lucky hikers spot the elusive mountain goats recently introduced into these mountains or the signs of mountain lions or black bears.

Timpanogos Cave National Monument❖, on Route 44 northeast of American Fork, is literally a jewel of the National Park System. Three linked limestone chambers high on the south wall of American Fork Canyon are encrusted with translucent crystals and flowstones in the shape of stalagmites, soda-straw stalactites, and sparkling helictites—delicate, randomly twisting filaments of calcite or aragonite. Trace minerals lend a bit of color—pink and copper, green and lilac—and a crystalline pool in Timpanogos Cave shimmers with light. These exquisite caves are

ABOVE: *The largest accipiters, or short-winged hawks, northern goshawks roam old-growth forests, swiftly pursuing prey— birds as large as ruffed grouse and pheasants as well as squirrels and snowshoe hares.*

RIGHT: *In the Uinta National Forest, bright green leaf buds clothe slender aspens in May, even as late snow lingers in the avalanche chutes of Mount Nebo.*

remarkably well preserved because they were placed under government protection soon after their discovery. Although visitors must often wait an hour or more before joining a cave tour, the entrance to the caves is 1,065 feet up a 1.5-mile paved trail from the visitor center, and the wait allows time to make this strenuous hike at a leisurely pace.

Nestled among slopes of Gambel oak and aspen that are gloriously golden in the fall, the **Cascade Springs Interpretive Site❖** is a refreshing oasis on the other side of the mountains from Timpanogos Cave via winding mountain roads (Route 92 to Forest Road 114). Here, three short trails lead around travertine pools fringed with watercress, cattails, Scouler's willows, and yellow monkeyflowers. Butterflies float in sunbeams above the pools, where brown trout introduced from Europe in the 1880s drift in the clear water. The terraced pools are white bowls of

calcium carbonate dissolved from the surrounding limestones by percolating groundwater, then redeposited as the water emerged from the rock. Wild roses bloom among the stinging nettles, and yellow warblers swoop between box-elder branches hung with paper wasp nests.

East of I-15 between Santaquin and Nephi lies the **Mount Nebo Wilderness Area❖,** which embraces 11,877-foot Mount Nebo, the highest peak of the Wasatch Range. Although there are access routes to the area from I-15, a better alternative is to take the Mount Nebo Scenic Loop (Forest Road 15), which begins just outside Payson and meanders south as it climbs through picturesque apple orchards and foothills covered in oak woodland to a forest of aspens, fir, and spruce and finally to views of the mountain. Mount Nebo, standing a little apart south of the rest of the Wasatch Range, is a good place to become familiar with a whole mountain—its summit, its foothills, its forests and meadows. From its heights, there are spectacular views of the surrounding ranges and valleys. In summer, meadows on its flanks brighten with blue columbine, purple lupine, vermilion paintbrush, and giant green gentian, while Clark's nutcrackers and other jays squawk noisily at picnickers seeking shady spots in the foothills.

Many gentle hiking trails lead off the scenic drive through this part of the **Uinta National Forest❖**, from the Bennie Creek Trail up a narrow stream canyon lined with maples and cottonwoods, to the Nebo Bench Trail, which winds into the high tundra wilderness. On the south side of Mount Nebo, a short paved trail passes through chokecherry and big sage to the **Devil's Kitchen Geologic Area❖**, where 80-million-year-old sandstone has been eroded into deep red columns and canyons. Black and orange crescent-spot butterflies waver in the warm, fragrant air on this sunny side of the mountain, making the stop a pleasant respite from the twisting mountain byway as it descends to Route 132 just east of Nephi.

THE SOUTH-CENTRAL HIGHLANDS

In the southern half of the state, faults along the Wasatch Line have produced the **Canyon, Pahvant,** and **Tushar** mountain ranges, as well as the long, narrow tablelands of the **Wasatch, Aquarius, Paunsaugunt,** and **Markagunt** plateaus. These south-central highlands, a geologic transition zone between the corrugated Great Basin province to the west and the Colorado Plateau province of sculpted sedimentary rock to the east, share certain characteristics with their neighbors on either side. Volcanic rocks protect much of the young sedimentary strata of this high country from erosion. Some of the sedimentary rocks are colorful—sometimes deep red, but mostly multihued pastel—freshwater limestones deposited in freshwater lakes 60 million years ago. Uplifted and cloaked in lava flows, they now form isolated tablelands with varicolored bluffs above down-dropped valley blocks called grabens.

Altogether, these mountains and plateaus—mostly federal land managed as national forests, with particularly scenic areas incorporated into the National Park System—cover an area greater than the state of Maryland. Beginning with an optional drive east to see the Wasatch Plateau, the itinerary continues south on Route 132 to Route 89, which provides the main access to the rest of the south-central highlands.

Travelers driving south on Route 132 who wish to hike or mountain-bike on the Wasatch Plateau in the **Manti–La Sal National Forest❖** can

ABOVE: *While cattle graze in the well-watered valley below, fast-moving winds force moist air upward over the Sevier Plateau. Here the elongated profiles of the resulting "wave clouds" echo the rolling terrain.*

turn north at Pigeon Hollow Junction on Route 89 to Fairview and there turn east on Route 31, the Huntington Canyon Scenic Byway. This road climbs over the mostly treeless, grassy top of the Wasatch Plateau, an uplifted block fissured from north to south by numerous faults. The plateau reaches 11,300 feet in elevation, and the resulting rain and snow supply many lakes, reservoirs, and streams popular with anglers. Ponderosa pines grow in protected side canyons, which are especially long and deep on the eastern side of the plateau, while dense aspens cloak the upper slopes. From the summit of the plateau, travelers can continue east on the scenic byway to Huntington or turn south along the top of the plateau on the Skyline Drive Scenic Backway, a bumpy, unpaved track recommended only for high-clearance vehicles. Although even those with four-wheel drive must proceed slowly, Skyline Drive provides good views of distant cliffs, mesas, and valleys stretching into infinity in the clear air. Many slopes of the Wasatch Plateau are badly scarred and artificially terraced because heavy grazing by domestic livestock destroyed their vegetative cover, causing erosion of the soil on the plateau and flooding in the valley and towns below.

Those travelers who wish to bypass the Wasatch Plateau can drive south at Pigeon Hollow Junction on Route 89—which converges with I-70 at Salina—through the rustic Sanpete and Sevier valleys. The Sevier (locally pronounced "severe") Valley is a chunk of the earth's crust that dropped down along faults between the Sevier Plateau on the east and the Pahvant Range to the west. On either side of the sagebrush-bunchgrass rangeland of the Sevier Valley, slopes and bluffs expose pink, white, and vermilion strata. In this active geothermal area, warm springs are tapped for their therapeutic properties in spa communities such as Monroe.

At the town of Sevier, I-70 and a smaller road signposted for the **Fremont Indian State Park❖** both dive west into a pass between the Pahvant Range to the north and the Tushar Range to the south. This pass is the narrow valley of Clear Creek, where Fremont people lived a thousand years ago. Only six miles from Sevier, the state park contains 500 panels of petroglyphs—mysterious figures tapped into the stone by the Fremont people and their predecessors. Interpretative trails lead to the panels and to a reconstructed pit house (a roofed-over subterranean dwelling) through areas supporting plants once used by the Fremont. Although they farmed, the Fremont also depended upon plants they gathered and animals they hunted here and in the marshes of Clear Creek. They stored their food in dozens of stone "granaries" in a substantial settlement of more than 80 pit houses. An excellent visitor center provides ranger programs, exhibits, films, and a bookshop.

A delightful place to take a walk on a warm summer day is **Clear Creek Canyon,** whose walls are gold and buff-colored tuff, layers of volcanic ash varnished by trace minerals that look like drips of dark honey. Aromatic sagebrush and dark-green snakeweed harbor sparrows, rabbits, and lizards. It is easy to understand the Paiutes' traditional reverence for this lovely, lively canyon.

From I-70 near Fremont Indian State Park, the Kimberly–Big John Scenic Backway leads south through the Tushar Mountains in the **Fishlake National Forest❖.** In good weather, passenger cars can negotiate this dirt and gravel road without problems, but there are some rough spots where low-clearance vehicles might scrape. Wet weather makes the road slick, and it is closed in winter and spring. Alternatively, Route 153 runs into the mountains from either side. The Beaver Canyon Scenic Byway, the paved portion of Route 153 from the town of Beaver to the **Elk Meadows Ski Area❖** below Mount Holly, is open all year. The eastern portion of Route 153, a good gravel road from the town of Junction on Route 89, is open as snow permits.

Rising more than 6,000 feet above the valleys on either side, the Tushars are some of the highest mountains between the Sierras of California and the Rockies of Colorado and the only range in Utah's southern highlands that supports tundra. A popular day-hiking route leads up 12,173-foot Delano Peak, the highest in the Tushars. This splendid climb passes through dry tundra offering breathtaking views of the whole range, including the Tushars' second highest peak, 12,139-foot Mount Belknap to the north. South of Puffer Lake, the top of the Tushar Range is gently rolling, almost level, featuring many small lakes and meadows and forests of aspens and mixed conifers. Ospreys fish in the lakes, and blue grouse strut about in the spruce-fir forest. In the fall, the mountains are popular with hunters pursuing the many elk and mule deer.

Just south of the town of Junction, Route 62 runs east from Route 89 and cuts through the Sevier Plateau, which like the other high country in the region is a tableland of small lakes and forests interspersed with meadows. Travelers with four-wheel drive can explore the network of dirt and gravel roads on its undulating, deeply ravined surface.

Seven miles south of Panguitch, Route 12 leads east from Route 89 to Route 63 into one of Utah's most famous scenic attractions, **Bryce Canyon National Park❖**. Approaching the park, visitors traverse high rangelands and a ponderosa forest, and then suddenly an altogether improbable spectacle yawns before them: a sloping labyrinth of powdery pink, fanciful rock pillars called hoodoos.

Aided by frost wedging and landslides, the branching tributaries of several creeks have carved amphitheaters cluttered with hoodoos into the eastern flank of the Paunsaugunt (Paiute for "place of the beavers") Plateau. About 70 to 65 million years ago, the soft pastel sediments of the Claron Formation, a thousand feet of friable, freshwater limestones and siltstones, were deposited in a huge shallow lake that formed between the uplifting Rocky Mountains to the east and the Sevier Mountains to the west. Between about 35 and 12 million years ago, continued uplifting of the Colorado Plateau caused major faulting in the area, which isolated the Paunsaugunt Plateau. The erosion at Bryce began perhaps as recently as half a million years ago, when the Paria River and its tributaries began to claw at the edge of the Paunsaugunt in earnest. Erosion here is rapid— about one foot per 65 years on average.

The park is long and narrow, its 56 square miles embracing about 20 miles of the scenic Pink Cliffs on the edge of the plateau. The north-south main road runs the length of these cliffs for 18 miles, to 9,105-foot

LEFT: *In Bryce Canyon National Park, a watchful mule deer pauses under a snowy ponderosa pine along the Navajo Loop Trail.*

RIGHT: *An intricately eroded limestone spire called Thor's Hammer balances gracefully below Bryce's Sunset Point.*

OVERLEAF: *Sunrise gilds the rock pinnacles of the Silent City at Bryce Canyon, which Mormon settler Ebenezer Bryce called "a hell of a place to lose a cow."*

Rainbow Point at the park's southern end. Just inside Bryce's northern boundary, a side road leads east to Fairyland Point, a fabulous scenic overlook and the trailhead into Fairyland Canyon. The visitor center, containing a bookshop and explanatory exhibits, is another mile farther south on the main road, next to the entrance station. Rangers offer interpretative programs here, at the campground, and along park trails during the summer. Continuing south, turnoffs from the main park road lead to views (including Sunset, Inspiration, and Bryce points) and trailheads.

Trails into the canyon zigzag across slopes of creeping, unstable soil that proves precarious for aspens and ponderosa, limber, and bristlecone pines. Here these usually robust trees are dwarfed and twisted, clinging with exposed roots to the shifting, sunset-colored dirt and adding the impression of a giant's bonsai garden to an already uncanny scene. On the more stable slopes, manzanita and curlleaf mountain mahogany thrive, and a few wildflowers dot the chalky soil in spring and early summer. Bryce supports a high concentration of endemic plant species restricted to these unusual limestone substrates, and summer finds some 170 bird species in residence. Chickadees, Steller's jays, Clark's nutcrackers, and robins flutter and call from clusters of ponderosas in the ravines. On many trees, the bark has been stripped away by lightning or fire exposing strong, spiral trunks—a genetic adaptation enabling them to withstand heavy winds.

Most people who visit Bryce come to see the rose-, white-, and salmon-colored hoodoos that distinguish the park. A relatively level trail skirts the rim for a few miles in either direction from the lodge area, and a number of gentle trails wind from this rim trail down through the pretty pink formations. The names of these trails are appropriate: Fairyland

ABOVE: *There are many species of Indian paintbrush; the red (left) and yellow (right) survive in the driest areas. The colorful bracts are not actually flowers but showy leaves modified to attract pollinators.*

Loop, Queen's Garden (passing a pinnacle that resembles Queen Victoria in her later years), and a horse trail named Peekaboo Loop. Even a short walk among these fantastic spires is well worth the effort. On all the trails, be sure to carry water as it can be very hot, or plan a visit to the dream-like landscape at sunrise, under moonlight, or when it is covered with a light dusting of snow.

Cedar Breaks National Monument❖ is Bryce's cousin to the west, on the edge of the Markagunt Plateau. Reached via Route 143 southwest from Panguitch on Route 89, Cedar Breaks at 10,000 feet is higher than Bryce, and the Claron Formation is even more colorful here, with yellow and purple adding to its splendor. Although Cedar Breaks is smaller than Bryce, it encircles one stupendous amphitheater, more than three miles in diameter and 2,000 feet deep, formed where the plateau uplifted along a fault and the basin and range country dropped down to the west.

The high plateau country of Cedar Breaks receives enough snow and rain to keep it green and speckled with gorgeous wildflowers during the visitor season (the monument is closed to all but snowshoers and cross-country skiers from November well into May). Considering its high, breath-taking elevation, the Alpine Pond Nature Trail is mercifully short—two

LEFT: *In Dixie National Forest, Parry's primrose, a purple alpine flower, blooms in July on the ancient volcanic rock of Brian Head, the highest point on the uptilted western edge of the Markagunt Plateau.*

miles of flowery meadow and deep old-growth woodland where blue grouse pace among the tree trunks, with a midpoint stop at a quiet pond. In spring and autumn, temperatures fluctuate so drastically here from noon to night that butterflies sometimes freeze into the ice as it forms on the surface of Alpine Pond. Nonetheless, many creatures thrive here, as attested by persistent ground squirrels and Clark's nutcrackers at the picnic area.

The steep, colorful slopes north and west of Cedar Breaks, which are part of the Dixie National Forest, have been set aside as the **Ashdown Gorge Wilderness Area❖.** The trail through the Ashdown is strenuous and seldom used; hikers determined to take it on should ascertain the trail's current conditions and the location of the trailhead at the Cedar Breaks Visitor Center.

Much of this country is strewn with jumbled lichen-covered boulders of black basalt, which gushed as lava over this part of Utah from 35 to 25 million years ago. This erosion-resistant basalt caps **Brian Head,** a promontory visible to the north from Cedar Breaks that overlooks the western basin and range country. At 11,146 feet above sea level, Brian Head receives lots of snow, making it a very popular ski resort.

Gentle, accessible trails in the **Dixie National Forest❖** south of Cedar Breaks include the Bristlecone Pine Trail, on Route 14 west of Route 148 and just east of the Zion Overlook, which leads to a stand of huge bristlecone pines in less than a mile. The Cascade Falls Trail, also off Route 14 but east of Route 148, runs less than a mile through rosy-colored limestone formations to a waterfall that is the outlet of Navajo Lake. The Dixie contains countless such trails through coniferous forests and sunny meadows. District office staff members in all the national forests in Utah are happy to describe their own favorite trails to visitors.

Both literally and figuratively, the Wasatch Highlands and Uinta Mountains are the backbone of Utah, extending across the state like a spine and shoulder blade. Without these high elevations, there would be even less water in this second-driest of the United States, and many plants and animals would be unable to survive without the cool, moist shelter they find here. As retreats from the glare and stress of life in the lowlands, the mountains are important to people, too. They are Utah's green refuge, a domain of big trees, open meadows, and cool water.

RIGHT: *A bristlecone pine grows on Spectra Point at Cedar Breaks National Monument. The oldest dated trees on earth, bristlecones survive harsh winds, intense sun, and extreme cold in their timberline habitat.*

UTAH: BENEATH THE HIGH PLATEAUS

In the shadow of Utah's towering Wasatch Line curves an arc of landscape that is caught between two different worlds. Clear streams and cool air flow down on it from the forested highlands to the west, while to the east lies a scorched and stony desert. These two extremes overlap within a remarkable expanse of country that stretches diagonally from Utah's southwestern corner near Zion National Park to Dinosaur National Monument in the state's far eastern corner. The landscape in this transition zone is one of spectacular geologic features and diverse flora and fauna, combining elements of the lofty plateaus of Utah's spine with those of the rockbound Colorado Plateau. Here beneath the high plateaus, Utah can be shady or sunstruck, moist or arid, dark or open.

Perhaps in no other place in the United States are rocks so interesting. The color and character of the stone is eloquent, speaking clearly of its origins: soft, pastel limestones formed in prehistoric salt- and freshwater seas; tawny sandstones from ancient dune fields, now stained deep red by iron oxides and cemented as hard as concrete by percolating silica; mounds of weathered clays—subtle lilacs, grays, and chocolates—imbedded in debris deposited by long-dormant volcanoes. The bones of dinosaurs protrude from the rocky terrain; petroglyphs and pictographs incised and painted by early civilizations embellish cliff walls. Severe and intricately eroded, the topography often overpowered nineteenth-century

LEFT: *Along Clear Creek in Zion National Park, erosion exposes the edges of ancient sandstone. These layers were deposited by persistent winds that blew across a huge dune field during the age of dinosaurs.*

scientist-explorers such as the legendary John Wesley Powell, who traced the canyons of the Green and Colorado rivers in the 1860s and 1870s. Powell's protégé, geologist Clarence Dutton, noted lyrically: "the very air is...visible. We see it, palpably, as a tenuous fluid, and the rocks beyond it do not appear to be colored blue as they do in other regions, but reveal themselves clothed in colors of their own."

Travelers today find this land equally wondrous. The transition between the highlands and the lower plateau and basin country creates striking landscapes and provides a rich habitat for wildlife. Runoff from the adjoining uplands deeply erodes bent or down-dropped strata into fantastic spires, arches, pinnacles, and hoodoos. Plants and animals typical of various elevations mingle, especially along streams. The air is dry— as it is elsewhere in Utah—but the harshness of the climate is mitigated by the shade of cliffs and canyons and by cool running water.

This chapter's itinerary begins in Zion National Park and winds across the arid southern border of the state to Glen Canyon and Lake Powell. Turning north it heads generally northeast, stopping at Kodachrome Basin State Park, Escalante Canyon, and Capitol Reef National Park and along the San Rafael Swell. A scenic backway then leads northward to steep-walled canyons, a prolific wildlife refuge, the White and Green rivers, and Dinosaur National Monument.

ZION NATIONAL PARK

Below Utah's central highlands, the natural areas that rim the Colorado Plateau are characterized by the remarkably beautiful cross-bedded Navajo sandstone, the thickest, most spectacular sandstone in Utah. This streaky blond rock was formed in a vast windblown desert over millions of years during the Triassic and Jurassic periods. In time, the desert's sand compacted under the pressure of overlying layers and was cemented into rock with silica. Today, where erosion has exposed cross-sections of the fossilized dunes, fine, diagonally bedded layers of sand resemble wavy golden hair. In this dry region of the country, the extremely hard Navajo sandstone tends to resist colonizing by plants. Where sand is swept away from the mother rock by wind and rain, the resulting surface is known locally as slickrock.

Zion National Park✥, west from Route 89 on Route 9, is a wilderness of pink and white slickrock that has been cut in half by the deep, narrow canyon of the Virgin River and its tributaries. At Zion, the Navajo sandstone is 2,400 feet thick (elsewhere in Utah it is as much as 3,000 feet

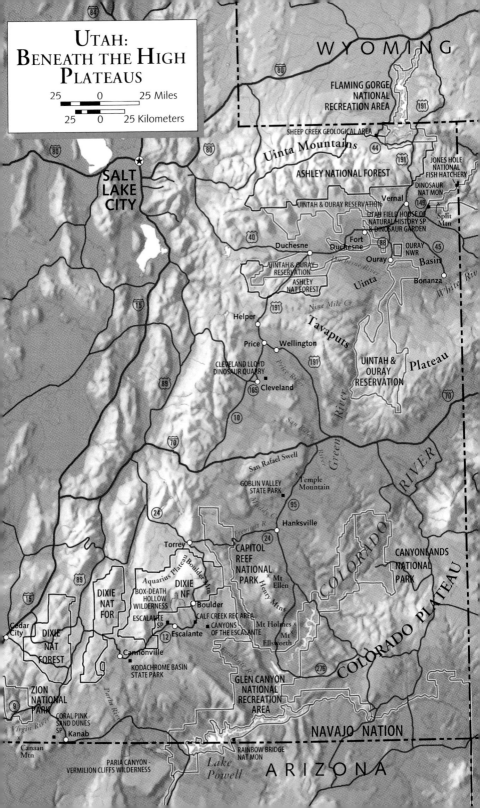

thick). As the Virgin River erodes softer rock beneath it, this massive sandstone falls away in great slabs in a process known as mass-wasting. Black and amber desert varnish—a deposit of manganese and iron oxides—stains the surface of the cliffs in long vertical streaks.

Most travelers to Zion begin at the visitor center, near the South Entrance on the main Park Road, an extension of Route 9, where exhibits outline the geologic story of the park and displays examine the natural and human history of the area. The center also contains one of the most extensive natural history bookshops in the region.

Zion's main attraction is the lovely sylvan canyon carved by the Virgin River, which was named for the Virgin Mary. The Zion Canyon Scenic Drive leads up this canyon to the lodge and several trailheads. Most of the land encompassed by the park, however, is about 2,000 feet above the canyon. Route 9—the Zion–Mount Carmel Highway—climbs up to the top of the plateau in the eastern portion of the park via the tributary canyon carved by Pine Creek, through two tunnels bored into the sandstone (one more than a mile long). On top, the road winds through a stunning, convoluted landscape—where exposed stretches of swirled, eroded sandstone form stone "beehives" and gorges—to Zion's eastern boundary. The Kolob Canyons section of the park, on the plateau west of Zion Canyon, is a higher, lesser-known, and more secluded area. The Kolob Canyons Road from Exit 40 on Interstate 15 leads to the deep red Finger Canyons along the edge of the Kolob Terrace. The 5.5-mile Taylor Creek Trail is a moderate hike in the Kolob; the 15-mile Kolob Arch Trail is strenuous. Both follow creeks, so there is cool water to splash on hot faces; but they are long walks in summer. In winter, deep snow shrouds the Kolob.

Probably the most popular walk in the park is the paved one-mile Riverside Walk, leading from the end of the Zion Canyon Scenic Drive to the beginning of the Zion Narrows. The path is cool and shady beneath the enormous cottonwoods and box elders draped with canyon grape that fringe the clear waters of the Virgin River. Sandstone walls support hanging gardens of maidenhair fern, magenta shooting stars, and golden columbine, and sooty little birds called American dippers bob on the rocks above the stream. The hike through the Narrows, 16 miles of wading in the waist-deep Virgin River between the precipitous walls of Zion

Left: *Called the "Sandstone Yosemite," Zion National Park boasts spectacular rock formations carved over eons by the Virgin River. The clear light of sunrise illuminates West Temple and Towers of the Virgin.*

Canyon, is a magical experience in May or June, but it is not recommended when rains or snowmelt could rush through the Narrows in a flash flood. Consult with staff at the visitor center before setting out.

Of the many shorter hikes in Zion National Park, one of the most pleasant is the loop to the lower and middle Emerald Pools. This trail winds through a woodland of Gambel oak and maples to shallow pools frequented by tadpoles and sister (*Adelpha*) butterflies and returns across a sunny slope of cliffrose, Mormon tea, and buffalo berry. A walk that gives a taste of the top of the plateau without requiring great exertion is the one-mile (round-trip) Canyon Overlook Trail, beginning just east of the first tunnel on the Zion–Mount Carmel Highway. This gentle path winds along a sandstone wall above a slot canyon (some walkers find the drop-off unnerving). Penstemon and manzanita bloom along the route, which ends at a breathtaking overlook a thousand feet above the canyon floor.

The more strenuous trail from Weeping Rock to Observation Point takes hikers four miles up switchbacks on cliff faces and through a high, sinuous slot canyon from the floor of Zion Canyon to its top, where the reward is expansive views of the canyon below and the plateau all around. Halfway to Observation Point, the East Rim Trail diverges to the northeast, leading 11.5 miles to Zion's east entrance. The East Rim Trail is very stren-

LEFT: *Red Indian paintbrush blooms in cracks in the weathered slickrock of Zion National Park. As they grow, probing plant roots chemically and physically break the layers of Navajo sandstone apart.*

RIGHT: *An American kestrel—at less than a foot the smallest and most common North American falcon—perches on a mullein stalk, a good vantage point to watch for grasshoppers, lizards, or mice.*

uous, climbs 2,400 feet, and contains steep drop-offs, as does the 14-mile West Rim Trail, which begins at the Grotto picnic area and climbs almost 3,600 feet to the Horse Pasture Plateau. Obviously, both trails are for fit and experienced hikers. The distances given are one-way: Most hikers traveling these trails park one vehicle at their destination point and then drive another car back to the trailhead to begin their hike.

For those who prefer tougher hikes in lesser-known areas, the Smithsonian Butte Scenic Backway leads from Rockville (just southwest of Zion on Route 9) to the BLM's 28,000-acre **Canaan Mountain❖,** between Zion and the Arizona border. Actually a plateau deeply grooved by canyons and trickling streams, 7,427-foot Canaan Mountain is a wonderland of pinnacles and balanced rocks hunted by hawks and coyotes that affords awe-inspiring 270-degree views of Zion and the Virgin River Valley. The unpaved backway, well maintained and suitable for a passenger car in dry weather, follows the general route taken by Captain Clarence Dutton—a protégé of the great geologist-adventurer John Wesley Powell—as he explored the Zion area in the 1870s. The Smithsonian Institution, established in 1846, was closely associated with Dutton and Powell's work of surveying and interpreting the landscape of the American West.

PARIA CANYON TO LAKE POWELL

Leading east from Zion on Route 9, the itinerary turns southeast on Route 89. The 12-mile paved Ponderosa–Coral Pink Sand Dunes Scenic Backway heads south on a signed road 10 miles southeast of Mount Carmel Junction. In **Coral Pink Sand Dunes State Park❖,** reminiscent of Zion 160 million years ago, wind has blown rosy-colored sand weathered from the Navajo sandstone into dunes like those formed in the distant Jurassic. Although this relatively small park is popular with dune-buggy

173

aficionados, hikers can spot tracks of bobcats, mice, beetles, and lizards. Big sunflowers called mule-ears bloom profusely in early summer. At 110,000 acres, the **Paria Canyon–Vermillion Cliffs Wilderness Area❖** is the largest BLM wilderness in the country. Half in Utah, half in Arizona, it straddles the border off Route 89 ten miles west of Big Water. The 38-mile hike through Paria Canyon finishes near Lees Ferry in Arizona. Trekking through this quintessential canyon country to the Colorado River in Arizona's Grand Canyon National Park means at least four glorious days of traipsing on rocky paths, wading in shin-deep water, and sleeping rough beneath soaring coppery cliffs. The world outside the narrow Paria is forgotten as canyon, stream, sunlight, and petroglyphs of bighorns and anthropomorphs with boomerang-shaped heads engage one's full attention. The journey is melodious—canyon wrens sing and the Paria River burbles and splashes—and colorful, as bright flowers peep from alcove gardens and from claret-cup cacti roasting in the sun. Flashing blue kingfishers swoop from tree to tree, and mule deer gaze from the shadows below the cliffs.

Farther east on Route 89 is the **Glen Canyon National Recreation Area❖.** The Colorado River carved Glen Canyon deep into Navajo sandstone, and tributary streams cut narrow, winding slot canyons on either side, creating an intricate pattern of sheer bronze cliffs and hidden beauty. Puebloan people built small cliff dwellings here and chipped petroglyphs into the desert tapestry streaking the canyon's walls. Today the deeper parts of Glen Canyon and its side canyons lie under the waters of Lake Powell, the second largest reservoir in the country, which stretches to the northeast behind Glen Canyon Dam at Page, Arizona. This cold, clear blue lake, narrow and almost 200 miles long, is very popular with anglers, houseboaters, water-skiers, and increasingly, kayakers. The reservoir was named for Major John Wesley Powell, the scientist-explorer who floated the Colorado in 1869 and 1871. Of Glen Canyon, one of the few placid portions of his remarkable journeys, he wrote: "So we have a curious ensemble of wonderful features—carved walls, royal arches, glens, alcove gulches, mounds, and monuments. From which of these features shall we select a name? We decide to call it Glen Canyon."

Glen Canyon NRA is most popular with boaters during the hot, 90-de-

---

RIGHT: *Running for miles in the Paria Canyon–Vermillion Wilderness Area, Buckskin Dive with its soaring walls is a lovely slot canyon—and particularly dangerous after storms because of flash floods.*

LEFT: *In Glen Canyon National Recreation Area, wild fleabane blooms on Romana Mesa overlooking Gunsight Butte in Lake Powell. Navajo Mountain, sacred to the Dine, or Navajo, rises on the horizon.* **RIGHT:** *Snowy egrets stir up sediments in shallow water to roust prey. Once hunted mercilessly for feathers, snowies now thrive as a protected species.*

gree-Fahrenheit summer. Boats from small skiffs to houseboats may be rented at Wahweap Marina, in the southern section, at Bullfrog Marina or Halls Crossing about halfway up the lake, and at Hite Marina at the lake's northeast end. Reservations for boats should be made well in advance.

On Lake Powell's almost 2,000 miles of shoreline, more than the total Pacific coastline of California, Oregon, and Washington, camping is permitted everywhere except near developed areas. Boaters and hikers find myriad opportunities for backcountry experiences here, because the land portion of Glen Canyon National Recreation Area exceeds one million mostly roadless acres. Bordered by public lands and on the south by the sparsely settled **Navajo Nation❖,** much of the landscape is almost naked slickrock, so many visitors take walks from the shoreline of the lake or from the roads without following a trail. Such walks, however, should be kept short because it is easy to get lost and also because the meager desert flora is extremely delicate and easily trampled.

Hikers may prefer the cooler days of spring and early fall. The Glen Canyon area receives only about ten inches of rain a year, and despite the deep lake, hiking here is very thirsty work. Serious hikers should phone or check in at the visitor center at Wahweap for more information, particularly if considering hiking on the Navajo side of the lake.

Glen Canyon NRA also offers good birding opportunities. A huge body of freshwater in the desert, Lake Powell has become an important wintering area for waterfowl. Snowy egrets and American avocets stalk the shallows, while eared grebes, white pelicans, and coots bob on the lake, and killdeer and spotted sandpipers scurry about on sandy beaches. As elsewhere in canyon country, white-throated swifts and violet-green swallows swoop about catching insects in morning and evening. Many sparrows, chickadees, and warblers sing from the streamside vegetation in spring. Birds that favor open country, such as horned larks and loggerhead

177

shrikes, are common here as well.

South of the Glen Canyon National Recreation Area, in Utah but surrounded by the Navajo Nation, rises the **Rainbow Bridge National Monument❖,** an extraordinary example of the gracefulness possible in natural features. No roads lead to this 290-foot-high arch of rosy sandstone, the largest natural bridge known, but it can be reached by boat—including tour boats from Wahweap, Halls Crossing, or Bullfrog marinas—or on foot through Navajo land from the Arizona side (permit required). Rainbow Bridge began as a barrier of rock extending across meandering Bridge Creek. When the velocity of the stream increased due to regional uplift, it scoured the base of this rock wall with sandy water, eventually wearing through it. As frost wedging and the tug of gravity cause slabs of sandstone to fall away, the opening enlarges. To the Navajo, this "rainbow-made-stone" is a sacred site because rainbows are symbolic of harmony, the essence of life.

SOUTH-CENTRAL CANYON COUNTRY

Tucked below the high plateaus are many little gems of Utah canyon country. Back on Route 89, 6 miles west of Big Water, the 46-mile mostly unpaved Cottonwood Canyon Scenic Backway leads north to Cannonville, providing access to **Grosvenor Arch❖** and **Kodachrome Basin State Park❖** en route. The backway is a popular summer route between Glen Canyon and points north that affords a look at the colorful, strangely eroded rock of Cottonwood Canyon. However, the unpaved stretch below Kodachrome Basin can be bumpy and dusty depending upon how recently it has been graded, and the road is impassable in very wet weather. Drivers who prefer can return through Kanab on Route 89 to the Route 12 Scenic Byway near Bryce Canyon and follow it to Cannonville, where an all-weather road leads south to Kodachrome Basin.

Worth a stop on the drive to Kodachrome Basin, Grosvenor Arch is a picturesque geologic whimsy: a natural double arch tucked into a butte like the bones of the inner ear. The main attractions in colorful Kodachrome Basin State Park are unusual rock formations known as sand pipes or petrified geysers. These erosional remnants, pillars of stone left standing as the surrounding rock eroded away, are composed of paler, coarser sandstone than their surroundings and are thought to have originated as liquefied sand squirted up into overlying sediments.

Petrified wood lies exposed at **Escalante State Park❖,** a mile west of the town of Escalante on the Route 12 Scenic Byway and about 30 miles

ABOVE: *Golden cottonwoods glow beside the Escalante River in the BLM's Box–Death Hollow area. Desert varnish, a stain of manganese oxides and other minerals, streaks the rusty walls of Canyons of the Escalante.*

northeast of Kodachrome Basin. Here stumps and trunks of trees that may have been blown down by a volcanic eruption were embedded in soft Morrison shale, where silica slowly replaced their organic material as water saturated with minerals dissolved from the volcanic ash percolated through them. Tree-ring patterns in the wood are colored red, yellow, and steely gray by the trace minerals. On Route 12 in the town is a multi-agency visitor center, an excellent place to stop for maps and information about exploring the public lands of southeast Utah.

The magnificent **Box–Death Hollow Wilderness Area**❖ awaits keen hikers just northwest of Escalante. Here the Death Hollow Creek, a tributary of the Escalante River, has clawed the golden sandstone of the Aquarius Plateau into deep, sheer-walled canyons musical with birdsong and trickling water. Dainty hanging gardens of ferns and yellow seep-spring monkeyflowers cling to massive cliffs that soar straight up to mere slits of bright sky. Hiking in Death Hollow is a considerable challenge requiring two to four days of wading, strenuous scrambling, and even climbing in some places, but it is a true retreat where nature dominates. The Box—the canyon of Pine Creek, west of Death Hollow—offers a less strenuous hike. An unpaved loop road called the Posey Lake Scenic Backway running north from Escalante leads into the wilderness, and the trailhead for the Box is about 7 miles north of town. Where the backway forks 13 miles from town, the right fork along Hell's Backbone, Forest Road 153, encircles the wilderness. The trailhead for Death Hollow is about 18 miles from Escalante along this backway, halfway to the town of Boulder.

The BLM's **Canyons of the Escalante❖** is an exquisite wilderness of about 600,000 acres, a maze of slickrock named for the river that sculpted its sinuous way southeast through the Navajo sandstone from Death Hollow into Glen Canyon. Although a few cattle graze here, the remote, golden-walled world of the Escalante River brings visitors very close to experiencing the canyon country as the people of centuries ago knew it—both the Fremont and the neighboring Puebloan people used the canyon as a passage. The Escalante area is locally famous because a young poet and artist named Everett Ruess disappeared here in 1934, after writing intensely emotional poems and letters inspired by the wild beauty of the Southwest. "Once more I am roaring drunk with the lust of life and adventure and unbearable beauty . . ," he wrote to a friend. "To live is to be happy; to be carefree, to be overwhelmed by the glory of it all."

The Canyons of the Escalante is such a rare and precious natural area that visitors should be careful to leave no trace. Hiking along the 100-mile river canyon—where willows and cottonwoods shelter timid mule deer, and great blue herons peer intently into the water—takes about ten days. There are also several access points that allow shorter visits, including several off the unpaved Hole-in-the-Rock Road (a 57-mile scenic backway running southeast from Escalante, named for the Mormon expedition that pioneered the route). Much of the hike is through very cold, ankle-deep water, and campers must beware of flash floods. Petroglyphs adorn boulders and cliffs along the route, and there are two notable rock formations—Escalante Natural Bridge (two miles from Route 12 where it crosses the Escalante River) and Escalante Natural Arch. Because of the complex topography of this remote area, visitors wishing to explore it should consult the BLM office in Escalante for detailed information.

In the BLM's **Calf Creek Recreation Area❖,** south of Boulder on Route 12, is a delightful natural pool below a 126-foot waterfall in the canyon of Calf Creek, a tributary of the Escalante River. Requiring a hike of five and a half miles round-trip, this pool is a popular spot for cooling off on a hot, dusty summer afternoon. The walk is surprisingly strenuous because the path is on sand eroded from the Navajo sandstone of the canyon's walls. On the cliffs are Fremont pictographs of elaborate anthropomorphs, as well as ancient stone granaries. Beaver dams form pools in the stream, where in early morning or at dusk hikers may spot ringtail cats and other mammals coming to drink. Birders enjoy Calf Creek, where hummingbirds hover above gilias and red penstemon.

CAPITOL REEF TO THE SAN RAFAEL SWELL

From Boulder, the Route 12 Scenic Byway climbs over the Aquarius Plateau, which towers a mile above the surrounding lowlands and covers about 70 square miles, most of the easternmost unit of the **Dixie National Forest❖.** Boulder Mountain, this forest's 50,000-acre, basalt-capped highland, is mostly above 10,000 feet, in a region where abundant summer rains supply many clear streams. A subalpine forest of spruce and fir spaced between wet meadows covers much of the Aquarius Plateau, and there are also large stands of aspens, which turn vivid yellow and orange in the autumn. Views of Capitol Reef, the San Rafael Swell, and the Henry Mountains appear between the trees and at scenic pullouts on this inviting drive. The Forest Service's Wildcat Visitor Information Station near the Pleasant Creek Campground can provide maps and advice about camping, fishing, and hiking in the area.

Capitol Reef❖ is a lovely lesser-known national park on Route 24 between Torrey and Hanksville. The reef is an imposing 100-mile line of massive, multicolored cliffs eroding along a north-south geologic dip known as the Waterpocket Fold, one of the largest monoclines in North America. The rocks of this buckled reef, its multicolored cliffs, eroded arches, domes, monoliths, and canyons, represent about 200 million years of earth history. Originally, the cliffs' multiple layers of sedimentary rock lay nearly horizontal, built up over time from deposits in ancient seas, marshes, and deserts. When the Colorado Plateau began its massive uplift, however, these rock layers draped over a fault to create an enormous fold, which wind and water have sculpted over time.

OVERLEAF: *As it slices through the flexed rock strata on the western side of the Waterpocket Fold in Capitol Reef National Park, Sulphur Creek Canyon exposes rock layers that are a quarter billion years old.*

Because of its great size, the Waterpocket Fold (named for its many potholes that collect rainwater) is considered geologically unique, and Congress established Capitol Reef National Park in 1971 to preserve the area. The name Capitol comes from one of the park's most conspicuous features, a white dome of Navajo sandstone that resembles the dome of the United States Capitol building. Pioneers called the massive ridge a "reef," a term that derives from *rif,* an old northern European word for a rocky escarpment. The narrow, almost 70-mile-long park encloses the most scenic section of the Waterpocket Fold. Route 24 follows the Fremont River along its cut through the northern third of the park, a green, shady oasis on the sun-hammered, rockbound Colorado Plateau. The visitor center is at the junction of Route 24 and the unpaved 12-mile scenic drive, which leads south along the west face of the Waterpocket Fold into sheer-walled Grand Wash and Capitol Gorge.

The Hickman Bridge Trail is a rewarding two-mile (round-trip) walk to a natural bridge from Route 24, two miles east of the visitor center. Along the trail (which climbs 400 feet) are numbered posts keyed to a brochure explaining details in the natural surroundings. In a short trip to a quiet place like this, such walks make all the difference; once out of the car, visitors can hear the birds and the purling of the water, observe the flowers, and touch the patterns in the rock.

Along with a number of day-hiking pathways around the visitor center and scenic drive, more rigorous trails lead into the rugged backcountry of Capitol Reef. High-clearance vehicles are needed to get to the South Desert (in the northern section of the park) from River Ford, just outside the park's eastern boundary. To reach the trails and scenic attractions in the southern half of Capitol Reef, take either the Burr Trail Scenic Backway east from Boulder to approach the fold from the west or the unpaved Notom Road Scenic Backway from just east of the park boundary to reach the fold from the east. Although they can be bumpy and dusty in dry weather and are subject to flash floods during the summer thunderstorm season, these backways offer awe-inspiring scenery along slickrock crests and down into deep, cool sandstone canyons.

Fabulous scenery—long parallel ridgelines eroded by streams into scallops of buff, brown, gray, and vermilion—is not the only reason to visit

LEFT: *Near the Capitol Reef Visitor Center, erosion has eaten away at the soft Chinle and Moenkopi formations below the Castle, leaving its hard sandstone "turrets" to rise against a cloudless desert sky.*

185

Capitol Reef. As it cuts through the park, the Fremont River creates a garden where early Mormon settlers planted orchards that still bear fruit and attract deer, marmots, skunks, and hundreds of birds. The Fremont people (so named because their culture centered on the river and its tributaries) also found this a hospitable place, farming here for centuries and leaving behind petroglyphs and pictographs, as well as grinding mortars that they may have used to prepare herbs or pigments for ceremonies. Although somewhat remote, Capitol Reef National Park is one of the most pleasant and inviting places to learn about the land, life, and human history that make the Colorado Plateau unique.

Southeastern Utah is known for its sandstone formations—arches, canyons, mesas, hogbacks, and hoodoos—but southeast of Capitol Reef rise some interesting knobby stocks and laccoliths called the **Henry Mountains.** Stocks are mountains formed when cylindrical masses of igneous rock push up overlying sedimentary layers, whereas laccoliths are similar but on a smaller scale—dome shapes resulting from igneous rock that lifts overlying sedimentary layers.

Not surprisingly, in a region offering so many scenic slickrock areas, most travelers ignore the five stocks and numerous laccoliths of the lumpy Henrys and their surrounding desolate gray shale badlands. In fact, the Henry Mountains were the last range in the continental United States to be explored and mapped. Yet the Henrys are significant as the largest of the seven laccolithic mountain groups on the Colorado Plateau.

The Henry Mountains are high and cool. Travelers seeking shady forests and green meadows may take any of several dirt roads from Notom Road or Burr Trail or Route 95 south of Hanksville to hike or camp among ponderosas, Douglas fir, or open grassy slopes. From Route 95, the unpaved Bull Mountain Scenic Backway, which may require four-wheel drive

ABOVE: *In the purple twilight of a cool October evening, moonlit hoodoos haunt Goblin Valley State Park. The infinitely varied shapes of these brick red boulders are the random work of centuries of erosion.*

in places, heads west 21 miles south of Hanksville, climbing from the desert at 5,000 feet to 10,500-foot Bull Creek Pass below Mount Ellen, where bristlecone pines grow. Two of the Henry Mountains, Mounts Ellsworth and Holmes, rise east of Route 276. Mountain lions and bighorn sheep live in these remote "Little Rockies." In 1941 the government established a bison herd in the Burr Desert east of Mount Ellen. After a few years, the bison found summer range in the Henry Mountains, and today they are the only free-ranging, hunted wild bison herd in the United States.

Twenty-two miles north of Hanksville, roads lead both east and west off Route 24. To the east lies the Maze District of **Canyonlands National Park❖,** one of the most inaccessible places in Utah. To reach the maze, most visitors take the 46-mile graded dirt Maze District access road from here. River rafters can access the maze via the Colorado or Green River (see Chapter 7). Some of the most haunting ancient rock art in North America is preserved in the Maze District's Horseshoe Canyon, a four-mile hike from the marked trailhead along the access road. Archaeologists are not sure who painted these eerie pictographs of humanlike figures with heads and long, triangular bodies—some of them six feet tall—but without arms or legs. Some contend that these red ocher pictures date back centuries; others believe that they may be 3,000 years old. Usually, the pictographs are attributed to foraging people of the Desert culture and dated between 500 B.C. and A.D. 500.

On the drive north from Hanksville, travelers will note the colorful, conspicuous **San Rafael Swell** rising over the flat desert terrain to the northeast. Flowing water eroded the rock layers on the edge of this upwarped part of the earth's crust into triangular plates known as flatirons, carving the San Rafael Reef—an escarpment—into the swell's eastern side. Muddy Creek on the south and the San Rafael River to the north have further dissected the swell, creating a very scenic but hot and dry collection of hogback ridges and rolling swales ornamented with arches, domes, pinnacles of sandstone, and prehistoric rock art. Desert bighorn sheep and wild horses browse on desert shrubs scattered over the grassland and pinyon-juniper woods. Most of the San Rafael Swell is BLM land open to camping and hiking. Temple Mountain, the highest point on the swell, was named for its resemblance to the Mormon temple in Salt Lake City.

The partly paved Temple Mountain–Goblin Valley Scenic Backway off Route 24 leads to **Goblin Valley State Park❖** at the eastern foot of the San Rafael Swell. Funny stone creatures carved by weathering and streams out of the San Rafael Reef inhabit Goblin Valley, and wandering about in this mob of orange and white sandstone hoodoos is like being lost in a cartoon. Some have little heads with big noses; others point nowhere in particular with great confidence. Chubby-pawed sphinxes and noodly-looking elephants are stuck in the sand. These fanciful gargoyles and their whimsical friends are made of alternating layers of hard and soft sandstone and siltstone, which erode differentially to produce odd shapes.

GREEN RIVER BASIN

North of I-70, the landscape is a series of bluffs and arid basins engraved by tributaries of the Green River, the lifeblood of this region. After rising in the Wind River Range in Wyoming and passing through Dinosaur National Monument, the Green continues southward through Utah in deeply entrenched meanders, gaining volume from numerous side streams until it also becomes a tributary, joining the Colorado River in Canyonlands National Park. En route, other streams—the Duchesne River, White River, Nine Mile Creek, Price River, and San Rafael River—add so much to its volume that the Green sometimes carries more water than the Colorado. The river supports rare, threatened Colorado squawfish, humpback chub, and humpback suckers, in addition to introduced game fish such as carp and bullheads. Despite its volume of water, the landscape drained by the

189

Green River is a dry expanse of cliffs, plateaus, and swales.

Sixty million years ago, this part of Utah was a bowl filling up with the sediments of Lake Uinta, the local portion of a vast lake system called the Green River Lakes. The basin gradually filled in, was uplifted, and is now eroding away. Today a smaller version of the Uinta Basin, centered on Ouray, Utah, survives between the Tavaputs Plateau and the Uinta Mountains. Pumps extracting oil from the Green River shale riddle the terrain.

In its plant communities, the country drained by the Green River is more akin to the Great Basin on the other side of the Wasatch Line than to the Colorado Plateau to the south and southeast. Most of its six to ten inches of annual rain falls in the autumn, not a very useful season for plant life. Consequently, this drought-adapted landscape is dominated by shrubs—shadscale and rabbitbrush mostly—and contains lots of prickly-pear cactus and bunchgrasses: bluebunch wheatgrass, needle-and-thread, and Indian ricegrass. In addition, the Green River and its tributaries support some high desert riparian areas.

The Tavaputs Plateau is a smile-shaped 10,000-foot-high upland north of I-70 between Price and the Colorado border. The Green River divides it into a western and an eastern portion. On its south side, the plateau begins abruptly with the **Book Cliffs** just north of I-70, and above them the **Roan Cliffs.** In these extensive lines of cliffs, both "retreating" to the north, each layer of rock tells a different story. Mine tailings and seams of dark deposits visible in road cuts reveal that this was once a shoreline environment where masses of organic material accumulated, were compressed, and became coal. Atop sandstones and shales lie colorful freshwater limestones like those of Cedar Breaks and Bryce, deposited here by rivers and the vast lake of 65 to 40 million years ago. Because these sediments are so easily eroded, few plants become established on the crumbly slopes and cliffs, but the flatter uplands of the plateau are forested and home to elk, bighorn sheep, black bears, and mountain lions.

From the turnoff to Goblin Valley, the itinerary exploring the edge of the Uinta Basin continues north on Route 24 and turns west on I-70 to see the **Little Grand Canyon** of the San Rafael River. Take Exit 129 and drive 29 miles north on the good gravel road designated the Wedge Overlook–Buckhorn Draw Scenic Backway. The last few miles follow

---

RIGHT: *Hikers can thread their way through a mile of narrows in Little Wild Horse Canyon. Tumbled boulders testify to the power of the occasional floods that cut through the San Rafael Swell near Goblin Valley.*

narrow, winding Buckhorn Draw, where a few pictographs and petroglyphs adorn the sandstone walls. At the signed junction, turn south for two miles and west again for seven miles to the Wedge Overlook, where there is a spectacular view over a sheer cliff 1,200 feet to the canyon floor and beyond to the magnificent San Rafael Swell. This stretch of the San Rafael River is popular for daylong "flat-water" (no rapids) raft trips in the spring. Check with the BLM office in Price for permits or information about companies that run the Little Grand Canyon.

Returning north on the dirt road from the Wedge Overlook, turn west for 13 miles to Route 10 at Castle Dale. Turn north for nine miles, then east on Route 155 through the town of Cleveland, for an interesting excursion to the BLM's **Cleveland Lloyd Dinosaur Quarry**❖, a national natural landmark. Take the Dinosaur Quarry Cedar Overlook Scenic Backway east from Cleveland to the quarry, where the Jurassic Morrison Formation is tilted up on edge on the northern slope of the San Rafael Swell. Erosion and excavation have exposed more than 12,000 dinosaur bones here, possibly the most extensive source of allosaurus, stegosaurus, camarasaurus, and other dinosaur relics in the world; but because of its remote location the Cleveland Lloyd Dinosaur Quarry Visitor Center is small, and its hours are limited.

Northeast of Price, Route 191—the Indian Canyon Scenic Byway—climbs from the old mining town of Helper in the canyon of the Price River up Willow Creek through the Book and Roan Cliffs to 9,100-foot Indian Creek Pass. The road then descends via Indian Canyon through desert terrain in the **Ashley National Forest**❖ and then the **Uintah and Ouray Ute Nation**❖ to the town of Duchesne on Route 40.

The Uintah and Ouray Ute Nation—composed of several separate blocks totaling more than a million acres and including everything from high mountain forests and lakes to sagebrush flats—is popular with hunters and anglers. Tribal offices in Fort Duchesne, just south of Route 40/191 about 35 miles east of Duchesne, can supply the necessary permits and information.

An alternative route through the Book Cliffs—the BLM's Nine Mile Canyon Scenic Backway—starts two miles east of Wellington (which is southeast of Price on Route 191). This partly paved backway wanders through the countryside for 78 miles, 40 of them alongside Nine Mile Creek through Nine Mile Canyon, which was named for a spot used in a mapping procedure involving nine-mile triangulations. Visitors can easily imagine the Fremont here, gathering seeds, berries, and roots and hunting the mule deer and elk that come to the stream. Every mile or so along the canyon is a panel of Fremont pictographs or petroglyphs, depicting snakes, bighorn, hunters with bows and arrows, and other mysterious symbols. The Fremont also farmed a little corn and beans here, storing their harvests in almost inaccessible granaries tucked into nooks and crannies in the canyon walls. Obscure remains of Fremont pit houses, as well as the crumbling stone walls of their granaries, may still be seen on ledges above the creek.

UTAH'S NORTHEAST CORNER

Flaming Gorge National Recreation Area❖ is in the Ashley National Forest on Routes 191 and 44 (known as the Flaming Gorge–Uintas Scenic Byway) north from the town of Vernal. The Green River, which cut this dramatic canyon through the northeast corner of the Uintas, is now impounded within Flaming Gorge for water storage and recreation. Fishing and boating are popular here, and boats may be rented at Buckboard, Cedar Springs, and Lucerne Valley. Of the several campgrounds, some are accessible only by boat.

As its name suggests, the walls of Flaming Gorge are bright red quartzite of the Uinta Uplift, vermilion shales, and other sedimentary layers ranging from gray to golden. The lake is 90 miles long and very narrow, its metallic blue water contrasting dramatically with its naked stone walls. The surrounding highlands are forested with ponderosa pines and aspens, and elk, deer, and bighorn sheep introduced by the U.S. Forest Service roam sunny openings of grass and sagebrush, sprinkled with pinyons and junipers on the lower slopes.

The steep and shady canyon of the **Sheep Creek Geological Area**❖, an interesting part of the national recreation area, is accessible via the Sheep Creek Loop Scenic Backway off Route 44. Willows, cottonwoods, and box elders line the creek, and fanciful spires and wedges of various rock strata border the road. Where these strata fall over Sheep Creek Fault, multicolored stone draperies—rust, maroon, buff, and gray—compose a fascinating perpendicular cross-section of the Uinta Uplift, an upwarped part of the earth's crust resulting from the compression of its tectonic plates. In the Uinta Uplift, strata of all ages are bent into a somewhat crumpled arch, with the most ancient—the distinctive rusty-colored quartzite—at its core.

Dinosaur National Monument❖ is downstream on the Green River, on Route 149 east from Vernal. Although there are four-wheel-drive

---

OVERLEAF: *Sunrise glances off the cliffs of the Green River in the Flaming Gorge National Recreation Area. Periodic fires there, often caused by lightning, burn debris shed by ponderosas, restoring nutrients to the soil.*

roads—the Island Park, Jones Hole, Yampa Bench, and Echo Park, as well as the paved roads to Harpers Corner, Gates of Lodore, and Deerlodge Park—river trips are one of the most popular ways to see this hot country. Eleven companies offer one- to five-day rafting trips on the Green and Yampa rivers, which converge in the heart of the national monument. River-runners drift past a fascinating array of different-colored rock strata peppered with tenacious desert shrubs and tufts of grass, the haunt of coyotes and lizards. Passengers hold on for dear life through Upper Disaster Falls, Lower Disaster Falls, Triplet Falls, and Split Mountain, delighted to be splashed with cold water after baking in the sun.

At the end of their adventure, river-runners emerge not far from the **Dinosaur Quarry,** the focal point of Dinosaur National Monument. For those intrigued by paleontology, this unusual structure may be the most exciting building in the country. One huge wall is a massive quarry where dinosaur bones lie exposed but in place, a Jurassic bas-relief that is fascinating and in a strange way beautiful. About 145 million years ago, a river deposited a layer of sand, gravel, and dinosaur bones here. More sediments accumulated on top of this layer, compacting it. Silica-laden water percolated down, cementing the earlier layer and mineralizing the dinosaur bones within it. After the Uinta Uplift squeezed up these deposits, the elements began to pluck at them, revealing a dense jumble of enormous, well-preserved bones of stegosaurus, apatosaurus, and allosaurus, among

RIGHT: *Although common, mallard drakes with their brilliant metallic-green feathers are nonetheless a dazzling sight.*

LEFT: *In Split Mountain Canyon, the Green River flows by the once-level layers of the Moenkopi Formation, now tilted into a striking array of vertical pastel stripes.*

others. The exhibits and staff of the quarry are up-to-date with the latest research on Jurassic dinosaurs and the ecosystem in which they lived.

In addition to the monument's roads and rivers, trails wind through Dinosaur. From the visitor center on Route 40, a 30-mile scenic drive leads to Harpers Corner, where a mile-long trail wends its way to a spectacular viewpoint above Echo Park at the confluence of the Green and Yampa rivers. There is also a pleasant 3-mile trail to the Green River from the **Jones Hole National Fish Hatchery✿,** on the paved 40-mile Jones Hole Scenic Backway, which begins 4 miles east of Vernal with a left turn off Route 149. Backpacking is somewhat limited at Dinosaur because of the heat and dissected terrain, but information is available at the visitor center.

For those who just can't get enough paleontology, the **Utah Field House of Natural History State Park and Dinosaur Garden✿**—in the town of Vernal on Route 191/40—conveys a vivid picture of the geology, paleontology, ecology, and human history of the Uinta Basin and Mountains. Dioramas, paintings, and other exhibits illuminate each of these subjects, and the rock and mineral hall with its fluorescent mineral room displays specimens from throughout Utah. In the Dinosaur Garden, 16 life-size prehistoric animals stand in re-created settings suggesting the nature of the earth as each experienced it.

Farther downstream on the Green River, just north of Ouray off Route 88, is the **Ouray National Wildlife Refuge✿,** an important stop for waterfowl migrating through this arid country. Here the U.S. Fish and Wildlife Service has enhanced or created five bottomland marshes of cattails and bulrushes between the meanders of the Green River by channeling and diking it. These wetlands nourish and provide ideal nesting spots for grebes, ducks, geese, and white-faced ibis. Great blue herons and double-crested cormorants nest in the cottonwood groves at the north and south ends of the refuge. Grains are grown and left standing in the fields so that fall migrants can "fuel up" for their long flights. In the spring, sandhill and whooping cranes pass through, as do several different gulls. Along with the many waterfowl, raptors, and perching birds here are colonies of white-tailed prairie dogs. Visitors may walk or drive (cars tend to make good blinds) a nine-mile, brochure-guided tour of the refuge.

Much of the public land surrounding the Green River is administered by the BLM, which has developed a number of hiking and bicycling trails in the vicinity. At the agency's office in Vernal, visitors can get details about these trails and about the White River, a gentle tributary of the Green that is suitable for canoes as wells as rafts and kayaks. Cowboy Canyon—upriver or east of Bonanza on Route 45—is a popular launch site; to the west there are two takeout sites on the Uintah and Ouray Ute Nation before the White flows into the Green River near Ouray. The shallow White River is best traveled during spring runoff because there is more water, the weather is cooler, and lots of birds may be seen and heard among the cottonwoods just leafing out in brilliant green on the riverbanks.

Fantasy Canyon, north of the White River before the boundary of the Uintah and Ouray Ute Nation, may be reached from the river or via a maze of dirt roads serving the oil and gas fields southeast of Bonanza. Ask at the BLM office in Vernal for detailed directions to this bizarre, monochromatic landscape of wildly improbable, snaky hoodoos eroded from soft lakebed sediments. Just enough pattering rain falls here to shape these weird, delicate formations without collapsing them.

More than 50 exhilarating rapids in mile-deep **Desolation Canyon**— Utah's deepest—make it a popular rafting experience. River-runners put in at Sand Wash, 30 miles downriver from Ouray, and take out four to seven days later, either 75 miles downstream at Nefertiti Rapid or 84 miles below at Swaseys Rapid. One- or two-day trips from Nefertiti Rapid to Swaseys Rapid are also popular, especially with organized groups. As they drift downriver in the calm periods between rapids, rafters may see black-crowned night herons, sandpipers, and mergansers among the more than 80 birds known here. Ringtail cats and bushy-tailed wood rats rob campsites at night. The high walls of Desolation Canyon reveal that other people have been here before: the Fremont and Ute embellished the desert-varnished rock with petroglyphs and pictographs, especially at the mouths of tributaries. The immensely rugged surrounding country is cleft by many gorges and barricaded by rock walls carved into arches and pinnacles and caves. For most of the way on this trip, the center of the river is the boundary between BLM land and the Hill Creek Extension of the Uintah and Ouray Ute Nation. The required permits for trips through Desolation Canyon on the Green River, as well as more information about group trips and routes to launch and takeout points via the tangle of un-

ABOVE: *Even in a state known for its eccentric geological formations, nowhere is the whimsy of erosion more eloquently expressed than in the badlands of Fantasy Canyon on BLM lands near Bonanza, Utah.*

paved roads in the area, may be obtained from the Price office of the BLM. Permits to hunt, fish, or camp on Ute land are available from the Ute Tribal Council in Fort Duchesne.

For the time being, strong public advocacy for the preservation of western rivers has defeated proposals to dam the Green River below Desolation Canyon. Many areas on the Colorado Plateau are threatened by similar schemes from time to time—plans to make the region's resources more useful and productive in the quantifiable sense of those words. But the plateau country is already immeasurably productive. It is a refuge for rare plants, a critical migration corridor for millions of birds, a wild place where creatures denied space elsewhere still live free. It is, as well, a sanctuary for the human spirit.

199

SOUTHEAST UTAH: CANYON COUNTRY

U tah's southeast canyon country is an airy realm of piercingly blue skies above a landscape of rocks, mostly golden sandstone. Rolling away to the horizon are luminous dunes of pale, cemented sand sliced by a million gullies and canyons, the offspring of eons of summer cloudbursts. The light here is extraordinary—the sun spills over the land with dazzling excess, drenching the bare slickrock. Every gnarled little tree, every scrubby little bush, stands apart from every other in lambent dignity. The wing beats of ravens are audible in the encircling stillness.

Utah's canyon country occupies most of this state's portion of the Colorado Plateau, the 130,000 square miles of tableland centered over the Four Corners, where the state lines of Utah, Colorado, New Mexico, and . Arizona meet. Named for the Colorado River, which drains it, the Colorado Plateau in Utah is bordered by the Uinta Mountains on the north and the Wasatch Line on the west. This chapter tours the part of the plateau that lies astride and east of the Colorado River.

The Colorado Plateau, which averages more than a mile above sea level, began to rise during the Laramide orogeny, the same geologic phenomenon that created the present Rocky Mountains about 65 million years ago. Although a series of subsequent events boosted and broke the plateau in places, its colorful sedimentary layers remained mostly intact instead of

---

LEFT: *Near the Colorado River on BLM lands north of Moab, the Fisher Towers shimmer in the sunset. The Titan, tallest of these erosional remnants, soars 900 feet above the surrounding Professor Valley.*

crumpling or folding. Erosion has been attacking the plateau ever since, exposing and etching the rocks as it strips away one layer after another. Rain pools on the flat plateaus, then pours down cracks and depressions in the rock, deepening them and using the grit it collects to scour out gullies, ravines, and canyons downstream. Water and wind scoop out the softer strata underneath hard layers, which then shear off in slabs to form cliffs. Ice freezing in cracks expands to pry rock apart, sculpting graceful arches.

Canyon country is prey to the "monsoons," late-summer thunderstorms that bring flash floods. More than half of the precipitation of southeast Utah falls from July to October, which is not to say that it rains much. Average annual precipitation ranges from only 9 to 18 inches here. Average lows are in the single digits, average highs in the 90s, and temperatures typically vary 30 to 40 degrees from day to night. Plants and animals here, as in much of the West, have thus adapted to dryness and extremes of temperature.

Most life in canyon country is based on the pinyon-juniper woodland, sometimes called the pygmy forest because of its small trees. Pinyons and junipers can grow in cracks in bare rock because their roots and small leaves are able to collect and conserve water very effectively. Pygmy forests colonize new areas quickly, although these trees need many decades to reach maturity. Berries of the juniper tree nourish many creatures, particularly birds such as cedar waxwings and even jackrabbits and coyotes. Pinyon and scrub jays and various rodents collect and store the succulent and nutritious nuts of the pinyon pine, and seeds that are not retrieved germinate in the sheltered, often buried caches, where it is moist enough for them to survive desert conditions.

Never lush, a pinyon-juniper woodland is often rich in its variety of grasses and shrubs. Several fragrant members of the rose family flourish here, scarcely recognizable as cousins of the garden rose. Cliff rose, Apache plume, mountain mahogany, antelope bitterbrush, and blackbrush all grow in southeast Utah as scraggly shrubs with narrow, skimpy leaves. Pack rats are the archivists of slickrock country, collecting big piles of twigs, seeds, and debris from their surroundings and inadvertently preserving them with their concentrated, resinous urine. By examining these middens and radiocarbon-dating their still-identifiable contents, scientists have been able to describe the environment of the last Ice Age.

OVERLEAF: *From the Colorado River Overlook in Canyonlands National Park, a dramatic panorama unfolds, a wilderness labyrinth of slickrock promontories, gorges, buttes, and spires that tantalize the imagination.*

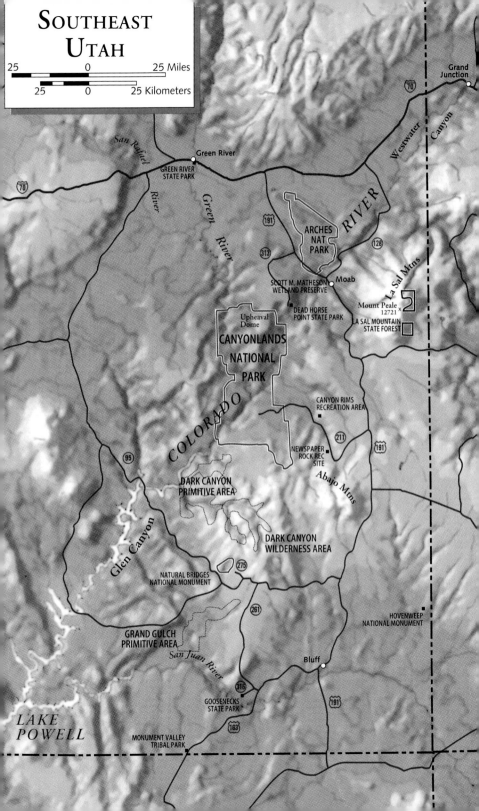

LEFT: *Talons extended, bald eagles snatch fish from Utah's lakes, rivers, and wetlands, invaluable habitat in this desert state.*
RIGHT: *At sunset, Delicate Arch, teetering on the edge of a 400-foot cliff in Arches National Park, frames the snowy La Sal Mountains rising to the east.*

This itinerary begins in Westwater Canyon, on Utah's border with Colorado, and then visits Arches National Park and the area around Moab. For a cool respite, it heads into the high mountains of Manti–La Sal National Forest before exploring Canyonlands National Park. Next, it examines the ruins of Hovenweep, and then loops south to the Arizona border to experience Monument Valley. Finally, the route turns north to Grand Gulch, Natural Bridges, and White Canyon.

ARCHES NATIONAL PARK AND MOAB

Negotiating canyon country is tricky. A hiker can be rimrocked, sidetracked, or bamboozled into climbing cliffs or sliding down ravines or going in circles around monuments of stone. Slickrock isn't slick, of course—hikers can walk up steeply sloping knobs of it without slipping because its gritty surface grips the soles of their boots. Nothing sticks to slickrock for long, though: Winds sweep any soil or seeds away, leaving miles of naked sandstone that dwarf every living thing. Hiking here is exhilarating because the sense of freedom—of being able to stretch out and follow the beckoning landscape—makes up for any tricks canyon country might play.

As might be expected in a land of sun and rock, one of the most enjoyable ways to explore the region is by river. The Colorado River enters Utah through steep-walled **Westwater Canyon,** a sensational setting for a one- or two-day river trip from the Westwater Ranger Station, about 4 miles from the Colorado border, to the Cisco Takeout 17 miles downstream. This exciting white-water dash passes through 11 rapids, among them Funnel Falls, Skull, and Sock-It-to-Me. The BLM office in Moab issues the required permits to experienced river-runners; the average traveler's best bet is to take the trip with one of the commercial companies in Grand Junction.

206

ABOVE: *Utah junipers grow near the North Window formation in Arches National Park; their blue "berries" (actually modified cones) were an important food for the Puebloan people who lived here centuries ago.*

The rocks of Westwater Canyon, very different from slickrock, are black, very hard metamorphic rocks dating from the Precambrian of nearly two billion years ago, far more ancient than the local sandstone. They have eroded, slowly yielding to the scouring sands of the river, to form glassy, fluted patterns like the ornamentation on some dark Gothic cathedral.

The itinerary continues down the course of the Colorado River via Route 128, the Colorado River Scenic Byway, where there is a pullout for **Fisher Towers.** These erosional remnants of the 225-million-year-old Organ Rock Tongue of the Cutler Formation jut above the surrounding Richardson Amphitheater along the Colorado River. The rock here is weak and crumbly, making it very dangerous for climbing. Stick to the 2.2-mile hiking trail that leads around the base of the towers to a scenic overlook. Fisher Towers is a welcome respite from the long drives typical of canyon country travel, a pleasant opportunity to walk, watch for lizards, and listen to the birds.

Continuing to the Moab area, travelers have a delightful treat in store. **Arches National Park❖,** just north of Moab off Route 191, is a stone phantasmagoria, a rococo dreamscape of more than a thousand arches poking up among long, slender fins, spires, and balanced rocks. Like the landscape of nearby Canyonlands, Arches is the finely wrought handiwork of powerful forces acting over unimaginably long periods of time. Cracked by the shifting of underlying salt deposits, layers of sandstone hundreds of feet thick eroded first into upright slabs and then into an assortment of unlikely shapes.

The Arches Visitor Center, just inside the boundary of the park, offers information on trails, geology, and local flora and fauna and is the starting point for a .2-mile nature trail. The main road leads north, bisecting the roughly oval park. Visitors can see most of the more famous features of Arches without strolling very far from paved parking areas in sections of the park called Courthouse Towers, the Windows, the Fiery Furnace, and Devil's Garden. However, to take a longer walk here is to become enchanted with sand and slickrock, making time spent at Arches an unforgettable experience.

After working at Arches as a seasonal park ranger in the 1950s, Edward Abbey wrote *Desert Solitaire,* a passionate, rather polemical evocation of the Colorado Plateau and a powerful plea for conserving wilderness in the desert Southwest. In his book, Abbey reminds us that "a man on foot . . . will see more, feel more, enjoy more in one mile than the motorized tourist can in a hundred miles." To follow Abbey's advice, take one of the numerous trails leading through valiant desert flora to countless beguiling shapes carved by nature in the rough, warm rock. Come prepared for sun and heat: Wear a hat and carry several quart bottles of drinking water; there is little shade here. In summer, avoid walking too far during the hottest part of the day, which is between about noon and two o'clock.

The 1.5-mile trail to **Delicate Arch** from the trailhead at Wolfe Ranch passes an old pioneer homestead over Salt Wash, where pools of water support a few tiny minnows and leopard frogs. A side path leads to a panel of Ute rock art depicting figures on horseback. The final approach to Delicate Arch involves a long but fairly gentle climb past wall gardens of maidenhair ferns and seep-spring monkeyflowers. The reward is a glorious view of Delicate Arch perched beside a huge stone bowl, with spectacular, 400-foot drop-offs on its far side and the La Sal Mountains visible in the distance.

The Devil's Garden Trail leads from the parking lot at the end of the park road (where drinking water is available) past several arches and stone fins and then loops back to the parking lot, a distance of 7.2 miles. Although scrambling up the slickrock to get a closer look around corners or at distant vistas is tempting, visitors should stay on the bare rock or on trails because the sandy ground below the rock formations is delicate.

To cool off, travelers may wish to take a river trip from **Green River**

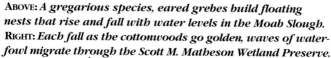

ABOVE: *A gregarious species, eared grebes build floating nests that rise and fall with water levels in the Moab Slough.* **RIGHT:** *Each fall as the cottonwoods go golden, waves of waterfowl migrate through the Scott M. Matheson Wetland Preserve.*

State Park❖, west of Arches near the town of Green River on I-70. In contrast to the dramatic cascades of the Colorado River as it slashes through Westwater Canyon, the Green River flows smoothly through the open desert south of I-70. After the San Rafael River joins the Green, in **Labyrinth Canyon,** the Green River begins to wind in tight loops between high cliffs and red, buff, and brown sandstone formations. River-runners usually take out at Mineral Bottom, 68 miles downstream, making this a three- to five-day trip.

Lining the Green River are feathery-leaved tamarisks, or salt cedars, "exotic" (nonnative) trees introduced into southern California for landscaping and erosion control that have since colonized most of the streams in the Southwest. Tolerant of alkali soils, they produce a great many tiny seeds easily carried by the wind, which take root in moist places and crowd out native willows and other plants. The riverside vegetation supports perching birds such as gray vireos, which trill sweetly at dawn and dusk. Canyon wrens often sing from high, rocky ledges along Labyrinth Canyon in the middle of the afternoon. Possible hikes up side canyons include a 14-mile trek to **Horseshoe Canyon,** in the Maze Unit of Canyonlands National Park, to see some of the most mysterious ancient rock art in North America.

Return to the town of Moab, now a major staging area for tourism in

southeastern Utah. It became the mountain-biking capital of the state with the establishment about 4 miles east of town of the 10.3-mile **Slickrock Bike Trail❖,** which follows paint dabs on undulating sandstone in a breathtaking scenic loop. Moab's northern section is also the starting point for **Kokopelli Trail❖,** a 128-mile mountain-bike path—marked every half mile by brown posts—that winds through shale and sandstone canyons from Moab to Grand Junction, Colorado. Other routes that the BLM has established for mountain bikes, four-wheel-drive vehicles, and hikes near Moab also meander over slickrock benches below cliffs streaked with syrupy-looking desert varnish, through pinyon-juniper woodlands and sagebrush flats. Detailed brochures describing these routes, as well as auto tours on paved roads, are available at the multiagency information center in Moab.

The Nature Conservancy's **Scott M. Matheson Wetland Preserve❖** protects more than 875 acres of wetlands in the Moab Slough in Moab. Bulrush wetlands, streamside habitat, uplands flooded by beaver dams, and a desert floodplain of the Colorado River mix here to provide a range of conditions—unique in southeast Utah—ideal for more than 175 species of birds. Great blue herons have established a rookery at the southern end of the slough, and white-faced ibis and snowy egrets stalk the shal-

211

ABOVE: *Harmless to humans, the exquisite mountain king snake reaches more than three feet in length and preys on a variety of rodents and insects. Babies emerge in early fall from eggs laid in early summer.*

lows and mudflats. Bald eagles and peregrine falcons haunt the marshes. Ducks, geese, and western grebes swim about in ponds, and river otters reintroduced to the Colorado River not far away have been seen here too. Short hikes in the preserve lead to good birding areas; some visitors paddle rafts or canoes in the Colorado River along the edge of the wetland.

Dead Horse Point State Park❖ is southeast off Route 313, which leads west from Route 191 just north of Moab. This promontory of stone, with its dramatic view into the gorge of the Colorado River 2,000 feet below, takes its name from the days when wranglers fenced it off to make a natural corral for trapping wild mustangs. A band of horses deemed unsuitable for taming are said to have died of thirst when they were left on the promontory with the gate closed. A number of short, relatively level trails lead from a campground and visitor center here.

CANYONLANDS NATIONAL PARK AND MANTI–LA SAL

Route 313 goes to **Canyonlands National Park❖**, the very heart of the Colorado Plateau. Converging in a Y, the Green and Colorado rivers have gouged 2,200-foot chasms into the sandstones and shales of the plateau. Their tributaries deeply dissect the surrounding pink-and-salmon slickrock into walls and ledges, buttes, and pinnacles separated by ravines and

RIGHT: *As thick, fluid layers of salt moved beneath it, the sandstone of Canyonlands National Park fractured, in some cases producing shafts that weathered into pinnacles such as these near Chesler Park.*

gorges, making overland travel very difficult. A major influence on this landscape has been the shifting far beneath its surface of layers of salts as much as half a mile thick. These salts, evaporated from a Paleozoic sea, ooze about under the pressure of overlying layers. As the soft deposits shift, the harder sandstones above crack, sometimes along narrow parallel lines. Blocks of rock drop in relation to those around them, forming grabens (from the German word for "trench") and further complicating the water-etched topography.

At Canyonlands, visitors find not only stirring vistas of a slickrock wilderness but also collared lizards, rattlesnakes, and ravens. In this warm, still area, the air is sharp with sage. Annual rainfall is less than ten inches, and as a result the vegetation is mostly bunchgrass, stunted shrubs, pinyons, and junipers. A walk here feels like an immersion in sun and stone, a visit to an infinite labyrinth. Dwellings and petroglyphs scattered throughout the park indicate that the Puebloan people were here too—and visitors can only marvel at the exuberance of their rock art in such a daunting environment.

In the more than 500 square miles of Canyonlands, one of the least de-

---

RIGHT: *In Canyonlands National Park, colorful layers of eroded sedimentary rock surround Upheaval Dome, where an ancient meteorite is believed to have struck the earth.*

215

ABOVE: *In the fall a blaze of amber cottonwoods traces a wash near Cave Springs in Canyonlands National Park. Usually dry, such sandy stream-beds may churn with violent flash floods after summer cloudbursts.*

veloped national parks in the lower 48 states, hikers can choose short and mild strolls or long and arduous backpacking trips. Because they can easily become lost or dehydrated in this baking-hot, confusing topography, they should consult park staff about specific routes and trails, especially when planning overnight trips.

North of their convergence, the Green and Colorado rivers enclose a broad mesa called Island in the Sky, on Route 313 off Route 191. At the visitor center, travelers can ask about walks or hikes appropriate to current weather conditions and about four-wheel-drive roads and river trips. Past the visitor center the park road forms a Y—the northern fork leads to Upheaval Dome and the south to Grand View Point Overlook. The White Rim Trail is a 100-mile four-wheel-drive road running along a ledge about 1,200 feet below Island in the Sky, a thousand feet above the rivers.

Geologists aren't sure what created **Upheaval Dome,** but walkers can take a 500-yard trail to look for themselves and choose their favorite hypothesis. Earlier scientists assumed that erosion had scooped out the top of a dome produced by the movement of underlying salts. Now many believe that a meteorite struck this point. In either case, erosion has attacked the edges of the turned-up sedimentary layers of Upheaval Dome, revealing concentric rings of multicolored rock.

ABOVE: *A member of the ubiquitous sunflower or aster family, orange sneezeweed blossoms among drifts of purple lupine and white yarrow in a moist wildflower meadow near Geyser Pass in the La Sal Mountains.*

Because the cliffs and slopes below **Grand View Point Overlook** are ideal habitat for desert bighorn sheep, sharp-eyed visitors will probably see some of these symbols of the western wilderness, muscular tan animals that look so different from domesticated sheep. Grand View Point also offers a sense of infinity. Nothing seems urgent under the vast blue sky, where the expanse of elaborately carved buff, orange, and chocolate rock owes its magnificence to the patient trickling of water.

Back on Route 191 heading south, travelers can see two separate mountain ranges dominating the landscape—the La Sal Mountains southeast of Moab and the Abajo Mountains farther to the southwest (northwest of Blanding)—both within the Manti–La Sal National Forest. As the mountains rise darkly more than a mile above the surrounding flat plateau, they are so high that they often create their own weather, wearing woolly clouds like Russian hats on their summits. The highest peak in the La Sal Mountains, the second highest range in Utah after the Uintas, is 12,721-foot Mount Peale. The national forest shares this range with **La Sal Mountain State Forest❖.** Both the Abajo and La Sal ranges are laccolithic, formed when molten matter within the earth pushed up against overlying sedimentary layers, cooling to form masses of rock later exposed by the erosion of those overlying strata.

217

Both mountain masses have shed considerable rock debris, which now forms skirts of rocky foothills around them. Climbing up their roads, travelers notice that the vegetation changes from sagebrush to pinyon-juniper woodlands, to conspicuous stands of Gambel oak, to ponderosa pine and Douglas fir with aspens in sunny spots, and eventually to sub-alpine fir-spruce forests, meadowed shoulders, and bald peaks of loose rock. White, three-petaled sego lilies, designated the state flower of Utah because their bulbs nourished early Mormon settlers, nod in the shade where meadows meet the lower forests. Grassy slopes flower with purple lupines, white yarrow, and lots of yellow sunflowers between long earthen snakes of "castings" pushed up by gophers tunneling beneath winter snows. At higher elevations, elderberry bushes, bistort, mertensia (blue-bells), buttercups, wild pink geraniums, and skyrocket gilia flower among lush grasses. Clark's nutcrackers and flickers glide from tree to tree, and chickadees and nuthatches hop about among the branches.

As in the other highlands of Utah, the difference between a protected national park and a multiple-use national forest is well illustrated here. Tree stumps and slash piles of discarded tree limbs are scattered throughout the mountain forests, as are cow manure and places where cattle have churned the ground into squelchy mud. However, wildlife is also conspicuous here, and not particularly shy. Whirring hummingbirds hover over scarlet flowers and hikers' red hats. Woodpeckers knock loudly on tree trunks, chickarees ratchet irritably from the branches, and marmots chirp and whistle from granitic boulders. Deer wander close at dusk, nuzzling the ground for forage, and at night, coyotes yowl and great horned owls swoop soundlessly over the meadows.

South of the La Sal Mountains on Route 191, several outstanding viewpoints lie outside Canyonlands National Park, within the BLM's **Canyon Rims Recreation Area✣.** The Needles–Anticline Overlook Scenic Backway runs west from Route 191 south of Moab. Its paved left fork goes to the Needles Overlook; a graveled right fork goes to Anticline Overlook.

Farther south on Route 191, turn west on Route 211 for 12 miles to **Newspaper Rock Recreation Site✣** and the Needles District of Canyonlands National Park. At Newspaper Rock, travelers can see densely carved panels of petroglyphs right by the highway or take a short, level nature

---

RIGHT: *Golden prince's plume, a spectacular desert mustard whose yellow bottle brush–shaped flowers top slender stems, flourishes on the rocky slopes at Anticline Overlook in the BLM's Canyon Rims Recreation Area.*

ABOVE: *Each rock monolith in Monument Valley Tribal Park, which straddles the Utah-Arizona border within the Navajo Nation, has a name and an associated story in the oral tradition of the Dine, or Navajo people.*

trail to learn about the geology, plants, and animals of the area. Although most of the petroglyphs date from the ancient Puebloan culture, depictions of riders on horses show that people were still tapping pictures into the desert-varnished sandstone after Europeans introduced horses to North America in the sixteenth century.

Route 211 continues to the **Needles District** of Canyonlands National Park, where the staff of the visitor center provides updated information on trails and the weather, and visitors can see clusters of thin rock spires as well as arches, bowls, alcoves, and a top-heavy feature called Molar Rock that looks like a giant's extracted tooth.

In the Needles District, a web of unpaved four-wheel-drive roads and trails leads to various vistas, including the **Confluence Overlook.** From this point, visitors can see the dendritic, or treelike, pattern of the tributaries that begin at higher elevations as small "twigs," converging into larger and larger branches lower down before they flow into the main "trunks": the appropriately named Green (colored by algae) and Colorado (colored by red silt) rivers. Although they are relatively calm where they separately enter the northern end of the park in deeply entrenched meanders, the two rivers increase in volume and velocity when they meet in Cataract Canyon, a 14-mile stretch of furious rapids both feared and beloved by river-runners. At this point, the single river is called the Colorado, and from here it flows into Glen Canyon and Lake Powell. The western side of Canyonlands borders Glen Canyon National Recreation Area.

PUEBLOS, MONUMENTS, GOOSENECKS, AND HOODOOS

On Utah's border with Colorado, east on unpaved Hovenweep Road from Route 191 just north of Bluff, is **Hovenweep National Monument❖**, a lesser-known Puebloan site that offers visitors a sense of personal discovery in encountering this ancient culture. Brooding in lonely, sunbaked isolation on the slickrock above sandy washes are six groups of ruined towers and villages of shared walls. A self-guided trail leads around Square Tower Ruins, the easiest to reach, where a ranger is stationed all year to answer questions about Hovenweep.

At the little town of Bluff, visitors can arrange one-day trips down the **San Juan River,** a BLM-administered area (noncommercial rafters must obtain advance reservations). Most of the cliffs beside the river are low and the water is muddy, making this a trip not for spectacular scenery but rather for the pleasure of communing with canyon country. Drifting along the river in the hot sun, watching for great blue herons wading in the shallows and buntings perched in the cottonwoods, is relaxing and somehow also invigorating. Iridescent dragonflies and violet-green swallows swoop over the river in pursuit of insects, and toads waddle across its muddy banks. The Puebloan people were here once too, leaving petroglyphs, grinding stones, and other evidence of their lives.

The itinerary now leads west from Bluff on Route 163 to **Monument Valley Tribal Park❖,** which echoes with an ancient Navajo chant: "Beauty before me, With it I wander; Beauty behind me, With it I wander. . . . Beauty all around me, With it I wander." Here travelers explore a sandy red desert below thousand-foot-high needles, or monuments, carved from the Permian DeChelly sandstone. The DeChelly is a hard rock fissured by cracks. As the fierce rains of summer thunderstorms hammer down, running water widens these cracks and begins to isolate enormous mesas, or tablelands, of sandstone. Water also erodes the much

OVERLEAF: *As a full moon descends over the horizon to the west, the rosy glow of dawn tints the ancient eroded terrain and spectacularly entrenched meanders of the San Juan River at Goosenecks State Park.*

Despite the difficulty they have in rooting in the soft, loose sediments, colorful wildflowers such as buckwheats and asters (above) and lark-spurs (right) bloom at the BLM's Valley of the Gods after wet winters.

softer Organ Rock Formation beneath them, causing great slabs of DeChelly sandstone to shear off the sides of these mesas and crumble into rubble at their feet. Over time, more and more rock spalls off the mesas, reducing them to buttes and finally to monuments.

Monument Valley Tribal Park headquarters is on the Utah-Arizona border. Most people drive or take a guided tour on a bumpy loop road through the heart of the park, but it is also possible to obtain a permit for hiking or horseback riding. Scattered throughout the park are hogans, the traditional eight-sided, one-room homes of the Navajo people, or Dine, who herd sheep here. These remarkable people revere this powerful landscape, where every rock feature, every life-form, and every weather phenomenon has character and meaning. Here visitors can see and imagine lives intimately intertwined with the forces of raw nature in twentieth-century America. The residents of Monument Valley do ask, however, that travelers respect their privacy.

Returning up Route 163, turn north on Route 261. **Goosenecks State Park❖,** just off Route 261 on Route 316, is a picnic area and viewpoint from which to see the San Juan River's amazing "goosenecks"—the back-and-forth windings of the riverbed established by the San Juan long ago as it flowed sluggishly across a more level plain. When renewed regional uplift caused the gradient and consequently the velocity of the river to increase about 20 million years ago, it continued in its old, meandering channel, but its sediment-laden waters acted as "liquid sandpaper" to scour deep into the limestone. The river is now a thousand feet below tear-shaped lobes of stair-stepped limestone and shale cliffs.

A few miles farther north on Route 261, a signed, unpaved spur road leads to the **Valley of the Gods,** a collection of rusty-colored hoodoos. This 14-mile road runs east off 261 through formations that resemble huge chess pieces and mythological monsters. The figures are the products of erosion, which in this region of faulted rock and flash floods often produces strange shapes. If rain fell here more consistently, such formations would soon erode away, and the landscape would be smooth and rolling rather than angular and hoodoo-ridden. Route 261, the paved Moki Dugway Scenic Backway, continues north to the Moki Dugway, a three-mile unpaved series of hairpin turns dug into the southeast edge of Cedar Mesa and given a name once used for the Hopi people. It ascends a thousand feet.

Carved into Cedar Mesa, the BLM's **Grand Gulch Primitive Area❖** is yet another place for an adventure. Hikers in Grand Gulch, a 50-mile-long tributary of the San Juan River, might tramp for several days without seeing anyone else. The walls of the main gulch and its extensive side canyons are full of nooks and crannies, numerous places to explore and infinite discoveries to make—from stone arches to Puebloan cliff dwellings, from painted handprints to chorusing frogs in sedge-lined pools. The difference in elevation from the rim of Grand Gulch to its floor, combined with the microclimates created by shade and water, nurture a cornucopia of natural resources that once provided the Puebloan people with a rich living. Grand Gulch is an extremely sensitive area, however, a delicate environment highly vulnerable to damage from thoughtless hikers. The privilege of visiting Grand Gulch carries with it the responsibility to tread very lightly here, and visitors should check with the BLM to learn how to access and respect this primitive area.

Natural Bridges National Monument❖, north on Route 275 four miles off Route 95, protects three bridges formed the same way that Rainbow Bridge was created but now at different stages of their development. Kachina Bridge (rock art on it inspired its Hopi name, meaning "spirit intermediaries") is in the early stage: Its opening is small and still being widened by floodwaters. Sipapu, the largest (named for the Hopi place of emergence into this world from a lower one), is narrower. Owachomo (Hopi for "rock mound") Bridge is near the end of its life—so thin that it looks as though it could collapse at any time. Day-hiking trails lead through the pinyon-juniper woodland to these bridges, to views of small Puebloan shelters in rock alcoves, and to a few of the ever mysterious Puebloan petroglyphs.

North of Natural Bridges and accessible via forest roads from Route 275 is a sprawling wilderness centered on Dark Canyon, which descends 5,000 feet in 30 rough miles to join the narrow upper reaches of Lake Powell. At its eastern, higher end, the canyon falls within the **Dark Canyon Wilderness Area❖** of the Manti–La Sal National Forest and supports ponderosas. Farther downstream, the canyon dives deeper between its walls as it enters the BLM's **Dark Canyon Primitive Area❖.** Because of its shade and water, the canyon is blessed with flowery rock gardens and lots of animals—black bears and mountain lions prowl here. Dark Canyon is so remote that hikes usually last several days and are best taken in June or July because snow blocks earlier access and flash floods are a danger in August.

Dark Canyon is but one of many remote and difficult to reach places in Utah's southeast canyonlands. Some people might find it strange that so many choose to brave the hardships and dangers of hiking in the wilderness when they could cover more ground in an automobile. Perhaps Everett Ruess said it best, "As to when I shall visit civilization, it will not be soon, I think . . . . I prefer the saddle to the streetcar and star-sprinkled sky to a roof, the obscure and difficult trail, leading into the unknown, to any paved highway, and the deep peace of the wild to the discontent bred by cities. Do you blame me then for staying here, where I feel that I belong and am one with the world around me?"

RIGHT: *In the BLM's Grand Gulch Primitive Area, prickly pear cactus now blossoms in Bullet Canyon, where eight centuries ago Puebloan farmers grew corn for thriving stone villages that were tucked up under the cliffs.*

CHAPTER EIGHT

WESTERN UTAH: BASIN AND RANGE

I n western Utah, narrow desert basins and long mountain ranges alternate to create a corrugated landscape, which nineteenth-century geologist Clarence Dutton compared to an army of caterpillars marching to Mexico. Twentieth-century naturalist and writer John McPhee described basin-and-range country as "a cloudless immensity with mountains in it," and indeed landforms dwarf the life-forms here.

In this remote, sparsely populated region, open terrain stretches as far as the eye can see, awash in sunlight and melodious with the sounds of birds and breezes. The air is a tonic: clear, warm, and scented with resinous shrubs. Rocks—fine green shales and coarse pink granites, crumbly red ochers and hard gray limestones—shift and clink underfoot. Jackrabbits bolt, big eyes staring, long ears glowing translucent with red veins. Pronghorn thunder across hardpan basins.

About 17 million years ago, the earth's crust began to bulge between the Sierra Nevada and the Wasatch Line. Geologists are still debating the cause, but the result was that a section of crust measuring 300 to 600 miles wide and 1,000 miles long stretched upward and cracked along faults running north-northeast. Huge blocks of crust slid relative to one another, tilting up on one side and dropping on the other. The edges of the blocks formed long, high ranges up to 15,000 or 20,000 feet above the intervening basins. Over the millennia, streams etched deep canyons and tributaries on the

LEFT: *At the north end of the BLM's Wah Wah Mountains, twisted ponderosas grow on the parched flanks of Crystal Peak; this sparkling mass of white rock, or rhyolite tuff, was formed by volcanic eruptions.*

sides of these ranges, carrying sand, gravel, and boulders down to fill the basins with as much as 10,000 feet of debris in some cases. From this practically level fill, the mountainsides jut up very suddenly.

In the Great Basin, the landlocked section of the basin and range, streams are blocked by the highlands around them and can find no outlet to the sea. Instead, creeks and rivers flow into lakes, and in spring, undrained desert basins flood with water that evaporates quickly, leaving concentrations of mineral salts. Great Salt Lake is the most famous of these bodies of briny water. Other lakes are only temporary, ephemeral sheets of shallow water that soon dry out completely to form playas—flat white salt crusts. During the cool, moist Ice Age, a vast lake submerged the basins of western Utah, eastern Nevada, and southern Idaho. Great Salt Lake, Little Salt Lake, Utah Lake, and Sevier Lake are all that remain of this earlier body of water, known to geologists as Lake Bonneville.

In some basins, springs support wetlands vital to many birds and plants. Animals come from miles away to drink at these springs, usually during the cool hours of darkness. Because western Utah is in the rain shadow of the Sierra Nevada, some parts of it receive a dozen or fewer inches of precipitation per year. Although grumbly black thunderstorms drift across the sky in August, they bring only intermittent and localized rain. Measurable moisture comes mostly in the winter, when plants are dormant in the intense winter cold and unable to use it.

And the wind! As one old-timer said, the snow doesn't melt in the basin-and-range country, "it just blows around till it wears out." Not surprisingly, the most common plants—grasses and sagebrush—are wind-pollinated. Temperatures tend to be extreme in both winter and summer, and the growing season is short.

The basins of western Utah are classified as intermountain grasslands. Grasses with distinctive flower heads—blue grama, squirreltail, needle-and-thread, and ricegrass—nod delicately in protected places, but sagebrush is now dominant. Botanists are uncertain about the natural balance of the plant community here because livestock grazing, fire suppression, and the introduction of exotic (alien) weeds have modified it.

Flowers of the basin-and-range country tend to be small. Because there is no carpet of green grass as a backdrop for them, even hundreds of blos-

---

OVERLEAF: *Based on a Thomas Moran watercolor, this delicate 1876 chromolithograph,* **The Great Salt Lake of Utah,** *illustrated F.V. Hayden's account of his pioneering geologic expedition to Yellowstone and the West.*

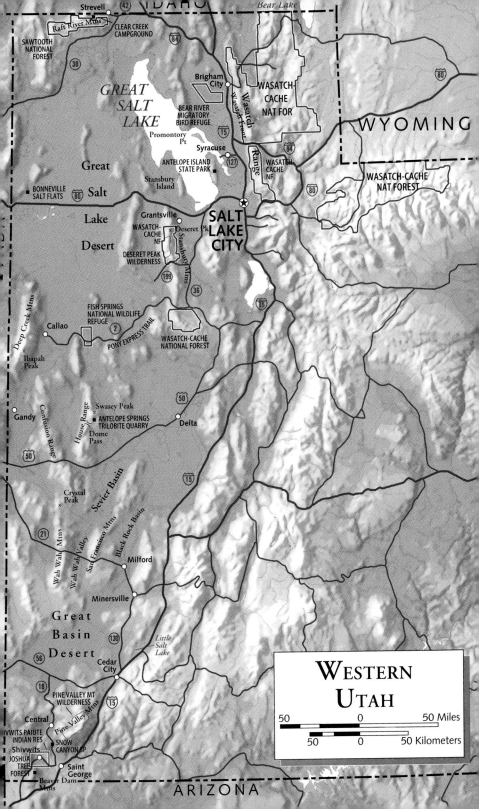

Species typical of the Mojave Desert populate Utah's southwest corner. In the BLM's Joshua Tree Forest, namesake trees (right)—actually big spiky yuccas—coexist with greater roadrunners (left), giant members of the cuckoo family.

soms only faintly tint the land. In spring, the desert blushes with scarlet gilias, globemallows, and paintbrush, then is gilded with hairy golden asters, blanketflowers, and hawk's beard. Dark blue larkspurs and lupines pop up where conditions permit, and papery-white prickly poppies line roadsides where rainwater runs off the pavement.

Low shrubs dot the flatlands and foothills. Rabbitbrush, Mormon tea, bitterbrush, greasewood, and winter fat share the range with pungent big sage, of which a dozen species and many subspecies are adapted to local conditions. Spiny pads of the ubiquitous prickly-pear cactus sprawl here and there. Alkali sacaton, salt-loving shadscale, and four-wing saltbush cope with the concentrated salts and alkali minerals of the playas.

Pretty little green-tailed towhees, lazuli buntings, and gray flycatchers enliven this intimidating landscape by scrabbling on the ground, picking among the shrubs, or performing exquisite aerobatics in pursuit of a mouthful. Although conditions are harsh, insects here include various ants, flies, beetles, and even butterflies and dragonflies. Arachnids—tarantulas, wolf spiders, and scorpions—are common.

For many people, reptiles characterize the western deserts, and this country contains plenty of evidence of snakes and lizards. Shed snakeskins blow among the rocks and greasewood, and lizard tracks meander everywhere in the dust. Silent except for the viper's menacing rattle, these creatures with their cold blood and scaly bodies make the desert seem dangerous despite its fragile beauty.

Most of western Utah is federal land administered by the Bureau of Land Management for mining and grazing cattle and sheep. Although trails are few, the open nature of the country makes hiking fairly easy in most places. Camping is permitted almost everywhere, except for the U.S. military testing ranges, which are off limits to the public. There are few paved roads, and visitors should follow maps and directions very carefully. An accurate odometer is essential, and never travel without water.

For the purposes of this book, Utah's basin and range is bordered by I-15 on the east and by the state's boundaries with Arizona to the south, Nevada to the west, and Idaho to the north. The itinerary follows scenic backways through the valleys and mountains here, visiting desert springs, wildlife refuges, and state parks. Ending with a loop around the Great Salt Lake, the route winds up near the Idaho border.

UTAH'S DIXIE: BELOW CEDAR CITY

Although it is mostly sunny plains and cliffs, Utah's southwestern corner lies on an ecotone, or overlap, of the Mojave Desert to the west and south and the Great Basin Desert to the north and east. The Mojave Desert extends only a little way into southwestern Utah (it covers the southern tip of Nevada, the northwest corner of Arizona, and part of southeastern California). Because the Mojave Desert is hot year-round, crops possible nowhere else in Utah may be grown here with the help of irrigation. In the nineteenth century, Mormon settlers planted cotton, giving the region the nickname Utah's Dixie.

Creosote bush—sprays of delicate black branches with pungent little olive-green leaves—freckles the flats of the Mojave, but not the Great Basin Desert. However, Joshua trees, barrel cacti, and other Mojave species do overlap into the Great Basin slightly. Roadrunners, cactus wrens, and the endangered desert tortoise may be spotted here too, although the latter has suffered greatly from competition with grazing animals, predation of its young by birds, and death under the wheels of cars. This area is transitional in more than the political sense of its boundaries with Nevada and Arizona and its mix of environments: It also lies on a geologic boundary. Mountains and mantles of igneous rock darken much of this region, pushing up under and breaking through colorful sedimentary rock layers. Stocks, laccoliths, and basalt flows reveal Dixie's place below the geologically active edge of the rotating Colorado Plateau. Nevertheless, some features—the Beaver Dam Mountains with their exposed core of Precambrian rock, for instance—are classic basin-and-range topography.

The BLM's **Joshua Tree Forest❖**—on the unpaved Mojave Desert–Joshua Tree Scenic Backway, which loops east from old Route 91 west of Saint George—lies at about 2,000 feet above sea level, the lowest land in Utah. At the foot of the Beaver Dam Mountains is a picturesque stand of the huge yuccas with uplifted limbs that are called Joshua trees for the biblical prophet who exhorted his people to victory in the desert. From 20 to 30 feet tall, with shaggy trunks, daggerlike leaves, and creamy clusters of flowers, Joshua trees are important nesting sites for birds, and their fruits and seeds nourish many desert creatures.

To reach **Snow Canyon State Park❖** from the Joshua Tree Forest, take Route 91 north into the **Shivwits Paiute Indian Reservation❖** and turn east through the hamlet of Shivwits to the intersection with Route 8. Turn north onto Route 8, the paved seven-mile Snow Canyon Scenic Backway. Named not for local weather conditions but for the Mormon apostles Lorenzo and Erastus Snow, Snow Canyon is a cleft in the white and red Navajo sandstone, which is ornamented with Puebloan petroglyphs of bighorn sheep, spirals, and humanlike figures. Flowing and freezing water has sculpted the exposed sedimentary rock into graceful shapes such as Johnson's Arch. The five-mile-long canyon is almost a thousand feet deep, making it a shady, though hot, place for a short walk. Snow Canyon State Park also encompasses a small dune field, a natural sandbox where visitors of all ages love to romp. In addition, Snow Canyon is surrounded by volcanic features including cinder cones, lava flows, and lava caves that formed as liquid rock drained from under a hardening crust. These caves are high enough for visitors to walk in upright and explore their rough, black interiors (bring a flashlight).

From Snow Canyon, continue north to join Route 18 to the town of Central, where Forest Road 35 leads into the Pine Valley Mountains in the **Dixie National Forest❖**. These mountains exhibit great plant diversity, not only because they are located in the Mojave–Great Basin ecotone but because their 6,000 feet of elevation above the valley embrace several life zones. Nearly 150 miles of trails wind through the **Pine Valley Mountain Wilderness Area✧,** accessible via Forest Road 35. The area includes 10,365-foot Signal Peak, which supports bristlecone and limber pine, spruce, Douglas fir, and aspen. The strenuous Summit Ridge Trail meanders up through forests and flowery meadows to the crest of the mountain, featuring spectacular views and a cool haven from the hot desert below.

The Pine Valley Mountains are a cluster of lumpy highlands that originated as massive intrusions of magma welling up between sedimentary rocks and sheets of volcanic basalt. Erosion later exposed the resulting laccoliths—submerged mounds of igneous rock—by removing the overlying layers. This region has been a very active mining district, and old silver mines may be seen west of Leeds in the Silver Reef sandstone member of the Triassic Chinle Formation, the only known instance of commercial quantities of silver ore to be found in sandstone in the United States. The colorful badlands of the Chinle are riddled with dinosaur fossils, petrified wood, and uranium.

NORTH THROUGH MOUNTAINS AND DESERTS

The country north of Cedar City is classic basin-and-range terrain: long mountain ranges—the Wah Wahs, the House Range, the Deep Creeks—and desert basins with names like Black Rock and Sevier (appropriately pronounced "severe"). Pale, perfectly flat strips of desert shimmer in the wavery silver air, through which dark escarpments resemble the menacing waves in some heroic Irish legend. Especially in the higher, more extensive ranges, a visitor could wander for days without seeing another person. Many of the places shown on maps are not actually towns; they are ranches that offer no services whatsoever. Visitors should prepare for travel in this part of Utah with water, food, and even extra fuel—such precautions are well worth the trouble.

This is magnificent country, honest and open, revealing its very bones. About 17 million years ago, long blocks of the earth's crust tilted up on their sides here to expose varicolored strata, while waves of runny black lava engulfed the countryside. Today the cool mountain ranges of western Utah are "sky islands" that support plants and animals isolated from others of their kind by the hot basins between them. During the Ice Age, when the climate even in the basins was cooler and wetter, these plants and animals mingled; but as the environment warmed, many species were forced to retreat up the slopes of the narrow mountains.

Although they may look barren through the heat-blurred air of the basins, these mountain ranges are often forested. In many, crystalline brooks bordered with mosses and wood nymphs (locally known as shy maidens) trickle through shady glens. Mountain lions roam steep slopes patrolled by hawks and eagles, and bighorn sheep pick their way among the lichen-covered rocks of the highest ridges. Few people visit these isolated places, which have a wild character even for the West.

The landscape between the mountains is powerful in its simplicity. Khaki-colored rangeland, perfectly flat but for gleaming white anthills, is accented with bluish big sage and lime green snakeweed. A closer look reveals red velvet and little black ants and bumbling darkling beetles with grooved carapaces. Afternoon clouds trace dappled patterns on the pale, dry dirt, and the dusty fragrance of sage gusts through the air. Pack-rat palaces under boulders or shrubs of Mormon tea are full of sticks, bones, and droppings. Dozens of galloping pronghorn vanish quickly into the distance; jackrabbits bound along on improbably long legs, their black-tipped ears alert.

Our journey continues north on Route 18 from Central to Route 56, then east to Cedar City. Fifteen miles north of Cedar City on Route 130, the

ABOVE: *Actually hares, black-tailed jackrabbits possess enormous ears that radiate excess heat and provide acute hearing to warn of such predators as coyotes, snakes, and hawks.*

LEFT: *In the Wah Wah Mountains in Utah's western desert, flat basins alternate with uptilted ranges of sedimentary rock.*

well-graveled Gap Road leads east to **Parowan Gap,** a passageway through the low cross-bedded sandstone Red Hills. Petroglyphs tapped into the rock here indicate that people have used this route for centuries. The Fremont and Paiute carved snakes and sunbursts, footprints and kilted humanlike figures with head ornaments resembling antennae. Geometric designs abound: rectangles filled with rows of dots, rows of triangles, meandering lines, concentric circles, "rakes," and ladderlike images. To see the petroglyphs, park in one of the pullouts beside the road and walk around the base of the

ABOVE: _Surrounded by sunset-reddened granite pinnacles, Notch Peak in the BLM's House Range soars 4,000 feet above the Tule Valley. The peak's 1,300-foot north face is the greatest vertical drop in Utah._

bluffs. Pioneer inscriptions from the 1880s show that Parowan Gap was important well into historic times. The ephemeral Little Salt Lake, which must have been an important place to collect salt and to hunt waterfowl in wet years, lies just on the eastern side of the Red Hills via Parowan Gap.

Return to Route 130 and turn north to Minersville, then take Route 21 to Milford (fill up with fuel and water here and note the odometer mileage before continuing). Route 21 to the northeast passes around the south end of the San Francisco Mountains. Twenty-five miles northwest of Milford on Route 21, turn north on a smooth, level gravel road up the **Wah Wah Valley,** which was once inundated by ancient Lake Bonneville. As in other basins in the region, caliche—sandy gravel cemented together with mineral salts—paves the valley floor. Miles of gray-green shrubs and bunchgrasses extend into the distance and up the slopes of dry foothills, where they mingle with widely spaced junipers. Northern harriers, and russet golden eagles larger than bald eagles, glide over the basin hardpan in pursuit of rodents and rabbits; kestrels hover and pounce on grasshoppers.

This landscape is as notable for its vastness beneath the open sky as for any particular feature. The noses of fault block mountains appear above a sea of scented sagebrush, their black and buff layers sharp in the clear air. The **Wah Wah Mountains** rise on the western side of the Wah Wah Valley. Encircled by paved and dirt roads, they are one of the more accessible ranges in this part of Utah. The west face of the Wah Wahs, a dramatic fault scarp, is much steeper than the east face. The lowest layer visible in

ABOVE: *Archaeologists believe that well-preserved petroglyphs in the BLM's Parowan Gap area were incised by several cultures—Desert Archaic, Fremont, Paiute—that used the pass during the past 1,000 years.*

the range dates from 500 million years ago, when a Cambrian sea invaded this area and deposited first sand (now metamorphosed as quartzite), then mud (now shale), then calcium carbonate (now limestone).

Crystal Peak, at the northern end of the slanting Wah Wah Range, can be reached by driving 18 miles to a T-intersection with Black Rock Road, then turning west for 18 miles to the pulloff on the south side of the road in the pass below the peak. A luminous pyramid of white volcanic ash that is visible from several miles away, Crystal Peak up close, with its blurry wind- and water-carved knobs and pockets, resembles a big, pale melting honeycomb. Rockmat and other persistent little plants have rooted in long cracks in the rock, creating a random pattern of intersecting lines. Cliffrose and gnarled pinyon pines scent the air below the peak, while ground squirrels scurry and scrub jays rasp and quarrel.

After continuing west on Black Rock Road for about 4 miles to a T-junction with a major north-south road, turn north and drive northwest for 13 miles to another major intersection. There, turn due north again for 6 miles to reach Route 50. (At this point, travelers should consider detouring west on Route 50 for 16 miles to the Nevada border to top off their fuel tank and water supply.)

ROUTE 50 TO GREAT SALT LAKE

At the junction of Route 50 and the road from Crystal Peak, note the odometer reading, then drive east on Route 50 for 21 miles, descending through the Confusion Range via scenic Kings Canyon to a spectacular view of the House Range, a 50-mile-long escarpment rising above Tule Valley. To visit Desert Springs, a fascinating quarry containing trilobites (ancient arthropods), and 9,669-foot Swasey Peak, turn north on the unpaved Notch Peak Loop Scenic Backway on the east side of Tule Valley. (This scenic backway, 43 miles west of Delta on Route 50, is passable for passenger cars except in very wet weather.)

Notch Peak is a sheer limestone cliff on the east side of the road. Good campsites are scattered among the weathered spires of pink granite at its foot, and nearby granite walls offer fine technical rock-climbing. From these foothills, alluvial fans—gently sloping, wedge-shaped masses of debris carried by streams down the canyons dissecting mountain ranges and dumped onto valley floors—are visible far across the valley.

With Notch Peak as a reference point blocking half the sky, the movements of the sun and stars seem more vivid. Sunlight advances west across the basin from dawn until afternoon, when it suddenly reverses and sweeps east, split by the clouds into rays that seem animate, numinous. Stars progress swiftly across the night sky, popping out from behind Notch Peak with amazing frequency.

A few miles farther north on the scenic backway is a side road signposted for **Painter Spring** to the east. Painter Spring is an oasis given the local name for mountain lion, and visitors can easily imagine a big cat stalking the wildlife that depends upon this perennial stream. Cottonwoods wound with twining wild grape exude a sharp, oaky scent, and dense thickets of wild roses and willows teeming with birds grow along the salty brook that emerges from rounded pink granite rocks. Blue damselflies skim over the soft green algae floating in the water, which is bordered by mosses, red paintbrush, and tall grasses. Leggy red-winged wasps called tarantula hawks seek out tarantula spiders in which to lay their eggs, while brown spiders spin horizontal webs over the stream to catch their prey. Rodents and snakes occupy the many burrows here, and sharp-shinned hawks patrol overhead, communicating in high-pitched cries.

At Dome Pass Road, follow the Notch Peak Loop Scenic Backway east up Dome Canyon over Dome Pass to a T-junction, turning north to the spur road for the **Antelope Springs Trilobite Quarry❖.** Here, prospectors mine fossils of what Arizona naturalist Edwin McKee called "the ancient and once world-ruling race of trilobites," ancient sea-dwelling arthropods thought to be related to today's horseshoe crabs. Trilobites, which had exoskeletons divided lengthwise into three lobes as well as a head, thorax, and tail, existed for more than a quarter of a billion years, but became extinct some 250 million years ago. At Antelope Springs, slabs and slivers of steely gray shale lie heaped and scattered everywhere, and hand-lettered signs indicate where commercial collectors have staked their claims (there are plenty of spots left where visitors may quarry for an hour or so). The 500-million-year-old shale is easy to split and contains innumerable trilobite fossils.

Return to the main road and continue up the good but very steep road marked for the **Sinbad Cliffs** and 9,669-foot Swasey Peak. The Sinbad Cliffs offer a stupendous view of practically all the precipitous House Range stretching out to the north and south, as well as of the Tule Valley, the Confusion Range, and the western horizon. White-throated swifts dart about at the edge of the reared-back escarpment. Douglas firs, ponderosas, and big, strapping bristlecone pines grow among forests of mountain mahogany and currants. White phlox, matlike buckwheat, and pinkish rockmat bloom underneath Mormon tea. Sapsuckers have drilled holes in the junipers, and chukars start up underfoot. Mule deer and their fawns make their way daintily along the ridgelines as chipmunks slip into hiding places among the loose rocks.

The top of **Swasey Peak** affords a breathtaking view in all directions of white playas in flat basins split by dark, sharp ranges. There is no trail to the top, just a route up the drainage at the end of the road near where visitors have established a rough campground (the walk takes about three hours round-trip). Birds—chickadees, jays, and sparrows—call continuously, and monarch butterflies, ladybugs, and fuzzy, bee-mimicking flies loop in the bright sunshine. In this dry place, slow-to-spread orange lichens and rockmat grow on fallen wood faster than the wood can rot.

To descend back to Tule Valley, retrace the route to Dome Pass, note the odometer reading there, and continue due west to **Tule Springs.** Named for the head-high rushes growing in pools fed by the springs, Tule Springs is in the middle of the alkali flats of Tule Valley, exposed to the full brunt of sun, wind, and grazing cattle. Although trampled and soiled by livestock, the springs have produced marshes fringed with potentilla and seep-spring monkeyflowers, and succulent pickleweed flourishes here as it would beside a saltwater lagoon at the seashore. Yellow-headed blackbirds perch among the dense rushes in the middle of the pools, croaking hoarsely and flapping to keep their balance as the tall wands bend in the breeze.

Beyond the springs—18 miles from Dome Pass—is an intersection with an unnamed road. Again noting the odometer reading, turn right for 12

miles through Cowboy Pass in the Confusion Range and take the right fork
(note odometer) for 18 miles to the T-junction at Gandy. Turn north and
drive 20 miles to the Trout Creek Ranch. After just under 8 more miles, turn
on the signed road leading west to Granite Creek Canyon at the base of the
Deep Creek Mountains. Follow the road up Granite Creek Canyon as far as
possible by car, then walk if necessary to the camping area, which is 3.8
miles from the turnoff. The Granite Creek road deteriorates as it enters the
foothills of the Deep Creeks and crosses back and forth over Granite Creek.

The **Deep Creek Mountains,** on the Nevada border northwest of
Tule Valley, are a pristine, sky-island wilderness of hawks and mountain
lions. Highest of the ranges in this part of Utah, they rise more than a mile
above the valley—high enough to reap significant rains from summer
clouds—and include two peaks more than 12,000 feet above sea level.
Their name is appropriate: Snow-fed brooks tumble between banks green
with mosses, mints, Parry's primroses, wild geraniums, and monkshood.
These streams are some of the few remaining habitats for Bonneville cutthroat trout, which have been virtually eliminated elsewhere by overfish-
ing. For the cutthroat, as for several unusual plants, the isolation of the
Deep Creek Mountains has proved a sanctuary.

The hike from the Granite Springs camping area to the summit of
12,087-foot **Ibapah Peak** is about six miles and climbs one mile in elevation. Although the trip can be made in a day, overnight is better. The
steep, nameless, unmaintained trail begins among weathered heaps of
granite in the draw carved by Granite Creek. At first, it leads through
scrublands and junipers to stands of aspens and firs. Clearings on south-
and east-facing slopes blossom with fragrant ceanothus buzzing with pollinating flies and clacking with grasshoppers. Farther on, in the cool forest
where delphiniums, roses, elderberries, and yarrow bloom, woodpeckers
rap noisily on dead trees. Eight different conifers live here, the greatest
variety anywhere in the Great Basin. On the exposed crest of the saddle
below the highest peaks are meadows carpeted with matlike tundra
plants—cushion buckwheat, yellow sedum, and saxifrage—and frequented by mule deer at dusk.

From the meadows, the trail ascends another steep, forested slope

---

Left: *In the long shadow of the House Range near Tule Springs, a briny
pool evaporates in the flat salt basin, or playa, of the Tule Valley.*
Overleaf: *The Deep Creek Mountains roll to the horizon below Ibapah
Peak, where alpine potentillas nestle among the lichen-splotched granite.*

Western Utah: Basin and Range

RIGHT: *Great Salt Lake stretches beyond Buffalo Point in Antelope Island State Park, a perfect vantage point to savor the grandeur of the sky, the beauty of the desert, and the largest lake west of the Mississippi.*

prowled by blue grouse to a narrow ridge leading to Ibapah Peak. The treeless summit is covered with loose rocks. Skypilot and moss campion flower in this harsh environment, and bighorn sheep are often sighted. In this thrilling, top-of-the-world view, flat basins extend to distant ranges in all directions. The crest of Deep Creeks rises along a major raptor migration route very important to hawks and eagles.

Returning to Granite Creek, take the road back out, turn left, and continue for about 9 miles to Callao. There turn east on Route 2, the Old Pony Express National Backcountry Byway, and follow it about 21 miles to the **Fish Springs National Wildlife Refuge❖**.

At Fish Springs, the U.S. Fish and Wildlife Service channels the water of a spring-fed marsh to create nine large ponds for wildlife (a brochure for a self-guided auto tour of several of the ponds is available). Encircled with meager, dusty shrubs and a few cottonwoods, the water impoundments shine like chrome in the middle of the stark desert. Skinny, green immature white-faced ibis stalk the shallow water in the company of snowy egrets, great blue herons, and American avocets. All sorts of shorebirds, perching birds, and raptors thrive here in spring and summer, and thousands of ducks and geese migrate through in the fall. The ponds are a magnet to mice, gopher snakes, bullfrogs, and their predators—short-eared owls hunch in the shrubbery, and coyotes pace restlessly around the pools. Since pre-Columbian times, people have also used the springs, which issue from a fault zone along the east side of the Fish Springs Range.

Fish Springs was a critical stop on the Pony Express Trail, as was **Simpson Springs,** 50 miles east. Pony Express riders galloped through this area delivering mail on their 1,900-mile route from Saint Joseph, Missouri, to Sacramento, California. Teams of riders usually covered the distance in ten days, although they carried Lincoln's inaugural address in seven and a half. The Pony Express lasted only 19 months from 1860 to 1861, but as this desolate spot on its route vividly illustrates, it was a triumph of physical courage and endurance. Today Simpson Springs, which features a restored

cabin and several explanatory panels, is a pleasant place to stop for a picnic and to contemplate the importance of water and its influence on human history in these forbidding deserts.

The Deseret Test Center and the Dugway Proving Grounds to the north are military testing ranges. They are not accessible to the public, and proving-grounds activities on the Great Salt Lake Desert are a military secret.

To reach the Stansbury Mountains in the **Wasatch-Cache National Forest❖** to the northeast, continue east on the Pony Express Trail from Simpson Springs to the intersection with Route 36 just before Faust Station. Turn north on Route 36, then west toward Rush Valley on Route 199 for about two miles. Turn north again on the road to Grantsville for about 15 miles, to South Willow Road west up South Willow Canyon into the Stansbury Mountains, a popular weekend retreat from the cities of the Wasatch Front. Hiking and horseback riding in the **Deseret Peak Wilderness Area❖** are usually cool and pleasant, offering the opportunity to enjoy a rich array of flowers and animals in a blending of the Rocky Mountain and Great Basin ecosystems. The higher elevations provide fabulous views of the Great Salt Lake to the north and surrounding mountain ranges.

The signposted trail to Deseret Peak from the head of South Willow Road climbs alongside a stream shaded by aspens and box elders.

Maidenhair ferns, snowberries, and mountain gooseberries with their prickly red fruit flourish in the moist soil. Lovage, yarrow, coneflowers, and lupines bloom in the meadows, and higher up, the forest supports many old-growth Douglas firs. Around tree line on the slopes below the summit grow towering monument plants, tiny white bladder campion, and stunted "banner" trees, with limbs extending away from the wind. Marmots chirp from boulder piles and turkey vultures teeter overhead; like other ranges of the area, the Stansburys are important raptor habitat.

GREAT SALT LAKE—HEART OF THE GREAT BASIN

The Great Basin encompasses a quarter of a million square miles with no outlet to the sea: about half of Utah, most of Nevada, and bits of California, Oregon, and Idaho. The terms *basin and range* and *Great Basin* are sometimes used interchangeably, and their eastern and western boundaries almost overlap, but they are not the same. The basin and range is a corrugated landscape—extending all the way from within Idaho and Oregon through Utah, Nevada, and California into Arizona, New Mexico, and Mexico—that formed as the earth's crust stretched.

Great Salt Lake so dominates the Great Basin of northwest Utah that it is quite noticeable from hundreds of miles up in space. Because its basin is very shallow, a relatively small difference in the lake's volume of water can extend its coverage considerably, from 1,000 to 2,300 square miles. On average, the lake covers about 1,500 square miles and is only 14 feet deep. It is surrounded by flat, salty land that slopes ever so gradually up to where

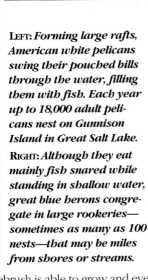

Left: *Forming large rafts, American white pelicans swing their pouched bills through the water, filling them with fish. Each year up to 18,000 adult pelicans nest on Gunnison Island in Great Salt Lake.*

Right: *Although they eat mainly fish snared while standing in shallow water, great blue herons congregate in large rookeries—sometimes as many as 100 nests—that may be miles from shores or streams.*

sagebrush is able to grow and eventually meets steep mountain ranges.

Flowing water—laden with a yearly average of two million tons of dissolved minerals—enters the lake, the lowest point on the landscape, and can flow no farther. As the water evaporates, it leaves behind mineral salts. Today, an estimated five billion tons of salts are concentrated in the waters of Great Salt Lake, making it up to eight times as salty as ocean water. As a result, the lake does not freeze in winter. Only a narrow range of plants and aquatic organisms can survive in it, most successfully the brine shrimp, a tiny nondescript crustacean that tickles swimmers and feeds hordes of birds. Swimmers find themselves extremely buoyant and float without effort, but they cannot swim underwater at all.

The **Great Salt Desert**—the former floor of Great Salt Lake's ancestor, Lake Bonneville—covers about 4,000 square miles of northwestern Utah west of Great Salt Lake. Its salty, hard mineral crust—from one-sixteenth of an inch to as deep as four feet—prevents plants from growing on it except in the very rare pockets where soil has accumulated. Water pools here in winter and spring, becoming saturated with salts flowing from the mountains and left behind by Lake Bonneville. As the water evaporates, the salt crust forms, leaving an eerie landscape of polygonal ridges of salt outlining pans of more salt. Little salt balls crunch under walkers' feet. Because virtually no plants can tolerate the concentration of salts here, the land is a moonscape bounded by dark, fault block mountain ranges. The waters of Lake Bonneville once lapped these ranges, eroding shorelines in them that can still be seen a thousand feet higher than the level of

ABOVE: *At the Bear River Migratory Bird Refuge, nesting platforms built for Canada geese stand above bulrushes and cattails. Each year millions of birds, mainly waterfowl, use the 65,000-acre freshwater marsh.*

Great Salt Lake, which lies about 4,200 feet above sea level today.

Probably the most famous part of this desert is the BLM's 30,000-acre **Bonneville Salt Flats❖** on the Nevada border due west of Salt Lake City via I-80. Vast, surreal, and lifeless, this place is so flat that a person gazing across it can perceive the curvature of the earth. Because these salt flats are so level and hard, they have been used for racing since 1911, when a fellow named W. D. Rishel convinced Fery Johnson to take his Packard for a spin. Automobile racers and test drivers from all over the world come to Bonneville, where they have set the land-speed records of 300, 400, 500, and 600 miles per hour. Speed trials take place in summer and fall, ending with the winter rains.

To the east, the interstate highways skirt the southern and eastern edges of the Great Salt Lake and serve the Salt Lake City metropolitan area. Like its mirror image on the far side of the Rockies—the Denver metropolitan area—this cluster of cities nestles at the foot of a fault-scarp, or front. Thirsty city dwellers tap the streams of the mountains for water, find a cool refuge in the peaks in summer, and ski the slopes in winter.

Great Salt Lake's long, narrow islands and shoreline peninsulas are the tops of ancient ranges exposed above the water that now fills their intervening basins. To visit one of these islands, take Exit 335 from I-15 and drive west on Route 127 through Syracuse and over the 7.5-mile causeway to Antelope Island State Park. The causeway is an excellent vantage point for watching the gulls, grebes, and rafts of white pelicans bobbing about in the salty, shallow waters nearby.

Experiencing **Antelope Island State Park**❖ is like visiting a desert sea. The largest of Great Salt Lake's ten major islands at almost 28,000 acres, the arid, rugged island lies surrounded by salt water shimmering in the sun. The air has the sulfurous scent of low tide, and there is even a swimming beach on the northwest coastline. The state park includes just the northern promontory of the island, where a short hike up to Buffalo Point affords a panoramic view of Stansbury Island to the southwest (a partially submerged extension of the Stansbury Range), of Promontory Point to the north (the landmark for the 1869 driving of the golden spike that united 1,776 miles of track laid by the Union Pacific and the Central Pacific railroads), and of the cities below the Wasatch Range to the east.

In the 1840s, U.S. Army explorer John C. Frémont named Antelope Island for the many pronghorn (wrongly called antelope) that lived there then. The pronghorn died out by the 1870s, because the cattle that local settlers brought to the island in 1848 competed with the pronghorn for forage and water. More livestock arrived in 1856, and the Antelope Island bison herd, established in 1893, now numbers 600 animals. Pronghorn were reintroduced in 1991.

On the fringes of Great Salt Lake, streams flowing down from the surrounding mountains form marshy deltas that are an excellent habitat for birds, particularly waterfowl, migrating along the Pacific and Central flyways. One of the best places to watch some of the more than 250 species of birds seen around Great Salt Lake is the **Bear River Migratory Bird Refuge**❖ (take I-15 north to Brigham City, then Forest Street west, which becomes the Bear River Migratory Bird Refuge Road). One of the most important bird preserves in the country, the refuge occupies the flat delta of the Bear River, a natural wetland enhanced by man-made dikes and channels whose blue waters are brilliant against the surrounding pastels of hills and valleys. Spring is the best time to visit, when the water is highest and birds are in breeding plumage.

The brochure-guided auto tour of the refuge around Unit 2 from the old headquarters area is best taken in early morning or evening, when the birds are more active and the light better for seeing colors. Although many birds leave the refuge in the fall, various ducks, Canada geese, and tundra swans arrive then. Mice live among the grasses of the refuge, attracting hawks, eagles, weasels, and coyotes, which also feast on the carcasses of birds. At the Bear River refuge, elegant, long-legged shorebirds—herons, ibis, avocets—share their habitat with perching birds such as marsh wrens and red-winged blackbirds. Various plovers and sandpipers poke about busily in the mudflats, while plump ducks of all kinds and colors quack contentedly. Centuries ago, the Fremont people hunted and gathered in the delta of Bear River, collecting eggs, birds, and plants. After many of the dikes and buildings in the refuge were destroyed by the high water of Great Salt Lake in 1983, staff and volunteers have restored the facilities as time and funds have permitted.

Almost lost in the northwest corner of Utah is another range, the **Raft River Mountains,** whose north side is in the **Sawtooth National Forest❖.** Classified as a "metamorphic core complex," the range is composed of 2.5-billion-year-old Precambrian rocks—the oldest rocks found in the Great Basin—that were once buried by sedimentary strata. Until about 11 million years ago, the mountains' sedimentary layers kept sliding off them like untucked blankets off a bed, to be deposited in the surrounding basins. How the layers were pulled remains a subject of debate among geologists, but the process appears to have been connected with the same kind of stretching, or extensional forces, that created the basin and range.

To visit the Raft Rivers, take Interstate 84 and then Routes 30 and 42 north and west from Brigham City over Utah's border with Idaho to Strevell. Turn west from Strevell and drive parallel to the border, following the signs to the **Clear Creek Campground❖** in the Raft River Mountains. Although there are no paved roads or maintained trails in the Raft Rivers, the open, meadowy higher slopes offer cross-country hiking and jeep roads. Hikers here are treated to breathtaking views of the interior of the range, the distant basin of the Great Salt Desert to the south, and Idaho's Snake River Range to the north.

Western Utah is stark country, wild and open, the most lightly inhabited region within all of Utah and Colorado. It is a place where the elements rule, a place to come to terms with heat and dust, space and light, fear and freedom. And like all natural areas, it is a place to come to terms with ourselves and the world around us.

RIGHT: *Extraordinary, unexpected scenes—such as the polygonal patterns of dried salt lit by the setting sun on the Bonneville Salt Flats—await those who seek out the region's sere and lovely landscapes.*

FURTHER READING ABOUT THE SOUTHERN ROCKIES

ABBEY, EDWARD. *Desert Solitaire: A Season in the Wilderness.* New York: Ballantine, 1968. One of the most influential books on the Southwest, this fierce, lyrical polemic by a former seasonal ranger at Arches National Park has inspired both appreciation of and radical advocacy for the desert wilderness.

AITCHISON, STEWART. *Utah Wildlands.* Salt Lake City: Utah Geographic, 1987. A knowledgeable, illustrated guide to Utah's wilderness areas, with discussions of their natural and political histories.

BIRD, ISABELLA L. *A Lady's Life in the Rocky Mountains.* Norman: University of Oklahoma Press, 1960. These letters, written by an adventurous Englishwoman in 1873 as she traveled alone in Colorado, provide a vivid picture of frontier America as well as insights into why pioneers left society for new lives in the Rockies.

BORLAND, HAL. *High, Wide and Lonesome.* Philadelphia: Lippincott, 1956. A memoir of the author's childhood on the plains of Colorado, where his family homesteaded from 1910 to 1915; this western classic captures the feel of the land and its effect on the human spirit.

CHRONIC, HALKA. *Roadside Geology of Colorado.* Missoula, MT: Mountain Press, 1980. The author clearly explains the origins of the landforms along the main roads of Colorado in a lively style interesting to beginners as well as experts in geology.

————. *Roadside Geology of Utah.* Missoula, MT: Mountain Press, 1990. Part of the same series as the volume described above, this book by the same author describes the landforms visible from the roads of Utah.

MUTEL, CORNELIA, AND JOHN EMERICK. *From Grassland to Glacier: The Natural History of Colorado and the Surrounding Region.* Boulder: Johnson Books, 1992. A concise description of Colorado's 15 ecosystems, with species listings of both plants and animals.

NATIONAL GEOGRAPHIC SOCIETY. *Birds of North America.* Washington: National Geographic Society, 1983. One of the better illustrated bird guides, with entries describing appearance, songs, migrations, and behavior.

RUSHO, W. L. *Everett Ruess: A Vagabond for Beauty.* Salt Lake City: Peregrine Smith Books, 1983. An intriguing account of the brief life of Everett Ruess, a young man who wandered in the West in the 1920s, wrote passionate poetry, prose, and letters home, and then disappeared without a trace.

SPELLENBERG, RICHARD. *The Audubon Society Field Guide to North American Wildflowers: Western Region.* New York: Knopf, 1979. A guide to the species most likely to be found in Colorado and Utah, with notes on their adaptations to diverse habitats and their interactions with other forms of life.

STEGNER, WALLACE. *Beyond the Hundredth Meridian: John Wesley Powell and the Second Opening of the West.* Lincoln: University of Nebraska Press, 1954. This history of Civil War veteran Powell's expeditions to the West and his struggles with Washington reveals that controversy about the conservation of natural resources goes back to the earliest days of the American presence in Colorado and Utah.

————. *Mormon Country.* Lincoln: University of Nebraska Press, 1970. A cheerful yet respectful collection of anecdotal essays, by a non-Mormon who once lived in Salt Lake City, which adds up to a very readable portrayal of the history and beliefs of these determined settlers of Utah.

WILLIAMS, TERRY TEMPEST. *Refuge: An Unnatural History of Family and Place.* New York: Vintage, 1992. Two tragedies are woven together in this nonetheless uplifting account of a loss in the author's family that is mirrored by a catastrophe in the natural world: the inundation of the Bear River Migratory Bird Refuge.

ZWINGER, ANN. *Wind in the Rock.* Tucson: University of Arizona Press, 1978. As the author savors the canyonlands of southeastern Utah, she gently educates her readers about the flora, the fauna, and the landscape of the stark yet lovely Colorado Plateau.

ZWINGER, ANN, AND BEATRICE WILLARD. *Land Above the Trees.* Tucson: University of Arizona Press, 1972. A delightful introduction to the surprisingly rich American tundra, where delicate flowers and birds flourish despite the harsh, unprotected conditions of the treeless reaches that lie two miles above sea level.

GLOSSARY

alluvial fan deposit of alluvium: gravel, sand, and smaller materials that have formed a fan shape, usually at the base of mountains; created by water rushing down a mountain

arête sharp-crested ridge

batholith large mass of igneous rock that has melted into surrounding strata and lies a great distance below the earth's surface

bog wetland, formed in glacial kettle holes, common to cool climates of northern North America, Europe, and Asia; acidic nature produces large quantities of peat moss

butte tall, steep-sided tower of rock formed from an eroded plateau; buttes delay inevitable erosional changes because of their hard uppermost layer of rock

cirque large, bowl-shaped depression hollowed out in a mountain by glacial movement

delta flat, low-lying plain that forms at the mouth of a river as the river slows and deposits sediment gathered upstream

dendritic referring to shapes or markings resembling the branching figure of a plant

dike vertical sheet of rock formed when molten rock cools on its way to the earth's surface and surrounding rock erodes

ecotone transition zone between two different plant communities

endemic having originated in and being restricted to one particular environment

escarpment cliff or steep rock face, formed by faulting or fracturing of the earth's crust, that separates two comparatively level land surfaces

fault break in the earth's outermost layer, or crust, along which rock may move against rock

fault block mountain characterized by steep walls on one side and gentler slopes on the other; formed when plate movement causes land on one side of the fault to rise higher than on the other side

faulted anticline upward fold in the earth's crust; when eroded, the oldest rocks are found in the center of the fold

hogback sharply defined ridge produced by the erosion of highly angled rock layers, one of which is more resistant than the others

hoodoo natural column of rock often formed into fantastic shapes; found in western North America

igneous referring to rock formed by cooled and hardened lava or magma

karst area of land lying over limestone that is dotted with sinkholes, underground streams, and caves formed by the erosion of the limestone by rainwater

laccolith underground body of lens-shaped igneous rock that has squeezed between rock layers forcing the strata above into a dome shape

lateral moraine hill or ridge of debris (rock, sand, gravel, silt, and clay) deposited along a retreating or advancing glacier's side

lek assembly area where birds, especially prairie chickens, carry on courtship behavior

magma molten rock within the earth that becomes igneous rock when it cools

mesa isolated, relatively flat-topped natural elevation more extensive than a butte and less extensive than a plateau

metamorphic referring to a rock that has been changed into its present state after being subjected to heat, pressure, or chemical change

monocline fold in stratified rock in which all strata dip in the same direction

montane relating to the biogeographic zone of relatively moist, cool upland slopes below timberline; dominated by evergreen trees

orogeny geologic process of mountain building and formation

petroglyph carving on rock, especially one made by prehistoric people

pictograph prehistoric painting or drawing on rock created with natural pigments applied with animal-hair brushes

plates thick slabs of rock that make up the earth's outer shell, including the ocean floor and the continental land masses; movement and interaction of the plates is known as plate tectonics

playa flat-floored bottom of an undrained desert basin that may become a shallow lake in wet times and may be encrusted with salt or other minerals when dry

rapids broken, fast-flowing water that tumbles around boulders; classified from I to VI according to increasing difficulty of watercraft navigation

riparian relating to the bank of a natural watercourse, lake, or tidewater

scarp line of steep cliffs formed by erosion

scree accumulation of loose stones or rocky debris lying on a slope or at the base of a hill

sedimentary referring to rocks formed from deposits of small eroded debris such as gravel, sand, mud, silt, or peat

sinkhole funnel-shaped hole formed where water has collected in the cracks of limestone, dissolved the rock, and carried it away; also formed when roofs of caves collapse

tableland large area of elevated, level land

talus rock debris that accumulates at the base of a cliff

tectonic referring to the deformation of the earth's crust, the forces involved, and the resulting formations

terminal moraine final deposit of rock and debris that has formed at a glacier's farthest leading edge, and is left behind as the glacier retreats

thrust fault fault in which one block is pushed up and over another; ancient metamorphic rock often ends up on top of newer sedimentary rock

travertine mineral formed by deposition from spring waters or hot springs creating (among other deposits) stalactites and stalagmites

tuff rock formed by small debris of a volcanic ash flow

wetland area of land covered or saturated with groundwater; includes swamps, marshes, and bogs

LAND MANAGEMENT RESOURCES

The following public and private organizations are among the important administrators of the preserved and protected areas described in this volume. Brief explanations of the various legal and legislative designations of these areas follow.

MANAGING ORGANIZATIONS

Bureau of Land Management (BLM) Department of the Interior
Administers nearly half of all federal lands, some 272 million acres, predominantly in the western states. Resources are managed for multiple uses: recreation, grazing, logging, mining, fish and wildlife, and watershed and wilderness preservation.

Colorado Division of Parks and Outdoor Recreation
Manages 40 state parks totaling some 170,000 acres. Responsible for registering all boats and licensing all river outfitters.

Colorado Division of Wildlife
Responsible for preservation, protection, and management of all state wildlife areas in Colorado, totaling approximately 450,000 acres. Maintains state hunting and fishing areas and licenses.

National Park Service (NPS) Department of the Interior
Regulates the use of national parks, monuments, and preserves. Resources are managed to preserve and protect landscape, natural and historic artifacts, and wildlife. Also administers historic and national landmarks, national seashores, wild and scenic rivers, and the national trail system.

U.S. Fish and Wildlife Service (USFWS) Department of the Interior
Principal federal agency responsible for conserving, protecting, and enhancing the country's fish and wildlife and their habitats. Manages national wildlife refuges and fish hatcheries as well as programs for migratory birds and endangered and threatened species.

U.S. Forest Service (USFS) Department of Agriculture
Administers more than 190 million acres in the national forests and national grasslands and is responsible for the management of their resources. Determines how best to combine commercial uses such as grazing, mining, and logging with conservation needs.

Utah Division of Parks and Recreation
Administers and maintains all state parks including natural scenic areas, cultural and historic areas, and water parks and reservoirs. Total acreage under management is approximately 103,000.

Utah Division of Wildlife Resources
Responsible for wildlife management areas that protect big game and waterfowl throughout the state. Manages approximately 400,000 acres in total. Also responsible for hunting and fishing licensing and regulation.

DESIGNATIONS

Archaeological Area
Area of significant archaeological interest and resources that may contribute to the study of prehistory. Managed by BLM or individual states.

National Backcountry Byway
Dirt or gravel road designated for its scenic, geologic, or historic attributes. Mainly for sightseeing and recreation via automobile. Managed by BLM.

National Forest
Large acreage managed for the use of forests, watersheds, wildlife, and recreation by the public and private sectors. Managed by the USFS.

National Grassland
Federal land where more than 80 percent of the canopy cover is dominated by grasses or grasslike plants. May encompass private holdings. Managed by USFS.

National Historic Landmark
Land area, building, or object preserved because of its historic importance. Managed by NPS.

National Monument
Nationally significant landmark, structure, object, or area of scientific or historic significance. Managed by NPS.

National Park
Spacious primitive or wilderness area with scenery and natural wonders so outstanding it has been preserved and designated by the federal government. Managed by NPS.

National Recreation Area
Site established to conserve and develop for recreational purposes an area of scenic, natural, or historic interest. Powerboats, dirt and mountain bikes, and ORVs allowed with restrictions. Managed by the NPS.

National Wildlife Refuge
Public land set aside for wild animals; protects migratory waterfowl, endangered and threatened species, and native plants. Managed by USFWS.

Reservation
Area of land held in trust by the federal government and reserved for use by Native Americans.

Wild and Scenic River System
National program to preserve selected rivers in their natural free-flowing condition; stretches are classified as wild, scenic, or recreational depending on the degree of development on the river, shoreline, or adjacent lands. Management shared by BLM, NPS, and USFWS.

Wilderness Area
Area with particular ecological, geological, or scientific, scenic, or historic value that has been set aside in its natural condition to be preserved as wild land; limited recreational use is permitted. Managed by BLM and NPS.

NATURE TRAVEL

The following is a selection of national and local organizations that sponsor nature-related travel activities or can provide specialized regional travel information.

NATIONAL

National Audubon Society
700 Broadway
New York, NY 10003
(212) 979-3000
Offers a wide range of ecological field studies, tours, and cruises throughout the United States

National Wildlife Federation
1400 16th Street NW
Washington, D.C. 20036
(703) 790-4363
Offers training in environmental education for all ages, wildlife camp and teen adventures, conservation summits involving nature walks, field trips, and classes

The Nature Conservancy
1815 North Lynn Street
Arlington, VA 22209
(703) 841-5300
Offers a variety of excursions based out of regional and state offices. May include hiking, backpacking, canoeing, horseback riding. Contact above number to locate state offices

Sierra Club Outings
730 Polk Street
San Francisco, CA 94109
(415) 923-5630
Offers tours of different lengths for all ages throughout the United States. Outings may include backpacking, hiking, biking, skiing, and water excursions

Smithsonian Study Tours and Seminars
1100 Jefferson Dr. SW
MRC 702
Washington, D.C. 20560
(202) 357-4700
Offers extended tours, cruises, research expeditions, and seminars throughout the United States

REGIONAL

Colorado Mountain Club
710 10th St., #200
Golden, CO 80401
(303) 279-3080
Private, nonprofit outdoor club; most day trips open to nonmembers

Colorado Tourism Information Services
c/o Denver Convention & Visitors Bureau
225 West Colfax
Denver, CO 80202
(800) COLORADO (265-6723)
Publishes state vacation guide and answers phone queries about nature travel and accommodations

Denver Museum of Natural History
2001 Colorado Blvd.
Denver, CO 80205
(303) 370-6304
Natural history museum that offers a variety of domestic, ecologically minded recreational travel and study tours

Four Corners School of Outdoor Education
P.O. Box 1029
Monticello, UT 84535
(800) 525-4456
Private, nonprofit group offering river tours, backpacking, van tours, and base-camp hiking at archaeological sites.

The Norwegian School of Nature Life
P.O. Box 4036
Park City, UT 84060
(800) 649-5322
Nonprofit organization that offers instruction in skiing, snowshoeing, mountaineering, and survival methods

Utah Travel Council
Council Hall Capitol Hill
Salt Lake City, UT 84114
(800) 200-1160
Publishes travel brochures and answers questions about travel and lodging

How to Use This Site Guide

The following site information guide will assist you in planning your tour of the natural areas of Colorado and Utah. Sites set in boldface and followed by the symbol ❖ in the text are here organized alphabetically by state. Each entry is followed by the mailing address (sometimes different from the street address) and phone number of the immediate managing office, plus brief notes and a list of facilities and activities available. (A key appears on each page of this section.)

Information on hours of operation, seasonal closings, and fees is often not listed, as these vary from season to season and year to year. Please also bear in mind that responsibility for the management of some sites may change. Call well in advance to obtain maps, brochures, and pertinent, up-to-date information that will help you plan your adventures in the Southern Rockies.

Each site entry in the guide includes the address and phone number of its immediate managing agency. Many of these sites are under the stewardship of a forest or park ranger or supervised from a small nearby office. Hence, in many cases, those sites will be difficult to contact directly, and it is preferable to call the managing agency.

The following umbrella organizations can provide general information for individual natural sites, as well as the area as a whole:

COLORADO

Bureau of Land Management State Director's Office
2850 Youngfield St.
Lakewood, CO 80215
(303) 239-3700

Colorado Department of Natural Resources
1313 Sherman St.,
Rm. 718
Denver, CO 80203
(303) 866-3311

Colorado Division of Wildlife
6060 Broadway
Denver, CO 80216
(303) 297-1192

Colorado State Parks
1313 Sherman St., Rm 618,
Denver, CO 80203
(303) 866-3437
(800) 678-2267 (for camping reservations)

UTAH

Utah Department of Natural Resources
1636 W. N. Temple
Ste. 316
Salt Lake City, UT 84116
(801) 538-7200

Utah Division of Parks and Recreation
1636 W. N. Temple
Suite 116
Salt Lake City, UT 84116
(801) 538-7221

Utah Division of Wildlife Resources
1596 W. N. Temple
Salt Lake City, UT 84116
(801) 538-4700

Utah State Office of the Bureau of Land Management
PO Box 45155
Salt Lake City, UT 84145
(801) 539-4010

National Park Service Regional Office
12795 W. Alameda Pkwy.
Box 25287
Denver, CO 80225
(303) 969-2000

COLORADO

ALAMOSA NATIONAL WILDLIFE REFUGE
U.S. Fish and Wildlife Service
9383 El Rancho Lane
Alamosa, CO 81101
(719) 589-4021
BT, BW, H, MB, I, MT, T

ALFRED M. BAILEY BIRD NESTING AREA
White River National Forest
Dillon Ranger District
PO Box 620, Silverthorne, CO 80498
(970) 468-5400
Participate in bird-banding demonstrations May–August **BW, H**

ANASAZI HERITAGE CENTER
Bureau of Land Management
27501 Rte. 184
Delores, CO 81323
(970) 882-4811; (970) 882-4825
BW, GS, I, MT, PA, T

ARAPAHO NATIONAL FOREST
U.S. Forest Service
240 W. Prospect
Fort Collins, CO 80526
(970) 498-1100
BT, BW, C, CK, DS, F, H, HR, I, MB, MT, PA, RC, T, XC

ARAPAHO NATIONAL RECREATION AREA
U.S. Forest Service,
Sulphur Ranger District
PO Box 10, Granby, CO 80446
(303) 887-3331
BT, BW, C, CK, DS, F, GS, H, HR, I, MB, MT, PA, RA, T, TG, XC

ARAPAHO NATIONAL WILDLIFE REFUGE
U.S. Fish and Wildlife Service
PO Box 457, Walden, CO 80480
(970) 723-8202 **BW, F, I, MT, PA, T**

ARKANSAS HEADWATERS RECREATION AREA
Colorado Div. of Parks and Outdoor Recreation /BLM
PO Box 126, Salida, CO 81201
(719) 539-7289
Get park passes at several self-service dispensers or Salida office; white-water rafting; private boats must be labeled
BT, BW, CK, F, H, HR, I, MB, PA, T

ASPEN CENTER FOR ENVIRONMENTAL STUDIES AT HALLAM LAKE
100 Puppy Smith St.
Aspen, CO 81611
(970) 925-5756
Call ahead for hours and program schedules; bike path to Northstar Nature Preserve **BW, GS, I, MT, RA, T, TG**

BEAR CREEK REGIONAL PARK
El Paso County Parks
245 Bear Creek Rd.
Colorado Springs, CO 80906
(719) 520-6387
Includes Nature Center
BT, BW, H, HR, I, MB, MT, PA, RA, T, TG, XC

BEAVER CREEK WILDERNESS
Bureau of Land Management
3170 E. Main, Canon City, CO 81215-0313
(719) 275-0631 **BW, F, H, HR, MT**

BLACK CANYON OF THE GUNNISON NATIONAL MONUMENT
National Park Service
2233 E. Main St., Suite A
Montrose, CO 81401
(970) 249-7036
North Rim Rd. closed during snow season; permit required for all inner canyon activities **BW, C, F, H, I, MT, RA, RC, T, XC**

BLUE RIVER CAMPGROUND
White River National Forest
Dillon Ranger District
PO Box 620
Silverthorne, CO 80498
(970) 468-5400
Seasonal operation; vault toilets; water not always available **BW, C, T**

BRISTLECONE PINE SCENIC AREA
U.S. Forest Service
South Park Ranger District
PO Box 219, Fairplay, CO 80440
(719) 836-2031
Do not remove even the smallest part of any tree, dead or alive **BW, H**

BROWNS PARK NATIONAL WILDLIFE REFUGE
U.S. Fish and Wildlife Service
1318 Rte. 318, Maybell, CO 81640
(970) 365-3613

BT	Bike Trails	**CK**	Canoeing, Kayaking	**F**	Fishing	**HR**	Horseback Riding
BW	Bird-watching			**GS**	Gift Shop		
C	Camping	**DS**	Downhill Skiing	**H**	Hiking	**I**	Information Center

Seasonal closures; mountain bikes limited to roads
BW, C, CK, F, H, HR, MB, I, PA, S, T, TG

CACHE LA POUDRE
WILD AND SCENIC RIVER
U.S. Forest Service
Estes-Poudre Ranger District
1311 S. College
Fort Collins, CO 80524
(970) 498-2775
BT, BW, C, CK, F, H, I, L,
MB, MT, PA, RA, RC, T, TG, XC

CASTLEWOOD CANYON STATE PARK
Colorado Div. of Parks and
Outdoor Recreation
PO Box 504
Franktown, CO 80116-0504
(303) 688-5242
Entrance fee; dogs must be on leashes;
fires in grills only
BW, GS, H, I, MT, PA, RA, RC, T

CAVE OF THE WINDS
PO Box 826
Manitou Springs, CO 80829
(719) 685-5444
BW, GS, H, I, MT, PA, T, TG

CHATFIELD STATE PARK
Colorado Div. of Parks
and Outdoor Recreation
11500 N. Roxborough Park Rd.
Littleton, CO 80125
(303) 791-7275; (303) 973-9401
Park pass required for vehicle
BT, BW, C, CK, F, H, HR,
MB, MT, PA, RA, S, T, XC

CHIMNEY ROCK ARCHAEOLOGICAL AREA
San Juan National Forest
Pagosa Ranger District
PO Box 310, Pagosa Springs, CO 81147
(970) 264-2268
Tours available May–October; be prepared for hot summers and high altitude
I, MT, RA, T, TG

CITY PARK
Denver Parks and Recreation
2300 15th St., Suite 100
Denver, CO 80202
(303) 964-2500
Paddle boats; permits required for large groups
BT, BW, F, MB, PA, T, XC

COALMONT LEK
Bureau of Land Management
PO Box 68
Kremmling, CO 80459
(970) 724-3437
Private land; BLM will provide information
BW, TG

COLLEGIATE PEAKS WILDERNESS AREA
U.S. Forest Service
216 N. Colorado
Gunnison, CO 81230
(970) 641-0471
BW, C, F, H, HR, XC

COLORADO NATIONAL MONUMENT
National Park Service
Fruita, CO 81521
(970) 858-3617
Bicycles must stay on roads; 23-mile
Rim Rock Drive
BW, C, GS, H, HR, I, MB,
MT, PA, RA, RC, T, XC

COLORADO STATE FOREST STATE PARK
Colorado Div. of Parks
and Outdoor Recreation
Star Route, Box 91
Walden, CO 80480
(970) 723-8366; (800) 678-2267
C, F, H, HR, I, L, MB,
MT, PA, RA, T, XC

COMANCHE NATIONAL GRASSLAND
U.S. Forest Service
PO Box 127
Springfield, CO 81073
(719) 523-6591—Springfield
(719) 384-2181—La Junta
Include Santa Fe National Historic Trail;
No motorized vehicles or camping in
Picket Wire Canyonlands
BT, BW, C, H,
HR, I, MB, MT, PA, T

CROSS CANYON
WILDERNESS STUDY AREA
Bureau of Land Management
701 Camino del Rio
Durango, CO 81301-5462
(970) 247-4082
BW, C, H, HR, XC

CROW CANYON
ARCHAEOLOGICAL CENTER
23390 County Rd. K
Cortez, CO 81321
(800) 422-8975
GS, TG

L	Lodging	**PA**	Picnic Areas	**RC**	Rock Climbing
MB	Mountain Biking	**RA**	Ranger-led	**S**	Swimming
MT	Marked Trails		Activities	**T**	Toilets

TG	Tours, Guides
XC	Cross-country Skiing

265

CROW VALLEY RECREATION AREA
U.S. Forest Service
Pawnee National Grassland
660 O St.
Greeley, CO 80631
(970) 353-5004   BW, C, H, MB, PA, T

CURECANTI NATIONAL RECREATION AREA
National Park Service
102 Elk Creek
Gunnison, CO 81230
(970) 249-4074 (Cimmaron Ranger
District)   BW, C, CK, F, H, I,
                   MT, PA, RA, S, T, XC

DENVER BOTANIC GARDENS
909 York St.
Denver, CO 80206
(303) 331-4000;
(303) 370-8018   GS, I, PA, T, TG

DENVER MUSEUM OF NATURAL HISTORY
2001 Colorado Blvd.
Denver, CO. 80205
(303) 322-7009
     Includes Gates Planetarium;
     Imax Theater   GS, T

DENVER ZOO
Denver Zoological Foundation
2300 Steele St.
Denver, CO 80205
(303) 331-4110   I, T

DINOSAUR HILL
Bureau of Land Management
Grand Junction District
2815 H. Rd.
Grand Junction, CO 81506
(970) 244-3000   H, MT, RA

DINOSAUR NATIONAL MONUMENT
National Park Service
4545 Hwy. E
Dinosaur, CO 81610
(970) 374-3000
     Permit required for canoeing or
     kayaking   BW, C, CK, H, I, MT, RA, T

ELDORADO CANYON STATE PARK
Colorado Div. of Parks
and Outdoor Recreation
PO Box B
Eldorado Springs, CO 80025
(303) 494-3943   BT, BW, F, GS, H, HR, I,
                   MB, MT, PA, RA, RC, T, XC

FLORISSANT FOSSIL BEDS NATIONAL MONUMENT
National Park Service
PO Box 185
Florissant, CO 80816
(719) 748-3253
     Tours and guides summer only
                   BW, GS, H, I, MT,
                   PA, RA, T, TG, XC

FOUNTAIN CREEK REGIONAL PARK
El Paso County Parks
320 Pepper Grass Lane
Fountain, CO 80817
(719) 520-6745   BT, BW, F, H, HR,
                   I, MB, MT, PA, RA, T, TG

GARDEN OF THE GODS
City of Colorado Springs, Parks and
Recreation Dept.
1401 Recreation Way
Colorado Springs, CO 80905
(719) 578-6939; (719) 578-6640
                   BT, BW, GS, H, HR, I,
                   MT, PA, RA, RC, T, TG

GARDEN PARK FOSSIL AREA
Bureau of Land Management
3170 E. Main
Canon City, CO 81215-0313
(719) 275-0631
     Information center at Dinosaur Depot
                   BW, H, I, MB, PA, TG

GOLD BELT NATIONAL BACKCOUNTRY BYWAY
Bureau of Land Management
3170 E. Main
Canon City, CO 81215-0313
(719) 275-0631
     Information center at Dinosaur Depot
                   BW, H, I, MB, MT

GOLDEN GATE CANYON STATE PARK
Colorado Div. of Parks and Recreation
3873 Rte. 46, Golden, CO 80403
(303) 592-1502   BW, C, F, GS, H, HR, I,
                   MB, MT, PA, RA, T, XC

GRAND MESA NATIONAL FOREST
U.S. Forest Service
2250 Rte. 50, Delta, CO 81416-8723
(970) 874-7691
     Includes Powderhorn ski area
                   BW, C, CK, DS, F, GS, H, HR,
                   I, L, MB, MT, PA, S, T, XC

BT Bike Trails
BW Bird-watching
C Camping

CK Canoeing,
        Kayaking
DS Downhill
        Skiing

F Fishing
GS Gift Shop
H Hiking

HR Horseback
        Riding
I Information
        Center

266

GREAT SAND DUNES NATIONAL MONUMENT
National Park Service
11500 Rte. 150
Mosca, CO 81146
(719) 378-2312
Tours and some activities limited to summer **BW, GS, H, HR, I, MB, PA, RA, T, TG**

GUNNISON NATIONAL FOREST
U.S. Forest Service
2250 Rte. 50
Delta, CO 81416-8723
(970) 874-7691 **BT, BW, C, CK, DS, F, H, HR, I, MB, MT, PA, RC, T, XC**

HOLY CROSS WILDERNESS AREA
U.S. Forest Service
Holy Cross District
PO Box 190
Minturn, CO 81645
(970) 827-5715 **BW, C, F, H, MT, TG, XC**

HORSETHIEF CANYON STATE WILDLIFE AREA
Colorado Div. of Wildlife
711 Independent Ave.
Grand Junction, CO 81505
(970) 248-7175
Mandatory check in; no charge **BW, F, H, HR, I, MT**

HOT CREEK STATE WILDLIFE AREA
Colorado Div. of Wildlife
0722 South Rd. 1 East
Monte Vista,CO 81144
(719) 852-4783
No motor vehicles December 1–April 30; no snowmobiling **BW, F, H, HR, XC**

INDIAN PEAKS WILDERNESS AREA
U.S. Forest Service
Boulder Ranger District
2995 Baseline Rd., Rm. 110
Boulder, CO 80303
(303) 444-6003
Permit required in summer for camping **BW, C, H**

INDIAN SPRINGS TRACE FOSSIL SITE
PO Box 405
Canon City, CO 81215-0405
(719) 372-3907 **BW, C, H, HR, I, MB, PA, S, T, TG**

KOKOPELLI TRAIL
Bureau of Land Management
Grand Junction District
2815 H Rd.
Grand Junction, CO 81506
(970) 244-3000
4WD and motorcycles allowed on certain sections, not on single track **BT, H, HR, MB, MT**

LA GARITA WILDERNESS
U.S. Forest Service
Divide Ranger District
PO Box 270
Creede, CO 81130
(719) 658-2556; (719) 655-2547
Includes Wheeler Geologic Area; no motorized vehicles; pit toilets at some trailheads **BW, C, F, H, HR, MT, RC, T, TG, XC**

LATHROP STATE PARK
Colorado Div. of Parks
and Outdoor Recreation
70 County Rd. 502
Walsenburg, CO 81089
(719) 738-2376 **BW, C, CK, F, H, I, MT, PA, RA, S, T, XC**

LITTLE BOOK CLIFFS WILD HORSE RANGE
Bureau of Land Management
Grand Junction District
2815 H. Rd.
Grand Junction, CO 81506
(970) 244-3000
Includes wilderness study area; seasonal closures; caution during fall hunting season **C, H, HR**

LIZARD HEAD WILDERNESS AREA
U.S. Forest Service
Norwood Ranger District
PO Box 388, Norwood, CO 81423
(970) 728-4211; (970) 967-2281 **BW, C, F, H, HR, MT, RC, XC**

LOST CREEK WILDERNESS AREA
U. S. Forest Service
South Park Ranger District
PO Box 219
Fairplay, CO 80440
(719) 836-2031
Groups, limited to 15 and need permit 60 days in advance **BW, C, F, H, HR, MT, RC, T, XC**

L	Lodging	**PA**	Picnic Areas	**RC**	Rock Climbing	**TG**	Tours, Guides
MB	Mountain Biking	**RA**	Ranger-led Activities	**S**	Swimming	**XC**	Cross-country Skiing
MT	Marked Trails			**T**	Toilets		

**LOWRY INDIAN RUINS NATIONAL
HISTORIC LANDMARK**
Bureau of Land Management
701 Camino del Rio
Durango, CO 81301-5462
(970) 247-4082   BW, H, MT, PA, T

**MAROON BELLS–SNOWMASS
WILDERNESS AREA**
U.S. Forest Service
PO Box 948, Glenwood Springs, CO 81602
(970) 945-2521   BW, C, F, H, HR,
                        MT, PA, RA, T, TG

MCDONALD CREEK
Bureau of Land Management
Grand Junction District
2815 H. Rd., Grand Junction, CO 81506
(970) 244-3000   H

MESA VERDE NATIONAL PARK
National Park Service
Mesa Verde, CO 81330
(970) 529-4475;
(970) 529-4461   BW, C, I, L, MT,
                        PA, RA, T, TG, XC

**MONTE VISTA NATIONAL
WILDLIFE REFUGE**
U.S. Fish and Wildlife Service
9383 El Rancho Lane, Alamosa, CO 81101
(719) 589-4021
    Marked trail for auto tour   BW, I, MT, T

MOUNT SNEFFELS WILDERNESS AREA
U.S. Forest Service
Ouray District
2505 S. Townsend
Montrose, CO 81401
(970) 249-3711   BW, C, F, H, HR, MT, XC

MUELLER STATE PARK
Colorado Div. of Parks
and Outdoor Recreation
PO Box 49, Divide, CO 80814
(719) 687-2366   BT, BW, C, F, H, HR,
                        MB, MT, PA, RA, T, XC

NORTH CLEAR CREEK FALLS
Rio Grande National Forest
Divide Ranger District
PO Box 270, Creede, CO 81130
(719) 658-2556
    Caution around falls; ice-climbing of
    falls in winter
                        BW, C, CK, F, MB, PA, T

NORTHSTAR NATURE PRESERVE
Aspen Center for Environmental Studies
100 Puppy Smith St.
Aspen, CO 81611
(970) 925-5756   BW, MT

PAWNEE NATIONAL GRASSLAND
U.S. Forest Service
660 O St.
Greeley, CO 80631
(970) 353-5004; (970) 346-5015
    Extreme weather conditions; carry water
                        BT, BW, H, HR, I, MB, PA, T

PIKE NATIONAL FOREST
U.S. Forest Service
1920 Valley Dr.
Pueblo, CO 81008
Includes Pikes Peak
(719) 545-8737   BT, BW, C, CK, F, GS, H,
                 HR, I, MB, MT, PA, RA, RC, T, XC

PUEBLO RESERVOIR
Colorado Div. of Parks and Outdoor
Recreation, c/o Lake Pueblo State Park
640 Reservoir Rd.
Pueblo, CO 81005
(719) 561-9320   BT, BW, C, F, GS, H,
                        I, MT, PA, RA, S, T

RABBIT VALLEY PALEONTOLOGICAL AREA
Bureau of Land Management
Grand Junction District
2815 H. Rd., Grand Junction, Co 81506
(970) 244-3000   H, I, MT, TG

RATTLESNAKE CANYON
Bureau of Land Management
Grand Junction District
2815 H. Rd., Grand Junction, CO 81506
(970) 244-3000   H, MT

RED CANYON CITY PARK
City of Canon City
PO Box 1460, Canon City, Co 81215
(719) 269-9028
                        BW, C, H, HR, MB, PA, T

RIDGWAY STATE PARK
Colorado Div. of Parks
and Outdoor Recreation
28555 Rte. 550, Ridgway, CO 81432
(970) 626-5822
    Includes the Confluence Nature Area
                        BT, BW, C, CK, F, GS,
                 H, HR, I, MB, MT, PA, RA, S, T, XC

BT	Bike Trails	**CK**	Canoeing, Kayaking	**F**	Fishing	**HR** Horseback Riding
BW	Bird-watching			**GS**	Gift Shop	
C	Camping	**DS**	Downhill Skiing	**H**	Hiking	**I** Information Center

RIFLE FALLS STATE PARK
Colorado Div. of Parks
and Outdoor Recreation
0050 County Rd. 219
Rifle, CO 81650
(970) 625-1607
  Limestone caves can be explored
                          BW, C, F, H, MT, PA, T

RIFLE GAP RESERVOIR
Colorado Div. of Parks
and Outdoor Recreation
0050 County Rd. 219
Rifle, CO 81650
(970) 625-1607
  Park pass required for vehicle

RIO GRANDE NATIONAL FOREST
U.S. Forest Service
1803 W. Rte. 160, Monte Vista, CO 81144
(719) 852-5941
  Ride through the Rockies and Animal
  Lovers Tour information
                  **BT, BW, C, CK, DS, F, H,
                  HR, L, MB, MT, PA, RA, T, XC**

**RIO GRANDE SPECIAL
MANAGENENT AREA**
Bureau of Land Management
3170 E. Main
Canon City, CO 81215-0313
(719) 275-0631
  Restrictions on rafting in April-May due
  to waterfowl nesting   **BW, CK, F**

ROARING FORK BRAILLE TRAIL
White River National Forest
Aspen Ranger District
806 W. Hallam
Aspen, CO 81611
(970) 925-3445   **H, MT**

ROCKY MOUNTAIN NATIONAL PARK
National Park Service
Estes Park, CO 80517
(970) 586-1206   **BW, C, F, GS, H, HR,
                       I, MT, PA, RA, RC, T, XC**

ROOSEVELT NATIONAL FOREST
U.S. Forest Service
240 W. Prospect, Fort Collins, CO 80524
(970) 498-2770
  Includes the Rawah Wilderness Area
  and Big Bend Campground
                       **BT, BW, C, CK, DS, F,
                       H, HR, I, MB, MT, PA, RC, T, XC**

ROUTT NATIONAL FOREST
U.S. Forest Service
29587 W. Rte. 40, Suite 20
Steamboat Springs, CO 80487
(970) 879-1722
  Includes Flat Tops and Mount Zirkle
  Wilderness Areas, Hahns Peak, North Park
                       **BT, BW, C, DS, F, H, HR,
                       I, MB, MT, PA, RA, T, TG, XC**

ROXBOROUGH STATE PARK
Colorado Div. of Parks
and Outdoor Recreation
4751 Roxborough Dr.
Littleton, CO 80125
(303) 973-3959
                       BW, GS, H, I, MT, RA, TG, XC

ROYAL GORGE BRIDGE
PO Box 549
Canon City, CO 81215
(719) 275-7507
  Open year-round; allow 2–3 hrs. for ex-
  ploration   **GS, I, MT, PA, T**

RUBY CANYON
Bureau of Land Management
2815 H Rd.
Grand Junction, CO 81506
(970) 244-3000   **BW, C, CK, F, S**

SAN ISABEL NATIONAL FOREST
U.S. Forest Service
1920 Valley Dr.
Pueblo, CO 81008
(719) 545-8737   **BT, BW, C, DS, F, H,
                        HR, MB, MT, PA, RC, T, XC**

SAN JUAN NATIONAL FOREST
U.S. Forest Service
701 Camino del Rio, #301
Durango, CO 81301
(970) 247-4874   **BT, BW, C, DS, F, H,
                        HR, I, MB, MT, PA, RC, T, XC**

SOUTHERN UTE NATION
Natural Resources Div.
S.Ute Indian Tribe
PO Box 737
Ignacio, CO 81137
(303) 563-0125
  Call for permit information

TABEGUACHE MOUNTAIN BIKE TRAIL
Bureau of Land Management
Uncompahgre Basin Resource Area

L	Lodging	**PA**	Picnic Areas	**RC**	Rock Climbing
MB	Mountain Biking	**RA**	Ranger-led	**S**	Swimming
MT	Marked Trails		Activities	**T**	Toilets

TG	Tours, Guides
XC	Cross-country
	Skiing

2505 S. Townsend Ave.
Montrose, CO 81481
(970) 249-6047
4WD allowed on all but single track section; 3 season trail, lower elev. spring and fall, higher elev. summer
BT, H, HR, MB, MT

TAMARACK STATE WILDLIFE AREA
Colorado Div. of Wildlife
6060 Broadway, Denver, CO 80216
(303) 297-1192
Camping and horseback riding limited to certain areas **BW, C, CK, HR, T**

TAYLOR PARK RESERVOIR
U.S. Forest Service
216 N. Colorado, Gunnison, CO 81230
(970) 641-1471; (970) 641-6817
BW, C, CK, F, GS, H, HR, MB, L, MT, T, XC

TRICKLE MOUNTAIN
WILDLIFE HABITAT AREA
Bureau of Land Management
3170 E. Main, Canon City, CO 81215-0313
(719) 275-0631 **BW, C, H, HR, MB, XC**

TRIMBLE HOT SPRINGS
6475 County Road 203
Durango, CO 81301
(970) 247-0111 **CK, L, S, T**

TRINIDAD LAKE STATE PARK
Colorado Div. of Parks
and Outdoor Recreation
32610 Rte. 12, Trinidad, CO 81082
(719) 846-6951
Park pass required for vehicle
BT, BW, C, CK, F, GS, H, I, MB, MT, PA, RA, T, TG, XC

UNAWEEP SEEP
Bureau of Land Management
Grand Junction Resource Area
764 Horizon Dr.
Grand Junction, CO 81506
(970) 243-6561
Restrictions; check with office

UNCOMPAHGRE WILDERNESS AREA
U.S. Forest Service
Ouray District
2505 S. Townsend, Montrose, CO 81401
(970) 249-3711
BW, F, H, HR, MT, RC, XC

UNCOMPAHGRE NATIONAL FOREST
U.S. Forest Service
2250 Rte. 50
Delta, CO 81416-8723
(970) 874-7691
BT, BW, C, CK, DS, F, GS, H, HR, I, L, MB, MT, PA, RC, T, XC

UTE MOUNTAIN TRIBAL PARK
General Delivery
Towaoc, CO 81334
(970) 565-3751
Advance reservations required
I, T, TG

WEMINUCHE WILDERNESS AREA
U.S. Forest Service
701 Camino del Rio
Durango, CO 81301
(970) 247-4874
Camp at least 100 ft. from streams and lakes; campfires banned at Needle Creek
BW, C, F, H, HR, MT, RC, XC

WEST ELK WILDERNESS AREA
U.S. Forest Service
Paonia Ranger District
PO Box 1030, Paonia, CO 81428
(970) 527-4131 **F, H, HR, MT**

WHITE RIVER NATIONAL FOREST
U.S. Forest Service
PO Box 948
Glenwood Springs, CO 81602
(970) 945-2521
BT, BW, C, CK, DS, F, GS, H, HR, I, L, MB, MT, PA, RA, RC, S, T, XC

WILLIAMS CREEK RESERVOIR
U.S. Forest Service, Pagosa Ranger District
PO Box 310
Pagosa Springs, CO 81147
(970) 264-2268
BT, BW, C, CK, F, H, HR, MB, MT, PA, RA, T, XC

UTAH

ALTA SKI RESORT
Wasatch-Cache National Forest
Salt Lake Ranger District
5944 South 3000 East
Salt Lake City, UT 84121
(801) 943-1794
Within Salt Lake City watershed area; no domestic animals
BT, BW, DS, GS, H, I, L, MB, MT, RA, T, TG, XC

BT	Bike Trails	**CK**	Canoeing, Kayaking	**F**	Fishing
BW	Bird-watching			**GS**	Gift Shop
C	Camping	**DS**	Downhill Skiing	**H**	Hiking

HR	Horseback Riding		
		I	Information Center

ANTELOPE ISLAND STATE PARK
Utah Div. of Parks and Recreation
4528 West 1700 South
Syracuse, UT 84075
(801) 773-2941   **BT, BW, C, CK, GS, H,
                     HR, MB, MT, PA, S, T, TG, XC**

ANTELOPE SPRINGS TRILOBITE QUARRY
Bureau of Land Management
Warm Springs Resource Area
PO Box 778, Fillmore, UT 84631
(801) 743-6811
     Rock hounding

ARCHES NATIONAL PARK
National Park Service
PO Box 907,
Moab, UT 84532
(801) 259-8161; (801) 259-5279
                     **BW, C, H, HR, I, MB,
                     MT, PA, RA, RC, T, TG**

ASHDOWN GORGE WILDERNESS AREA
Dixie National Forest
PO Box 580, Cedar City, UT 84721
(801) 865-3700   **H, HR, MT**

ASHLEY NATIONAL FOREST
U.S. Forest Servive
355 N. Vernal Ave.
Vernal, UT 84078
(801) 789-1181   **BT, BW, C, F, H, HR,
                     I, MB, MT, PA, RA, XC**

BEAR RIVER MIGRATORY BIRD REFUGE
U.S. Fish and Wildlife Service
806 S. Main, Brigham City, UT 84302
(801) 723-5887
     Seasonal road closures; fishing at entrance
     area only; self-guided auto tour route
                     BW, F, I, T

BONNEVILLE SALT FLATS
Bureau of Land Management
Salt Lake District
2370 South 2300 West
Salt Lake City, UT 84119
(801) 977-4300
     No improvements; no drinking water; area
     usually flooded November to March

BOX-DEATH HOLLOW WILDERNESS AREA
Dixie National Forest
Escalante Ranger District
PO Box 246, Escalante, UT 84726
(801) 826-5400   **C, H**

BRIGHTON SKI RESORT
Wasatch-Cache National Forest
Salt Lake Ranger District
5944 South 3000 East
Salt Lake City, UT 84121
(801) 943-1794
     Within Salt Lake City watershed area; no
     domestic animals   **BT, BW, DS, F, GS,
                     H, I, L, MB, MT, PA, RA, T, TG, XC**

**BRYCE CANYON
NATIONAL PARK**
National Park Service
Bryce Canyon, UT 84717
(801) 834-5322   **BW, C, GS, H, HR, I,
                     L, MT, PA, RA, T, TG, XC**

CALF CREEK RECREATION AREA
Bureau of Land Management
Escalante Resource Area
PO Box 246
Escalante, UT 84726
(801) 826-5499   **BW, C, F, H, PA, T**

CANAAN MOUNTAIN
Bureau of Land Management
Dixie Resource Area
345 E. Riverside Dr., Suite 102
St. George, UT 84770
(801) 673-4654   **BW, C, H, RC**

CANYONLANDS NATIONAL PARK
National Park Service
2282 S.W. Resource Blvd.
Moab, UT 84532
(801) 259-7961;
(801) 259-4351, reservations
     Mountain bikes restricted to 4WD rds.
                     **C, CK, H, I, MB, MT,
                     PA, RA, RC, T, TG**

CANYON RIMS RECREATION AREA
Bureau of Land Management
Grand Resource Area
82 East Dogwood, Suite G
Moab, UT 84532
(801) 259-6111
                     BT, BW, C, H, HR, MB, MT, PA, T

CANYONS OF THE ESCALANTE
Bureau of Land Management
Escalante Resource Area
PO Box 246
Escalante, UT 84726
(801) 826-5499
                     BW, C, F, H, HR, I, MB, MT, PA, T

L	Lodging	**PA**	Picnic Areas	**RC**	Rock Climbing	**TG**	Tours, Guides
MB	Mountain Biking	**RA**	Ranger-led	**S**	Swimming	**XC**	Cross-country
MT	Marked Trails		Activities	**T**	Toilets		Skiing

CAPITOL REEF NATIONAL PARK
National Park Service
HC 70, Box 15, Torrey, UT 84775-9602
(801) 425-3791
  Weather extremes; knowledge of desert
  survival skills helpful
              BW, C, F, GS, H, HR, I, MB,
              MT, PA, RA, RC, S, T, TG, XC

CASCADE SPRINGS INTERPRETIVE SITE
Uinta National Forest
Pleasant Grove Ranger District
PO Box 228, Pleasant Grove, UT 84062
(801) 785-3563   **BW, H, MT, T**

CEDAR BREAKS NATIONAL MONUMENT
National Park Service
82 North 100 East, Suite #3
Cedar City, UT 84720
(801) 586-9451
  Rte. 148 into park closed from late
  November until mid-May
              BW, C, H, I, MT, PA, RA, T, XC

CLEAR CREEK CAMPGROUND
Sawtooth National Forest
Burley Ranger District
Rte. 3, 3650 Overland Ave.
Burley, ID 83318
(208) 678-0430   **C, H, T**

CLEVELAND LLOYD DINOSAUR QUARRY
Bureau of Land Management
125 South 600 West
Price, UT 84501
(801) 637-4584   **GS, H, I, MT, PA, T, TG**

CORAL PINK SAND DUNES STATE PARK
Utah Div. of Parks and Recreation
PO Box 95, Kanab, UT 84741
(801) 874-2408
  Off-hwy. 4WD vehicle riding
              C, GS, H, HR, I, MT, PA, RA, T

DARK CANYON PRIMITIVE AREA
Bureau of Land Management
San Juan Resource Area
PO Box 7, Monticello, UT 84535
(801) 587-2141   **BW, C, H**

DARK CANYON WILDERNESS AREA
Manti-La Sal National Forest
Monticello Ranger District
PO Box 826, Monticello, UT 84535
(801) 587-2041
              BW, C, H, HR, MT, RC

DEAD HORSE POINT STATE PARK
Utah Div. of Parks and Recreation
PO Box 609, Moab, UT 84532
(801) 259-2614
              BW, C, GS, H, I, MT, PA, RA, T

DEVIL'S KITCHEN GEOLOGIC AREA
Uinta National Forest
Spanish Fork Ranger District
Spanish Fork, UT 84660
(801) 798-3571   **BW, I, MT, PA, T**

DESERET PEAK WILDERNESS AREA
Wasatch-Cache National Forest
Salt Lake Ranger District
5944 South 3000 East
Salt Lake City, UT 84121
(801) 943-1794   **BW, C, F, H, HR, MT, XC**

DINOSAUR NATIONAL MONUMENT
National Park Service
PO Box 128, Jensen, UT 84035
(801) 789-2115
(800) 845-3466—Dinosaur Nature Assoc.
  Permit required for canoeing or kayaking
              BW, C, CK, H, I, MT, RA, T

DIXIE NATIONAL FOREST
U.S. Forest Service
PO Box 0580, Cedar City, UT 84721-0580
(801) 865-3700
  Includes 3 wilderness areas
              BT, BW, C, CK, DS, F, H,
              HR, I, L, MB, MT, PA, S, T, XC

ELK MEADOWS SKI AREA
PO Box 511, Beaver, UT 84713
(801) 438-5433
              DS, L, T, XC

ESCALANTE STATE PARK
Utah Div. of Parks and Recreation
PO Box 350, Escalante, UT 84726
(801) 826-4466
  Hike in to see Petrified Forest; examples
  can be viewed in visitor center
              BW, C, CK, F, H, I, MT, PA, S, T

FISHLAKE NATIONAL FOREST
U.S. Forest Service
115 East 900 North
Richfield, UT 84701
(801) 896-9233
  Includes 240-mile Paiute ATV trail
              BT, BW, C, DS, F, H, HR,
              I, L, MB, MT, PA, RA, RC, S, T, XC

BT Bike Trails	**CK** Canoeing,	**F** Fishing	**HR** Horseback
BW Bird-watching	Kayaking	**GS** Gift Shop	Riding
C Camping	**DS** Downhill	**H** Hiking	**I** Information
	Skiing		Center

FISH SPRINGS NATIONAL WILDLIFE REFUGE
U.S. Fish and Wildlife Service
PO Box 568
Dugway, UT 84022
(801) 831-5353   BW, CK, H, MB, PA, T

FLAMING GORGE NATIONAL RECREATION AREA
U.S. Forest Service
PO Box 279, Manila, UT 84046
(801) 784-3445
Raft rentals and guide services for the
Green River in the Dutch John area
BT, BW, C, CK, F, GS, H, HR, I,
L, MB, MT, PA, RA, S, T, TG, XC

FREMONT INDIAN STATE PARK
Utah Div. of Parks and Recreation
11550 W. Clear Creek Canyon Rd.
Sevier, UT 84766
(801) 527-4631
BT, BW, C, F, GS, H, I, MB, MT, PA, RA

GLEN CANYON NATIONAL RECREATION AREA
National Park Service
PO Box 1507
Page, AZ 86040
(520) 645-8404   BW, C, CK, F, GS, H, I,
L, PA, RA, S, T, TG

GOBLIN VALLEY STATE PARK
Utah Div. of Parks and Recreation
c/o Green River State Park
PO Box 637
Green River, UT 84525
(801) 564-3633;
(800) 322-3770, reservations   C, H, PA, T

GOOSENECKS STATE PARK
Utah Div. of Parks and Recreation
PO Box 788
Blanding, UT 84511
(801) 678-2238   BW, C, H, HR, PA, T

GRAND GULCH PRIMITIVE AREA
Bureau of Land Management
San Juan Resource Area
PO Box 7
Monticello, UT 84535
(801) 587-2191
Permits required for groups of 8 or
more at least 3 wks. in advance; maxi-
mum group size 12
BW, C, H, HR, I

GREEN RIVER STATE PARK
Utah Div. of Parks and Recreation
PO Box 637, Green River, UT 84525
(801) 564-3633;
(800) 322-3770, reservations
BW, C, CK, F, H, I, PA, T

GROSVENOR ARCH
Bureau of Land Management
Kanab Resource Area
318 North First East, Kanab, UT 84741
(801) 644-2672
Primitive camping; vault toilets
C, H, MB, T

HARDWARE RANCH GAME MANAGEMENT AREA
Utah Div. of Wildlife
PO Box 301, Hyrum, UT 84319
(801) 245-3131; (801) 479-5143
Moonlight sleighrides   H, I, T, TG

HIGH UINTAS WILDERNESS AREA
U.S. Forest Service
355 N. Vernal Ave.
Vernal, UT 84078
(801) 789-1181
Groups limited to 14 people, 15 animals
BW, C, F, H, HR, I, MT, TG

HOVENWEEP NATIONAL MONUMENT
National Park Service
McElmo Route
Cortez, CO 81321
(970) 749-0510   BW, C, H, I, MT, PA, T

JONES HOLE NATIONAL FISH HATCHERY
U.S. Fish and Wildlife Service
266 West 100 North, Rte. 2
Vernal, UT 84078
(801) 789-4481
BW, C, F, H, I, MT, PA, T, XC

JOSHUA TREE FOREST
Bureau of Land Management
Dixie Resource Area
345 E. Riverside Dr., Suite 102
St. George, UT 84770
(801) 673-4654   BW, C, H, HR, RC

KODACHROME BASIN STATE PARK
Utah Div. of Parks and Recreation
PO Box 238
Cannonville, UT 84718
(801) 679-8562   BT, BW, C, GS, H,
HR, I, MB, MT, PA, T, TG

L Lodging	**PA** Picnic Areas	**RC** Rock Climbing	**TG** Tours, Guides
MB Mountain Biking	**RA** Ranger-led	**S** Swimming	**XC** Cross-country
MT Marked Trails	Activities	**T** Toilets	Skiing

KOKOPELLI TRAIL
Bureau of Land Management
Grand Resource Area
82 East Dogwood, Suite G
Moab, UT 84532
(801) 259-8193
4WD and motorcycles allowed on certain
sections, not on single track; no potable
water **BT, H, HR, MB, MT**

LA SAL MOUNTAIN STATE FOREST
School and Institutional
Trust Land Administration
3 Triad, Suite 400
Salt Lake City, UT 84180-1204
(801) 523-5508
Avalanche risk
BT, BW, C, F, H, HR, MB, RC, XC

LONE PEAK WILDERNESS AREA
U.S. Forest Service Service
Salt Lake Ranger District
5944 South 3000 East
Salt Lake City, UT 84121
(801) 943-1794
Within Salt Lake City watershed area; no
domestic animals
BW, C, F, H, MT, RC, TG, XC

MANTI–LA SAL NATIONAL FOREST
U.S. Forest Service
599 W. Price River Dr.
Price, UT 84501
(801) 637-2817 **BT, BW, C, F, GS, H,
HR, I, MB, MT, PA, T, XC**

MONUMENT VALLEY TRIBAL PARK
PO Box 360289
Monument Valley, UT 84536
(801) 727-3287
Admission fee; permits required for hik-
ing and horseback riding
C, GS, H, HR, I, T, TG

MOUNT NAOMI WILDERNESS
Wasatch-Cache National Forest
Logan Ranger District
1500 East Rte. 89, Logan, UT 84321
(801) 755-3620 **BW, C, H**

MOUNT NEBO WILDERNESS AREA
Uinta National Forest
Spanish Fork Ranger District
44 West 400 North
Spanish Fork, UT 84660
(801) 798-3571 **BW, C, H, HR**

MOUNT OLYMPUS WILDERNESS AREA
Wasatch-Cache National Forest
Salt Lake Ranger District
5944 South 3000 East
Salt Lake City, UT 84121
(801) 943-1794
Watershed restrictions south side only;
horseback riding on Millcreek Canyon side
only **BW, H, HR, MT, RC, TG, XC**

MOUNT TIMPANOGOS WILDERNESS AREA
U.S. Forest Service
Pleasant Grove Ranger District
PO Box 228, Pleasant Grove, UT 84062
(801) 342-5240 **BW, C, H, HR, I, MT**

NATURAL BRIDGES NATIONAL MONUMENT
National Park Service
PO Box 1, Lake Powell, UT 84533
(801) 259-5174
C, GS, H, I, MT, PA, RA, TG

NAVAJO NATION
Dept. of Tourism
PO Box 663, Window Rock, AZ 86515
(520) 871-6436
Check with office for permission to visit

NEWSPAPER ROCK RECREATION SITE
Bureau of Land Management
San Juan Resource Area
PO Box 7, Monticello, UT 84535
BW, C, H, HR, MB, MT, PA, T

OURAY NATIONAL WILDLIFE REFUGE
U.S. Fish and Wildlife Service
266 West 100 North, Vernal, UT 84078
(801) 789-0351
Large numbers of mosquitoes late May
to late August **BW, CK, F, H, T**

**PARIACANYON–VERMILLION CLIFFS
WILDERNESS AREA**
Bureau of Land Management
Kanab Resource Area
318 North First East
Kanab, UT 84741
(801) 644-2672 **H**

**PINE VALLEY MOUNTAIN
WILDERNESS AREA**
Dixie National Forest
Pine Valley Ranger District
345 East Riverside Dr., St. George, UT 84770
(801) 652-3100
Group limit 12 **BW, C, H, HR, I, MT**

BT	Bike Trails	**CK**	Canoeing, Kayaking	**F**	Fishing	**HR**	Horseback Riding
BW	Bird-watching			**GS**	Gift Shop		
C	Camping	**DS**	Downhill Skiing	**H**	Hiking	**I**	Information Center

RAINBOW BRIDGE NATIONAL MONUMENT
National Park Service
PO Box 1507, Page, AZ 86040
(520) 645-8404   BW, H, MT, T, TG

SAWTOOTH NATIONAL FOREST
U.S. Forest Service
2647 Kimberly Rd., E.
Twin Falls, ID 83301
(208) 737-3200   BT, BW, C, CK, F, GS, H,
                    HR, I, MT, PA, RA, RC, S, T, XC

**SCOTT M. MATHESON
WETLAND PRESERVE**
The Nature Conservancy
Great Basin Field Office
PO Box 11486, Salt Lake City, UT 84147
(801) 531-0999; (801) 259-4629
    Includes observation sites
                    BW, CK, H, I, MT

SHEEP CREEK GEOLOGICAL AREA
Ashley National Forest
Flaming Gorge
National Recreational Area
PO Box 278, , Manila, UT 84046
(801) 784-3445
    Self-guided tours   BW, C, F, GS, HR,
                         I, PA, RC, T, TG

SHIVWITS PAIUTE INDIAN RESERVATION
Bureau of Indian Affairs
Southern Paiute Field Station
PO Box 720,
St. George, UT 84771
(801) 674-9720
    Check with office for permission to visit

SLICKROCK BIKE TRAIL
Bureau of Land Management
Grand Resource Area
82 East Dogwood, Suite G
Moab, UT 84532
(801) 259-8193   BT, H, HR, MB, MT

SNOW CANYON STATE PARK
Utah Div. of Parks and Recreation
PO Box 140, Santa Clara, UT 84765
(801) 628-2255; (800) 322-3770
    Very hot summers   BT, BW, C, H, HR,
                         I, MB, MT, PA, RA, T

TIMPANOGOS CAVE NATIONAL MONUMENT
National Park Service
RR 3, Box 200, American Fork, UT 84003
(801) 756-5238   H, I, PA, RA, TG

TWIN PEAKS WILDERNESS AREA
Wasatch-Cache National Forest
Salt Lake Ranger District
5944 South 3000 East
Salt Lake City, UT 84121
(801) 943-1794
    Within Salt Lake City watershed area; no
    domestic animals
                    BW, C, F, H, MT, TG, XC

UINTA NATIONAL FOREST
U.S. Forest Service
88 West 100 North, Provo, UT 84601
(801) 377-5780   BT, BW, C, CK, F, H, HR,
                    I, MB, MT, PA, RA, RC, S, T, XC

UINTAH AND OURAY UTE RESERVATION
PO Box 190, Fort Duchesne, UT 84026
(801) 722-5141; (801) 722-0877
general information, permits
(801) 722-5511
birds and wildlife information   BW, I, TG

**UTAH FIELD HOUSE OF
NATURAL HISTORY STATE PARK
AND DINOSAUR GARDEN**
Utah Div. of Parks and Recreation
235 East Main St., Vernal, UT 84078
(801) 789-3799   GS, I, PA, T

WASATCH-CACHE NATIONAL FOREST
U.S. Forest Service
Rm. 8236, Federal Bldg.
125 S. State St., Salt Lake City, UT 84138
(801) 524-5030
          BT, BW, C, CK, DS, F, GS, H, HR, I, L,
          MB, MT, PA, RA, RC, S, T, TG, XC

WELLSVILLE MOUNTAIN WILDERNESS
Wasatch-Cache National Forest
Logan Ranger District
1500 East Rte. 89
Logan, UT 84321
(801) 755-3620
    Includes major western flyway for rap-
    tors each fall   BW, H

ZION NATIONAL PARK
National Park Service
Springdale, UT 84767-1099
(801) 772-3256 BT, BW, C, GS, H, HR, I, L,
MT, PA, RA, T, TG

L	Lodging	**PA**	Picnic Areas	**RC**	Rock Climbing	**TG**	Tours, Guides
MB	Mountain Biking	**RA**	Ranger-led	**S**	Swimming	**XC**	Cross-country
MT	Marked Trails		Activities	**T**	Toilets		Skiing

PHOTOGRAPH CREDITS

All photography by Tom Bean except for the following:

ix, right: Stephen J. Krasemann/DRK Photo, Sedona, AZ

xiv–xv: Amon Carter Museum, Fort Worth, TX (1967.27)

10: Library of Congress, Washington, D.C.

11: American Philosophical Society, Philadelphia, PA

20: Wendy Shattil/Bob Rozinski, Denver, CO

54: John Cancalosi, Tucson, AZ

62: Michael H. Francis, Billings, MT

66: Bates Littlehales, Arlington, VA

80: Colorado Historical Society, Denver, CO (F33111)

90: Barbara Gerlach, Chatham, MI

93: John Hendrickson, Clipper Mills, CA

94: John Shaw, Colorado Springs, CO

99: Jeff Foott, Jackson, WY

102, 120: Arthur Morris/Birds as Art, Deltona, FL

124: Stephen J. Krasemann/DRK Photo, Sedona, AZ

144: Michael H. Francis, Billings, MT

146: Glenn Van Nimwegen, Jackson, WY

148: Tom and Pat Leeson, Vancouver, WA

152: Michael S. Quinton, Macks Inn, ID

173: John Hendrickson, Clipper Mills, CA

177: Robert Villani, Merrick, NY

186: Thomas D. Mangelsen/Images of Nature, Jackson, WY

197: Dr. Scott Nielsen, Superior, WI

206: Tom and Pat Leeson/West Stock, Seattle, WA

210: Tim Fitzharris/Masterfile, Toronto, Canada

212: George H.H. Huey, Prescott, AZ

232–233: Yale Collection of Western Americana, Beinecke Rare Book and Manuscript Library, Yale University, New Haven, CT

234: Tim Fitzharris/Masterfile, Toronto, Canada

250: Wendy Shattil/Bob Rozinski, Denver, CO

Back cover: John Shaw (bobcat), Tom Bean (columbine, aspens)

ACKNOWLEDGMENTS

The editors gratefully acknowledge the professional assistance of Susan Kirby and Patricia Woodruff.

The following consultants also helped in the preparation of this volume: Professor Joseph Gordon, Hulbert Center for Southwest Studies, Colorado College; John E. Grassy; Dallas Rhodes, Professor and Chair of Geology, Whittier College, CA; and Joel S. Tuhy, Public Lands Director, The Nature Conservancy of Utah.